For Better
_____ or Worse

Contributions in American Studies
Series Editor: Robert H. Walker

"Ezra Pound Speaking": Radio Speeches of World War II
Leonard W. Doob, editor

The Supreme Court: Myth and Reality
Arthur Selwyn Miller

Television Fraud: The History and Implications of the Quiz Show Scandals
Kent Anderson

Menace in the West: The Rise of French Anti-Americanism in Modern Times
David Strauss

Social Change and Fundamental Law: America's Evolving Constitution
Arthur Selwyn Miller

American Character and Culture in a Changing World: Some
Twentieth-Century Perspectives
John A. Hague, editor

Olmsted South: Old South Critic/New South Planner
Dana F. White and Victor A. Kramer, editors

In the Trough of the Sea: Selected American Sea-Deliverance
Narratives, 1610-1766
Donald P. Wharton, editor

Aaron Burr and the American Literary Imagination
Charles J. Nolan, Jr.

The Popular Mood of Pre-Civil War America
Lewis O. Saum

The Essays of Mark Van Doren
William Claire, editor

Touching Base: Professional Baseball and American Culture in the
Progressive Era
Steven A. Riess

Late Harvest: Essays and Addresses in American Literature and Culture
Robert E. Spiller

Steppin' Out: New York Night Life and the Transformation of
American Culture, 1890-1930
Lewis A. Erenberg

For Better or Worse

THE AMERICAN INFLUENCE IN THE WORLD

Edited by ALLEN F. DAVIS

Contributions in American Studies, Number 51

GREENWOOD PRESS
WESTPORT, CONNECTICUT • LONDON, ENGLAND

Library of Congress Cataloging in Publication Data

Main entry under title:

For better or worse.

(Contributions in American studies ; no. 51 ISSN 0084-9227)
Papers originally presented at international conference sponsored by the American Council of Learned Societies, the American Studies Association, and the Smithsonian Institution, held in Washington, D. C., in Sept. 1976.
Includes bibliographical references and index.
1. United States--Relations (general) with foreign countries--Congresses. I. Davis, Allen Freeman, 1931- II. American Council of Learned Societies Devoted to Humanistic Studies. III. American Studies Association. IV. Smithsonian Institution.
E840.2.F67   303.4'82'0973   80-1048
ISBN 0-313-22342-4 (lib. bdg.)

Library of Congress Catalog Card Number: 80-1048
ISBN: 0-313-22342-4
ISSN: 0084-9227

First published in 1981

Greenwood Press
A division of Congressional Information Service, Inc.
88 Post Road West, Westport, Connecticut 06881

Printed in the United States of America

10 9 8 7 6 5 4 3 2 1

CONTENTS

TABLES AND ILLUSTRATIONS   vii

FOREWORD   ix

ACKNOWLEDGMENTS   xiii

1. *Allen F. Davis*, Introduction: The American Impact on the World   3

PART 1 CULTURE, MEDIA, AND THE ARTS   23

2. *Bruno Zevi*, The Influence of American Architecture and Urban Planning in the World   27

3. *Dušan Makavéjev*, Nikola Tesla Radiated a Blue Light   39

4. Maurice C. Horn, American Comics in France: A Cultural Evaluation   49

5. *Charlie Gillett*, Big Noise from Across the Water: The American Influence on British Popular Music   61

PART 2 TECHNOLOGY, BUSINESS, AND FOREIGN POLICY   93

6. *Isaias Flit Stern*, American Technology and Peruvian Development: Hopes and Frustrations   97

7. *Pehr G. Gyllenhammar*, The Impact of American Culture on Management Organization and the Transportation Industry   105

8. *Marina Menshikova*, The American Way in Agriculture and Its International Significance   111

9. *Eqbal Ahmad*, Political Culture and Foreign Policy: Notes
       on American Interventions in the Third World   119

PART 3 MISSIONARIES, EDUCATORS, AND WRITERS   **133**

10. *Sahair El Calamawy*, The American Influence on Education
       in Egypt   137

11. *Anthony Ngubo*, Contributions of the Black American
       Church to the Development of African Independence
       Movements in South Africa   145

12. *Mbulamwanza Mudimbe-Boyi*, African and Black American
       Literature: The "Negro Renaissance" and the Genesis
       of African Literature in French   157

13. *Sulak Sivaraksa*, American Influence on Books,
       Magazines, and Newspapers in Siam   171

    INDEX   187

    ABOUT THE CONTRIBUTORS   193

TABLES
AND ILLUSTRATIONS _____

TABLES

1. Ten Top Hits in the United Kingdom and the United States, 1955-1975   63

2. Ratio of British Ten Top Hits Between Two and Four Firms   68

3. U.S. and U.K. Share of British Ten Top Hits Market, 1965-1975   80

ILLUSTRATIONS

1. A Panel of Speakers at a 1976 Conference Session   84

2. An A & W Root Beer Stand in Kobe, Japan   85

3. Avis Advertisement in Germany   86

4. Heinz Ketchup Made in the Netherlands   87

5. Heinz Soup Billboard in Tokyo   88

6. Levi's Advertisement in Spanish   89

7. McDonald's Advertisement in Sweden   90

8. Purina Advertisement on a Truck in Mexico   91

FOREWORD_____

What difference have two hundred years of American history made? Much has been written on the influence of other countries on the development of the United States, but in the Bicentennial year of 1976 scholars and critics around the world instead considered the influence of American culture on the rest of the world. The essays in this volume were first presented at an international conference, "The United States in the World," held at the Smithsonian Institution in Washington, D.C., during the last week of September 1976. A nineteenth-century gift to the United States from an Englishman, the Smithsonian was a symbolic setting—a microcosm—within which America's legacy of imported and exported ideas and artifacts could be assessed. The conference was jointly sponsored by the American Council of Learned Societies, the American Studies Association, and the Smithsonian.

An impressive array of talent from more than forty nations assembled on the Mall in Washington. "A rare menagerie," Israel Shenker called the assembly in the *New York Times*.[1] Often an auditorium stage was occupied by participants from six countries and three continents. Many were "Americanists" who had devoted their lives to the study and teaching of American culture. More than a few professional and amateur "America-watchers" spoke, but most of the papers were prepared by film makers, agricultural experts, physicians, businessmen, musicians, architects, politicians, and scientists who had never systematically thought about the influence of American culture. From their vantage points they considered how American culture had influenced their work and their societies. Except for several special evening lectures, all of those who prepared papers came from outside the United States. They joined a long list of foreign visitors who have written about the United States. Unlike many of their predecessors, these visitors were concerned primarily about the American cultural impact on their own environments.

Some of these essays are quite favorable toward the United States and some are very critical, but most find points to praise and points to blame. Many of the essays deal with the influence of other countries and cultures on the United States, for cultural influence never flows in only one direction. Most of the authors have a hate-love relationship with the United States. By quoting frequently from the discussion, I hope to give some sense of the spirit of debate, fellowship, and discussion of the week-long conference.

In some ways the 1976 International Conference was the climax and culmination of a series of conferences on American Studies held during 1975-76 in various parts of the world. These conferences in Salzburg, Austria; Fujinomiya, Japan; Shiraz, Iran; San Antonio, Texas; and Abidian, Ivory Coast were attended largely by university professors who were teaching and writing about the United States in other countries. The 1976 International Conference, by contrast, included a large number of participants who were experts, practitioners, and observers from outside the world of the university. While the five world regional conferences dealt with many topics including methodological and pedagogical problems, the theme of the 1976 conference was the impact of American culture on the rest of the world.[2]

This collection makes no attempt to be comprehensive or inclusive. Left out are many possible topics such as the influence of American literature, American theoretical science, American abstract art, American jazz. Some of these essays do not have the usual scholarly footnotes, because they were written more from personal experience than from library research. Perhaps their real importance is that they are statements, some of them angry, some of them ambivalent, about the United States and its influence in various parts of the world. Written during the American Bicentennial year and dealing with diverse subjects, these essays present the opinions and the thoughtful analysis of an impressive group of foreign experts.

I made an effort to include essays that deal with various parts of the world: Europe, Latin America, Asia, and Africa. I tried to include statements about the American impact on developing countries as well as on the older, more mature nations. Here also there are omissions. This is a collection of essays that makes tentative explorations of an important topic, a topic that should be of vital concern to Americans and to people everywhere. For whether or not we like it, American culture, American foreign policy, and the American way of life have had a great influence on the rest of the world. That influence is likely to grow larger in the third century of United States history, as we also grow more cosmopolitan, more open, and more receptive to external influences on ourselves. Americans should take the criticism and the warnings in these essays seriously.

ALLEN F. DAVIS

NOTES

1. *New York Times*, September 30, 1976. The conference is also described in Allen F. Davis, "The 1976 International Conference, The United States and the World: 200 Years of American History—What Difference Has It Made?" *American Studies International*, 15 (Winter 1976): 19-27.

2. For an account of these regional conferences and a selection of papers read, see Robin W. Winks, editor, *Other Voices, Other Views: An International Collection of Essays from the Bicentennial* (Westport, Connecticut: Greenwood Press, 1978).

ACKNOWLEDGMENTS _____

Many people made the conference and this book possible. The committee that planned the conference consisted of Daniel Aaron of Harvard University representing the American Council of Learned Societies, William Goetzmann of the University of Texas representing the American Studies Association, Daniel J. Boorstin representing the Smithsonian Institution, Nathan Reingold who replaced Daniel Boorstin when the latter was appointed Librarian of Congress, and Frank Freidel of Harvard University representing the Council for International Exchange of Scholars. Of special assistance to the committee were Richard Downar, director of the American Studies program, American Council of Learned Societies; Charles Blitzer, assistant secretary of the Smithsonian Institution for history and art; Wilton S. Dillon, director of Smithsonian symposia and seminars; and Robin Winks of Yale University. Robert Walker of George Washington University believed that these papers were important enough to publish when some others did not. The conference and the book would not have been possible without the hard work and dedication of Carla M. Borden, program specialist, Office of Symposia and Seminars of the Smithsonian Institution, and Sally Benson, my assistant, guide, and collaborator at the American Studies Association. Frances Opher provided needed aid at crucial moments.

The conference was funded in large part by a grant from the National Endowment for the Humanities with other support coming from the American Council of Learned Societies, the Smithsonian Institution, and the United States Department of State. The conference was held in Washington, D.C., at the Smithsonian Institution, whose Office of Symposia and Seminars arranged for hospitality and special cultural events made possible by a grant from the Morris and Gwendolyn Cafritz Foundation. Additional contributions in support of the week's program were received from: Bendix Corporation, Bucyrus-Erie Company, Bunge Corporation, Champion Spark

Plug Company, Eaton Corporation, Fluor Corporation, Ford Motor Company Fund, I. U. International, Ingersoll-Rand Company, The Liberian Foundation, Inc., Massey-Ferguson Limited, Prudential Insurance Company of America, Sperry Rand Corporation, and Xerox International Center for Training and Management Development.

Grateful acknowledgment is also given to the following for their kind permission to include the illustrations presented in the book: A & W International, Inc., Avis Rent a Car System, Inc., H. J. Heinz Co., Levi Strauss & Co., McDonald's Corporation, Ralston Purina International, and the Smithsonian Institution.

INTRODUCTION: THE AMERICAN
IMPACT ON THE WORLD _____

Allen F. Davis

The American impact on the rest of the world began from the moment of its discovery. Indeed even before Columbus, the idea of a new land of riches and perfection had influenced European writers. Columbus reported that the New World was a kind of paradise, "a land to be desired, and once seen, never to be left."[1] Captain Arthur Barlowe, who visited the coast of Virginia in 1584, described a land of "incredible abundance." He called the natives "most gentle, loving and faithful, voide of all guile and treason, and such as live after the manner of the golden age." The new land, unspoiled and uncontaminated, filled with abundance, was to be the site of the new Golden Age. America was to lead the world toward an earthly paradise.[2]

But there was another image of the New World, that of a "hideous wilderness," a place of darkness, bareness, and fear, the very opposite of the bountiful garden. William Bradford described the land he saw in September 1620, as the *Mayflower* stood off Cape Cod, as a "hideous and desolate wilderness, full of wild beasts and wild men." Jacques Cartier remarked while off the coast of Labrador in 1534: "I am inclined to regard this land as the one God gave to Cain." The two contradictory images of America would persist for many centuries. As Leo Marx has written: "If America seemed to promise everything that men always had wanted, it also threatened to obliterate much of what they already had achieved."[3]

The discovery of the New World had an important impact on European political ideas and transformed international relations, but perhaps most significant was the American influence on the world economy. The New World contributed potatoes, corn (maize) (two of the world's most important staple foods), cocoa, tobacco, tomatoes, peanuts, peppers, squash, vanilla, and several varieties of beans. The discovery of America greatly expanded the production of coffee and sugar and increased the available supply of fish and the quantity of gold and silver. All of these products influenced the economy and the way people lived and functioned in the world. America also exported syphilis which was, next to tobacco, "the most harmful gift of the New World to the old."⁴ So from the very beginning America meant both hope and despair, both material progress and the threat of evil to the rest of the world.

Those who settled in America often thought of the new land as a special place ordained by God. The Puritans especially saw themselves as God-chosen people with a special mission to lead the world on a new and better path. Edward Johnson who emigrated to Massachusetts in 1630 saw the new land as "the place where the Lord will create a new Heaven and a new Earth, new churches, and a new Commonwealth together." Many of the early settlers decided that the New World was superior to the Old. The Reverend Francis Higginson after ten years at Plymouth wrote that "a swig of New England air is better than a whole flagon of English ale," and William Stoughton announced in 1668 that "God sifted a whole nation that he might send choice grain over into this wilderness."⁵

Those on the other side of the Atlantic were not quite so sure about the superiority of the New World, but they continued to be both fascinated and appalled by the new land. Yet the sense of destiny and the sense of superiority continued to be characteristic of Americans. "I have long been of the opinion," Benjamin Franklin wrote in 1760, "that the foundations of the future grandeur and stability of the British empire lie in America." John Adams, writing a few years later, was even more emphatic: "I always consider the settlement of America with reverence and wonder, as the opening of a grand scheme and design in Providence for the illumination and emancipation of the slavish part of mankind all over the earth."⁶ It was this sense of mission and destiny, shared by the leaders of the British colonies in America that helped to give them confidence to declare their independence from the world's greatest power in 1776.

The American Revolution had an influence around the world that is still reverberating two hundred years later. The war had an immediate impact on world trade and world politics, but it was the concept of the right of revolution as expressed in the Declaration of Independence, as well as the actual act of rebellion, that inspired those who stood for freedom, liberty, and independence everywhere. The impact was most immediate in France. The news of American independence was received with great enthusiasm by politicians and intellectuals. A street in Paris was renamed "Rue de l'In-dépendence Américaine" and many American books were translated into French. A tapestry called "America" was constructed by Jean-Jacques-François Le Barbier, and another artist did a drawing entitled "Liberty Crowning Franklin." The American Revolution also had a direct influence on the French Revolution, though the exact nature of that influence is still a matter of controversy. Yet it is undeniable that the Declaration of the Rights of Man of 1789 owed much to the Declaration of Independence and to the various state constitutions written between 1776 and 1782.[7]

The American Revolution also influenced other European countries—Holland, Italy, Greece, Belgium, even Poland. The fit was never exact, but as Robert Palmer has written: "The European idea of the American Revolution was more than a dream, or a myth, or mirage. It was indeed partly a myth or moral story which, in rising above mere facts, could inspire action in Europe and in any case reflected the discontents of a class-ridden and over complicated society. But it was also a kind of laboratory for observations in political science. . . . The American Revolution was the opening signal, raised on a distant shore, for a revolutionary outburst which in the next 30 years was to sweep through the world of Western Civilization."[8] The American Revolution and the continuing American revolutionary tradition, real or imagined, continue to have an influence today in Asia, Africa, and Latin America.

The revolutionary generation redefined the purpose and the mission of the new land. The United States was to serve as a model and as an example for the rest of the world to follow, a living proof that democracy, peace, and justice were possible. Thomas Jefferson announced that his generation, which had fought the Revolution, "acted not for ourselves alone, but for the whole human race," and he called the American experiment, "the last best hope of mankind." Albert Gallatin told his fellow citizens that their most important task was "to be a model for all other governments and all other less-favored nations, to adhere to the most elevated principles of political morality . . . , and by your example to exert a moral influence most beneficial to mankind."[9]

Many Europeans agreed. "They are the hope of the human race," Turgot remarked, "they may well become its model." But a French writer in 1788 discovered a flaw in the land of liberty—a flaw that would become larger and larger as time went on. "The friends of justice and humanity will perhaps be astonished to learn," he announced, "that in the United States in that asylum of peace, happiness and liberty, which has so often re-echoed to those sacred words 'all men are created equal,' there still are today nearly several hundred thousand slaves."[10]

Despite the flaw of slavery, the concept that American democracy and the American way of life could be exported to the rest of the world was a constant theme of American writers and politicians during the nineteenth century. It was America's destiny to lead the world toward a millenium. Speaking in 1832, Daniel Webster maintained that: "In our endeavor to maintain our existing forms of government we are acting not for ourselves alone, but for the globe. We are trustees holding a sacred treasure, in which all lovers of freedom have a stake. . . . The gaze of the sons of liberty everywhere is upon us, anxiously, intensely, upon us.'' Ralph Waldo Emerson decided that: ''The office of America is to liberate, to abolish kingcraft, priestcraft, caste, monopoly, to pull down the gallows, to burn up the bloody statute book. . . .''[11]

America's sense of mission included the genuine desire to help other, less fortunate people around the world. Part of this impulse to help was translated into the Christian missionary movement. The American Board of Commissioners for Foreign Missions was organized in 1810 by Samuel Mills, a Connecticut Congregationalist. Two years later the Board sent ten missionaries to Calcutta and Ceylon, the first of thousands of American missionaries of all denominations to go to Africa, Asia, and South America. These missionaries not only tried to convert foreigners to Christianity, but also, consciously or unconsciously, they tried to convince their subjects of the superiority of American democracy and the American way of life. American missionaries founded schools, colleges, hospitals, and churches in all parts of the world. Roberts College in Turkey became an outpost for American influence in the Middle East. American missionaries helped to establish an American foothold in China and Korea, and missionaries played an important role in preparing for the American annexation of Hawaii.[12]

The American nation, John Quincy Adams once proclaimed, would stand as ''a beacon . . . on the summit of the mountains to which all the inhabitants of the earth may turn their eyes.'' But America would not only be a beacon, it would also be a haven for the oppressed. Thomas Paine in *Common Sense* called America ''an asylum for the persecuted lovers of civil and religious liberty from every part of Europe.'' And seventy-five years later, Wendell Phillips announced to the world: ''Let every oppressed man come; let every man who wished to change his residence come—we welcome all.''[13]

The twin themes of the United States as a beacon or model and a haven for the oppressed were generally accepted and embellished by European observers during the nineteenth century. Michel-Guillaume Jean De Crèvecoeur, the Frenchman who moved to America and became one of the country's greatest defenders and admirers, reported that ''here individuals of all nations are melted into a new race of men whose labours and posterity will one day cause a great change in the world.'' The most famous of all foreign visitors, Alexis de Tocqueville, found much to praise in the United States as well as some things to question, but the main purpose of his *Democracy in America* was to demonstrate that Europe had much to gain by emulating America. ''I wished to show what a democratic people really was in our day,'' he remarked, and to show that ''under a democratic government the fortunes and rights of society may be respected, liberty preserved, and religion honored.''[14]

Not all the foreign visitors and observers were so impressed. Charles Dickens, for example, was distressed by the American customs of fighting duels and spitting on the floor. He was critical of the poor sanitation and the lack of culture. He was especially depressed by slavery. He agreed with Harriet Martineau who wrote: ''A walk through a lunatic asylum is far less painful than a visit to the slave quarter of an estate. . . . It is well known that the most savage violence that is now heard of in the world takes place in the Southern and Western States of America.'' ''I believe the heaviest blow ever dealt at liberty's head will be dealt by this nation in the ultimate failure of its example to the earth,'' Dickens announced.[15]

Other foreign observers were critical of the Americans' impatience and love of speed. ''An American wants to perform within a year what others do within a much longer period. Ten years in America are like a century in Spain,'' Francis Lieber decided. But it was the Americans' concern for acquiring money and their apparent disinterest in music, art and culture which angered most foreign visitors. Harriet Martineau concluded in 1836: ''The Americans appear to me an eminently imaginative people [but] . . . They do not put their imaginative power to use in literature and the arts. . . .'' But it was Sydney Smith, a British minister, doctor, and writer who, in 1830, most dramatically made the case for America's lack of influence around the world. ''During the thirty or forty years of their independence, they have done absolutely nothing for the Sciences, for the Arts, for Literature, or even for the statesman-like studies of Political Economy. . . .'' He announced: ''In the four quarters of the globe, who reads an American book? Or goes to an American play? Or looks at an American picture or statue? What does the world yet owe to American physicians or surgeons? What new constellations have been discovered by the telescopes of Americans? What have they done in mathematics? Who drinks out of American glasses? Or eats from American plates? Or wears American coats or gowns? Or sleeps in American blankets?''[16]

There was truth in Smith's charges, though time would soon alter some of his points. Yet America remained a land of opportunity and promise for many Europeans. A German immigrant living in St. Louis wrote home shortly after arriving, ''You must not think that America is a country which abounds in scenic beauty. But if you come you will find a *good* country. Here the farmer who has established himself lives in almost unbounded wilderness, happy and contented like Adam in the Garden of Eden.'' Carl Schurz, one of America's most famous nineteenth-century immigrants, recalled that his image of America before he came was of a ''land where everybody could do what he thought best, and where nobody need be poor, because everybody was free.'' The idea of America as a haven for the oppressed received its most permanent symbol when the French nation gave the Statue of Liberty to America. The poem by Emma Lazarus engraved on its side announced to the world:

> Give me your tired, your poor,
> Your huddled masses yearning to breathe free,
> The wretched refuse of your teeming shore.
> Send these, the homeless, tempest-tossed to me,
> I lift my lamp beside the golden door.[17]

Ironically even before the statue was completed in 1886, the United States was debating the desirability of immigration restriction. At first it did not close the golden door entirely, but restricted the opportunities for Chinese and gradually for other undesirable and un-American types. Some like Theodore Munger, a liberal Protestant clergyman, feared that the foreign migration was bringing "anarchism, lawlessness . . . labor strikes and a general violation of personal rights.'' Like many other observers, he blamed the Haymarket Riot of 1886, and other disturbances, on radical immigrants. The immigrants from southern and eastern Europe seemed to pose a special threat to American democracy. Francis Walker, the president of the Massachusetts Institute of Technology and a leading exponent of immigration restriction, reversed the old argument that the best and most energetic people came to America. The new immigrants, he argued, "are beaten men from beaten races; representing the worst failures in the struggle for existence. . . .''[18]

Almost all the immigrants who came to America met some prejudice and for many, the Catholic Irish and Italian, the Jew and the Oriental, the prejudice and discrimination were often overwhelming. Gradually the door of opportunity closed, culminating with the Restriction Act of 1924 which limited immigration to 2 percent of the total population of each national group in the United States in 1890. It was an act which clearly discriminated against eastern and southern Europeans, as well as Asians and Africans. The restrictions were made even tighter in most cases in the era after World War II, so that for practical purposes, with a few exceptions, the United States had ceased to be the haven for the oppressed.

Before the gates closed, however, millions came to America. This immigration to the United States was part of the largest migration of people the world had ever seen, bigger by far than the invasion of the Roman Empire by the Germanic tribes. Between 1846 and 1932, according to one count, over 63 million people migrated from Europe, and over 40 million of those came to the United States. Some became disillusioned, many failed, several million returned to their homelands, but most stayed. Despite prejudice and discrimination, despite the fact that the streets in America were not paved with gold, as some had been led to believe, the dream of America as a land of opportunity and as a haven for the oppressed persisted. Perhaps in the last analysis the most important impact of the United States on the rest of the world was that the new country created a place for the world's population at a time when growing industrialism and countless political problems were causing millions to migrate. And America provided a dream for millions to believe in.

By the end of the nineteenth century the United States was much more than a haven for the oppressed of the world. It was beginning to have a real impact on the world's economy, politics, and technology. In 1876, the year the United States celebrated its one hundredth birthday, its trade balance shifted. For the first time in that year the United States exported more than it imported, and that single statistic served notice to the rest of the world about the kind of influence the United States would have during its second century.

The Centennial Exposition, held in Philadelphia, included impressive displays of American ingenuity and growing industrial might. There were typewriters, adding machines, woodworking machinery, printing presses, locomotives, telegraphs and cables, footwear, clothing, tools of all kinds, and even the recently patented telephone invented by Alexander Graham Bell. But it was the huge Corliss steam engine, which dominated Machinery Hall and powered all the other machines at the Exposition, that captured the imagination of American and foreign visitors alike. It seemed to symbolize the dawn of a new mechanical age, and to represent American technological progress. Frederic Auguste Bartholdi, creator of the Statue of Liberty, was inspired by the huge machine. "The lines are so grand and beautiful, the play of movement so skillfully arranged, and the whole machine so harmoniously constructed, that it had the beauty and almost the grace of the human form."[19]

It was not the grace of the Corliss engine that fascinated most foreign visitors but its power. In fact, the Centennial helped to change the minds of many Europeans about the United States. No longer was it just the land of opportunity, potential, and wilderness, but now it was viewed by France, Britain, and Germany as a serious industrial rival. Big, bold, powerful, rapid, modern, efficient, energetic were words often used to describe the United States.

American technology and inventive genius had influenced the world even before the Centennial, and they would continue to do so at an accelerated pace in the second hundred years. Benjamin Franklin, David Rittenhouse, and other early Americans were well known in Europe for their inventions and their scientific knowledge. Samuel Slater's New England textile mills, a success based in part on Eli Whitney's cotton gin, also had their impact abroad. But it was Cyrus McCormick's reaper, Samuel Colt's revolver, and the sewing machine as perfected by Isaac Singer that were among the greatest technological advances of the nineteenth century. Robert Gilpin has written:

Ours has always been a technological civilization. The influence and inspiration that we have radiated throughout the world have been largely technological. . . . In contrast the Greek inspiration was political and cultural. The Romans were soldiers and law-givers. Though the British were the initiators of the Industrial Revolution and of industrial civilization, as the 19th century wore on, they gave up technology for finance and the political management of empire. The French and the Russians have given the modern world great literature, art, and science, but little technology. And although the Germans led the way with respect to the technologies of the second phase of the Industrial Revolution—electricity, organic chemistry, steel, and the internal-combustion engine—America achieved the full potential of these technologies for reshaping society and the lives of men. It has been from America that these technologies have made their continuing impact on the world.[20]

Advancing technology, expanding production, and growing confidence led Americans to think about exporting their products to other parts of the world in the last part of the nineteenth century. The National Association of Manufacturers, organized in 1895, devoted half of its ten-part program to the expansion of trade overseas. Even before this, American shipowners, investment bankers, and missionaries were pushing for greater American economic involvement with the rest of the world. Alfred Thayer Mahan, the leading advocate of a big American navy, announced in 1897:

Whether they will or no, Americans must now begin to look outward. The growing production of the country demands it. An increasing volume of public sentiment demands it. The position of the United States between the two old worlds and the two great oceans makes the same claim, which will soon be strengthened by the creation of the new link joining the Atlantic and the Pacific. The tendency will be maintained and increased by the growth of European colonies in the Pacific, by the advancing civilization of Japan and by the rapid peopling of the Pacific states with men who have all the aggressive spirit of the advanced line of national progress.[21]

Albert Beveridge, a senator from Indiana and a leading American imperialist, was even more direct:

American factories are making more than the American people can use. American soil is producing more than they can consume. Fate has written our policy for us; the trade of the world must and shall be ours . . . our institutions will follow our flag on the wings of our commerce. And American law, American order, American civilization and the American flag will plant themselves on shores hitherto bloody and benighted, but by those agencies of God henceforth to be made beautiful and bright.[22]

The American flag was indeed planted on foreign soils. After a brief war with Spain, in 1898, the United States took over the Philippines, Guam, and several other small islands in the Pacific, as well as establishing a protectorate over Cuba. Americans could brag like the British that the sun never set on their empire. But the true story of American influence around the world cannot be told in terms of territory acquired or colonies established, for the United States constructed an empire built on investment, influence, and trade, rather than on territory. The United States in the late nineteenth and early twentieth centuries became an economic force to be reckoned with in Asia, Latin America, and even in Africa. American businessmen invested money in banks and railroads in Manchuria, copper mines in Mexico, packing plants in Argentina, sugar plantations in Cuba and Hawaii. They loaned money to foreign nations, including Japan. They helped to convince the government to reorganize the consular service and improve and enlarge the navy. Occasionally American economic involvement in a country like Nicaragua led to sending in the marines to protect American interests. But usually the American influence was more subtle—a combination of a genuine desire to help other people and a sense that America's superior way of life could be shared with the rest of the world, mixed with a realistic need of American businessmen and bankers to increase their profits.[23]

It was not until the eve of World War I that American investments abroad surpassed foreign investments in the United States. But long before that, the presence of the United States was felt in world politics and world trade, as well as in the world's imagination. In 1901 William T. Stead, the British journalist and reformer, published a book which he called *The Americanization of the World*.[24] The United States still seemed to be the land of opportunity, the place of the future, but now it was open spaces, cowboys and Indians, combined with a mechanized civilization filled with skyscrapers, assembly lines, labor-saving devices, and bathrooms with an inexhaustible supply of hot water that intrigued foreign visitors. Alexander Bing, a German-born French citizen, remarked in 1895 that in America "yesterday no longer counts while today exists only as a preparation for tomorrow." As Europe erupted in war in 1914, America's tomorrow seemed close at hand.[25]

Most Americans were shocked when, on 28 June 1914, the assassination of Archduke Ferdinand of Austria catapulted Europe into war. They were shocked at first, and then they were relieved, for they felt that they had no vital stake in the war. They were three thousand miles away from the combat and they could remain neutral. But gradually the United States was drawn into the war; neutrality was not as easy in 1915 as it had been a hundred years earlier during the Napoleonic wars. It was not so much submarine warfare, blockades, and sunken ships that led the United States into the war in the spring of 1917, though those all played a part. It was more a growing sense that the United States' destiny and the fate of the world were tied to the fate of Britain and France. There were obviously some Americans who disagreed, including many of those with Irish and German backgrounds. But Woodrow Wilson articulated the feelings of many Americans when he announced that the United States was entering the war "to fight for the ultimate peace of the world and for the liberation of its people . . . for the rights of nations great and small, and the privilege of men everywhere to choose their way of life and of obedience. The world must be made safe for democracy." He went on to say: "We desire no conquest, no dominion. We seek no indemnities for ourselves, no material compensation for the sacrifices we shall freely make."[26]

But Wilson, though he said that the United States desired no conquest, no dominion, did want a place for the United States at the peace negotiation and a place for American trade in the world. When he said that the war was a war to make the world safe for democracy, he really meant safe for American democracy. Wilson and some other Americans felt it was the destiny of the United States to become the "justest, the most progressive, the most honorable, the most enlightened nation in the world," and he wanted to make the rest of the world over into the American image.[27]

The European powers and the United States Senate rejected Wilson's version of world peace. But the failure of the United States to join the League of Nations did not mean that the United States had cut itself off from the rest of the world. On the contrary, American trade increased all during the 1920s. American businessmen took Warren G. Harding seriously when he urged them to "operate aggressively; go on to the peaceful commercial conquest of the world."[28]

In the years after World War I American art, literature, music, architecture, and technology were taken more and more seriously by Europeans, even as some American writers and artists lived as expatriates in Europe. The skyscraper had always fascinated foreign visitors, but in the 1920s and 1930s Art Nouveau and Art Deco were the first European styles to which American artists and architects made significant contributions. As Hugh Honour has written: "European designers hankering after streamlined up-to-the-minute modernity naturally turned to America—their new chromium-plated land."[29] American jazz, partly because of the radio and the phonograph, also had a wide impact on Europe, and to a lesser extent on other parts of the world. A jazz band was playing at the Casino de Paris in November 1918. "I recall the shock, the sudden awakening this staggering rhythm, this new sonority brought," Darius Milhaud recalled. "It seemed to represent the spirit of a new era especially for the young." When jazz was banned by Hitler in 1933, it took on a new meaning as the symbol of the land of freedom. As Joachim-Ernst Berendt from Germany remarked at the

1976 International Conference, "opinion, tolerance, freedom, spontaneity, individuality and personal expression, that is the actual reason why jazz is suspicious to all dictatorial regimes on the left and right."[30]

American art and literature seemed to travel better than American sports. American baseball caught on in Japan in the 1920s, and to some extent in Latin America, but American football could not compete with what the rest of the world called football. Some foreign observers saw Lindbergh's lone flight to Paris in 1927 as a symbol of the triumph of American technology, but not all observers were pleased with American progress. The French novelist, Georges Duhamel, who published a book in 1931 called *America the Menace: Scenes from the Life of the Future*, called Chicago "the tumor, the cancer among cities, about which all statistics are out of date when they reach you. . . . America is devoted to its ephemeral works. It erects, not monuments, but merely buildings. . . . Should it fall into ruins tomorrow, we should seek in its ashes in vain for the bronze statuette that is enough to immortalize a little Greek village. Ruins of Chicago!—prodigious heap of iron-work, concrete and old plaster. . . . I evoke you with horror and weariness of spirit. . . ." But even Duhamel believed that American civilization was destined to spread around the world. "America may fall, but American civilization will never perish; it is already mistress of the world."[31]

Duhamel also commented at one point: "O painters, my friends and brothers, you can never make anything of Chicago! You will never paint this world, for it is beyond human grasp." But Fernand Leger, the artist and refugee from Nazi-occupied Europe, had another reaction to New York at night. "I was struck, by the illuminated advertisements that swept the streets. You were there, talking to someone, and suddenly he became blue. Then the colour disappeared and another came, and he became red, yellow. That kind of projected colour is free, it is in space. I wanted to do the same thing in my canvases."[32]

Leger was not the only refugee from war-torn Europe who looked on America as the land of promise and the country of the future in a world gone mad. Albert Einstein and Enrico Fermi, physicists; Peter Drucker, economist and management consultant; Hannah Arendt, political scientist; Erik Erikson and Erich Fromm, psychologists; Walter Gropius and Mies van der Rohe, architects; Claude Levi-Strauss, anthropologist; Herbert Marcuse, philosopher; Igor Stravinsky, composer; Arturo Toscanini, conductor; and Paul Tillich, theologian, were a few among the many intellectuals and creative artists who fled to America in the 1930s.[33]

As World War II approached many Americans also believed that the future belonged to the United States, but their viewpoint was often quite different from those refugees who were fleeing Europe. Henry Luce, then the publisher and owner of *Time-Life*, defined the war in 1940 in terms of the American mission. He echoed and amplified the words of Woodrow Wilson: "We are *not* in a war to defend American territory. We are in a war to defend and even promote, encourage, and incite so-called democratic principles throughout the world. . . ." Americans, he argued, had "to accept whole-heartedly our duty and our opportunity as the most powerful and vital nation in the world and in consequence to exert upon the world the full impact of our influence, for such purposes as we see fit and by such means as we see fit."[34]

It did not work out quite the way Henry Luce envisioned it, but after six tragic years of war the United States did emerge as the hope of the world, especially the world of Western Europe. "As Europe becomes more helpless the Americans are compelled to become farseeing and responsible," the British writer, Cyril Connolly, wrote with hope in 1947. "As Rome was forced by the long decline of Greece to produce an Augustus, a Virgil, *our impotence liberates their potentialities.*"[35]

In the years immediately after the war, the United States did step in to fill the vacuum left by the destruction of much of Europe and Asia. Massive amounts of foreign aid were granted first to Europe, then to Asia, Africa, and Latin America. "Democracy alone can supply the vitalizing force to stir the peoples of the world into triumphant action, not only against their human oppressors, but against their ancient enemies—hunger, misery, and despair . . . ," President Truman announced in 1949.[36] The Marshall Plan, Point Four, and other aspects of the Truman Doctrine were designed in large part to contain communism and to restrain revolution around the world, and not incidentally to stimulate American business. There was also an ingredient of the American sense of mission, the genuine desire to help those in need.

After World War II the United States emerged as the leader in what Zbigniew Brzezinski calls the technetronic era—"shaped culturally, psychologically, socially and economically by the impact of technology and electronics, particularly in the area of computers and communications."[37] In part because of the wartime experience, the United States pioneered in the systematic harnessing of science to the advancement of technology. American corporations supported giant research laboratories, and the federal government recognized the importance of basic science. Because of these factors, the presence in the United States of many scientists and technicians, and the combined efforts of government and industry, the United States took the lead in the postwar years in developing sophisticated technologies in electronics, atomic energy, aerospace, and computers, enabling it to become the chief exporter of the new systems of the technetronic era. The same factors led to the development of the large and successful multinational corporations based in the United States.

Since World War II American products have been shipped around the world in an ever-increasing stream. American corporations have become international in their drive to seek profits and to spread the American way of life to every corner of the globe. The largest 298 United-States-based international corporations in one year, in the early 1970s, earned 40 percent of their profits outside the United States. In 1972 one-third of the business of the top thirty American advertising agencies came from outside the United States. If we compare the annual sales of corporations with the gross national products of countries we discover that in 1973 General Motor's income was bigger than that of Switzerland, Pakistan, and South Africa, that Royal Dutch Shell's was bigger than that of Iran, Venezuela, and Turkey, and that Goodyear Tire's was bigger than that of Saudi Arabia.[38]

These companies export products and technology which are of great benefit to millions of people. But as Ferenc Probald of Hungary remarked at the 1976 International Conference these companies are primarily "motivated by seeking more profit, and therefore the technology transferred by them goes mostly to those countries that provide the most favorable conditions to obtain profit and not necessarily to those which most badly need the technology." Flit Stern of Peru told an amusing and pointed story illustrating this thesis: General Motors some years ago built an assembly plant in Peru which produced Chevrolet cars for the Latin American market. The manager of the plant soon got many complaints that the suspension system was not adequate for the rough mountain roads in Peru. The manager wrote to Detroit not only complaining but suggesting modifications which would solve the problem. After several months, when he had heard nothing, he went to see the vice president for Latin American operations at General Motors who finally told him that the number of cars sold in Peru did not warrant design changes.[39]

American military units are stationed in many parts of the world. The United States sends military assistance usually accompanied by advisors and technicians to dozens of countries. And, as a participant at the 1976 conference pointed out, American technology and American products are exported in largest volume to the countries "which are regarded as most crucial politically and strategically to the United States." During the last two decades the countries leading the list were South Korea, South Vietnam, and Iran.

American students and American tourists are spread around the world (over three million went to Europe in 1970). Wherever they go they discover an American presence that is hard to avoid. Richard C. Longsworth, a diplomatic correspondent for United Press International, described the overwhelming impact of American products and American popular culture as he arrived at the Brussels airport. He immediately noticed signs advertising Ramada Inn, Coca Cola and ITT.

I pass up Hertz and Avis, hail a cab and ride into the city past buildings owned by IBM, Goodyear, 3M, Culligan and Champion Sparkplugs, past a Holiday Inn, past the headquarters of American-dominated NATO, past the Shell garage, Kodak store and Levi's shop, past my neighborhood supermarket (owned by J. C. Penney), and I'm home: I'm a city dweller, unlike many Americans in Brussels who live in suburban Waterloo, near hamburger stands, The American Women's Clubhouse, American schools, Baskin-Robbins, and Pat McNall's doughnut shop. By the gory ground where Wellington and Blucher defeated Napoleon, the Pirates and Padres now struggle in Little League combat.[40]

At the 1976 conference much of the discussion centered around American "cultural imperialism." One participant defined it as "the export of American junk": comics, popular music, film, technology, advertising—the American way of life. "There is a danger, I suppose," Marcus Cunliffe of the University of Sussex warned, "about exaggerating the American influence, of making it appear that nothing in the world can exist, should exist without the voice of America. There is a tendency for the United States to claim that their experience sums up everything in the world." Other participants tried to make distinctions between what was an American influence and what was merely modern or post-industrial. John Ziman, a British physicist, remarked: "I think we should be careful not to equate totally the modern world with the American world. We might be confusing the American image, the American dream, the American fashion, the American style of life with a technological revolution with much wider sources than simply the United States."

Yet all participants agreed that the American influence had been great, especially since World War II. "What is stimulating in American culture," Jacek Fuksiewicz of Poland announced, "are those parts which are most American." And for him these were jazz, comics, and film. For others the most important American influences were in science and technology, especially "elementary particle research using large scale acceleration with large teams and space science." Another participant suggested more succinctly that the greatest American contributions were the pill and the computer. But nearly all agreed that often Americans have been naive in assuming that a simple technique or machine could change the world regardless of cultural differences. And almost all were ambivalent about the ultimate benefits of American technology and popular culture.

Gordon Stewart of Scotland cited the case of the American export of penicillin to Africa which virtually eliminated diseases that had ravaged the continent for more than a thousand years. But he also mentioned the

American export of large quantities of dried milk to Bangladesh, India, and Pakistan which created all kinds of medical problems because the artificial milk deprived the infants of the natural protection against disease they were receiving from their mother's milk. Sometimes American altruism and American technology have created more problems than benefits.

Francisco José of the Philippines was even more emphatic about the negative aspects of American technology in his country. "It is my belief that the American experience in architecture is irrelevant to us in the Philippines if not downright pernicious." The large American skyscrapers, massive buildings with air conditioning, suburban housing and shopping centers all patterned on the American models, designed by architects trained in the United States, were all unnecessary, overly expensive and completely unappropriate. "The American experience should be something that we should only dream about, but not follow," he argued.

Almost all the conference participants praised the American openness, spontaneity, and willingness to be criticized. Ivan Boldizsar of Hungary remarked: "In countries where personal freedom is more restricted people look up to America as the country of the still unlimited possibilities. It is good you criticize yourself," he continued, "but this strengthens your feeling of superiority, because you can say, 'Look, we are so strong, we are so good anything can be said about us.' "[41]

Where once it was possible to ask, "Who reads an American book?" now there are many who complain that in some parts of the world American books, magazines, comic strips, movies, television shows, records, and consumer goods overwhelm the native products. "Traditional national drama and folk music retreat before *Peyton Place* and *Bonanza*," Jeremy Tunstall has written. "So powerful is the thrust of American commercial television that few nations can resist."[42] American popular culture and American products have an enormous appeal and a great impact in almost every corner of the world. Even in countries where anti-American feelings run high, young men and women can be seen chalking hate-America slogans on walls while wearing blue jeans and Ohio State T-shirts. Doris Anderson, editor of *Chatelaine*, suggested at the conference that Canada was in a unique position to feel the influence of the United States: "We are overwhelmed by American culture. Ninety-five percent of the magazines sold in Canada, 98 percent of the paperback books, most of the records and even the school books and the comics come from the United States. There has been a resurgence of nationalism in Canada in the last ten years which puzzles our American friends. They don't understand why we seem to become grumpy and cranky, and why we want our own culture."[43]

There is a powerful irony that at a time when American popular culture dominates much of the world, the reputation of the United States (the sense that the United States means freedom, opportunity, and hope for the future) has declined. The last decade has changed the image that the United States has presented to the world. We are now a nation where presidents and other leaders are assassinated, where there is violence not only on television, but in the city streets and on the campuses. Our national leaders promote war, pollution, waste, and corruption. "The world sees an America at once brutal and violent, racist and hypocritical, pathetic, sick, and above all, threatening—to itself, civilization and perhaps the planet."[44] As Jacek Fuksiewicz of Poland remarked at the conference: "The view that the great mass audience throughout the world has is of the violence in America, not only the actual violence such as shooting and killing people, but violence as a value system. If you look at the American telefilm, and to some extent cinema, you see violence as the main way of solving conflicts among people and that affects the stereotypes that people around the world have of the United States."[45]

Since the establishment of the United States, its image abroad has been that of a liberating and revolutionary nation. More often than not that image reflected something less than reality, for more often than not and especially in the twentieth century, the United States has supported the side of the establishment, rather than the forces of revolution. But it was the war in Vietnam which finally eroded the image of a nation always on the side of liberty.

Some of the most caustic critics have been Americans. As Joseph Ben-David of Israel announced at the conference: "There is an interesting difference between us foreigners and you people from the United States. We tend to see the positive and you tend to see the negative side of the American experience." Another critic, Emmet John Hughes, wrote on the occasion of the Bicentennial:

The Republic dedicated from birth to the spread of universal ideas has become instead the nation more devoted than all others to the universal sale of arms. Within the last decade, the annual sum of these sales has soared from $2 billion to $11 billion. . . . Thus the self-appointed guardian of international peace has managed to make itself the munitions monarch of the world. From continent to continent the Republic's strategy for defending human freedom has incongruously dictated the supporting of inhumane dictatorship. In essence, the Vietnam War itself was fought to save a tyranny that was our ally. From South Korea and West Pakistan, through Latin America, and on to Spain and Greece, the Republic's policies, overt and covert, have treated governments contemptuous of liberty as the ramparts over which we watch most fondly.[46]

Even Henry Steele Commager, who has usually emphasized the positive aspects of the American experience, says flatly:

We are no longer a revolutionary people. We are no longer creative in politics and government: every major political institution that we have today was invented before the year 1800; none has been since then. We no longer open our doors to the poor and the oppressed of the world. We no longer think of our mission as primarily that of lifting the burdens from the shoulders of men, and when we undertake to spread our way of life, it is through force not through moral example.[47]

There are a few in the United States and in the rest of the world who see the United States as being responsible for all the world's evil; and there are a few like Jean-François Revel who in *Without Marx or Jesus* depict the United States as the only true revolutionary hope for the world.[48] Most observers are more complex in their analysis, more troubled in their conclusions. At the 1976 International Conference it was Eqbal Ahmad from Pakistan and Amsterdam who set the tone for much of the discussion and debate. He was torn between what he defined as "the decency, the strengths, the good in this civilization, and in this culture," and the evil and the terror which he witnessed the same civilization perpetuating around the world.

He described the "inexhaustible reservoir of good will for America" which he experienced as a young boy growing up during World War II in India. The United States represented "both the possibility and the promise of liberation" for the colonial people of the world.

You were the first people after all to have fought a war of struggle against colonialism and had succeeded, even before the Irish did. . . . Your example had been important. . . . It was important to us because in your Declaration of Independence and in your Constitution you had made an almost uncompromising commitment to a people's inalienable right to self-determination, not only that, but more—their obligation to exercise that right and revolt against a government that they considered unjust, and therefore unlawful. . . . Our view of America was confirmed further by the existence of a certain rivalry between the United States and the other colonial powers. . . . We understood American rivalry with the established imperial powers as somehow constituting anti-imperialism. . . . But the reality is actually in sharp contrast to our perceptions. Since 1945, United States forces have engaged more frequently, lost more lives, inflicted more suffering, expended greater amounts on suppressing social revolutions in poor countries than they have in defending American security from any means or rivals like the USSR or China. Between 1947 and 1970, American forces have intervened at the rate of once every 16 months, to overthrow either the popularly elected or a popular government or movement in the Third World. Against these realities we continued to believe that America was somehow on the side of freedom and justice, that the principles of 1776 were being honored by the leaders and the governors of this society. That particular illusion, contrasting continually with the realities, ultimately broke in the 60's under the impact of the war in Indochina.[49]

John Kennedy acknowledged in 1963 that the American sense of mission had to change. "The United States is neither omnipotent nor omniscient.

We cannot always impose our will on the other ninety-four percent of mankind. . . . There cannot be an American solution to every world problem.''[50] But Kennedy often did not heed his own advice, and those who have followed him in office seem to have forgotten the lesson he was trying to teach. "All Americans must understand that because of its strength, its history and its concern for human dignity, this nation occupies a special place in the world," Richard Nixon announced just before he ordered the invasion of Cambodia.[51]

Despite the tragic events of the last two decades most Americans and many foreigners, both friends and critics of the United States, still want to have faith in the American dream, the American sense of uniqueness, in the hope that is named America. But the American dream has faded, the beacon has at least dimmed. The United States still means both good and evil to the rest of the world. As American culture merges, in the last quarter of the twentieth century, into a postindustrial drabness, dominated by multinational corporations, as the world faces a time of scarcity rather than abundance, what does this mean for the future of the world?

NOTES

1. Quoted in Howard Mumford Jones, *O Strange New World: American Culture, the Formative Years* (New York: Viking, 1964), pp. 1-5.

2. Quotations from Leo Marx, *The Machine in the Garden: Technology and the Pastoral Ideal* (New York: Oxford University Press, 1964), pp. 34-37.

3. Ibid., pp. 40-41, 45. For the various images of America in Europe see Hugh Honour, *The New Golden Land: European Images of America from the Discoveries to the Present Time* (New York: Pantheon, 1975).

4. Earl J. Hamilton, "What the New World Gave the Economy of the Old" in Fred Chiapelli, ed., *First Images of America* (Berkeley: University of California Press, 1976), vol. 2, p. 853.

5. Quotations from Russel B. Nye, *This Almost Chosen People* (East Lansing: Michigan State University Press, 1964), p. 165; Merle Curti, *The Roots of American Loyalty* (New York: Columbia University Press, 1946), p. 5.

6. Quoted in Curti, *Roots*, pp. 6, 8.

7. Claude Fohlen, "The Impact of the American Revolution on France" in *The Impact of the American Revolution Abroad* (Washington, D.C.: Library of Congress, 1976), pp. 21-38; Honour, *New Golden Land*, pp. 138-52.

8. Robert R. Palmer, "The Impact of the American Revolution Abroad" in *The Impact of the American Revolution Abroad*, p. 16; Cedric B. Cowing, ed., *The American Revolution: Its Meaning to Asians and Americans* (Honolulu: East-West Center, 1977).

9. Quoted in Nye, *Almost Chosen People*, pp. 169-70.

10. Quoted in Honour, *New Golden Land*, pp. 150-52.

11. Quoted in Nye, *Almost Chosen People*, pp. 173-74.

12. Daniel Boorstin, *The Americans: The Democratic Experience* (New York: Random House, 1973), pp. 557-66.

13. Quoted in Nye, *Almost Chosen People*, pp. 174, 179-80.

14. Quoted in Henry Steel Commager, ed., *America in Perspective: The United States through Foreign Eyes* (New York: Random House, 1947), pp. 8-41.

15. Quotations from Gerald Emanuel Stearn, ed., *Broken Image: Foreign Critiques of America* (New York: Random House, 1972), pp. 48-49.

16. Quoted in Commager, *America in Perspective*, pp. 38, 78; Stearn, *Broken Image*, pp. 23-24.

17. Quoted in Curti, *Roots*, p. 83; Nye, *Almost Chosen People*, p. 181.

18. Quoted in John Higham, *Strangers in the Land* (New Brunswick: Rutgers University Press, 1955), pp. 138, 143.

19. Quoted in Robert C. Post, ed., *1876: A Centennial Exhibition* (Washington, D.C.: Smithsonian Institution, 1976), p. 31.

20. Robert Gilpin, "Exporting the Technological Revolution," *Saturday Review* (13 December 1975): 31. *Also see* William Woodruff, *America's Impact on the World* (New York: Halsted, 1975), pp. 104-29.

21. Alfred Thayer Mahan, *The Influence of Seapower on History* in Merle Curti, Willard Thorp, and Carlos Baker, eds. *American Issues: The Social Record* (Philadelphia: Lippincott, 1960), p. 906.

22. Claude Bowers, *Beveridge and the Progressive Era* (Boston: Houghton Mifflin, 1932), p. 69.

23. *See* William A. Williams, *The Tragedy of American Diplomacy* (Cleveland: World, 1959).

24. William T. Stead, *The Americanization of the World* (New York: Horace Markley, 1901).

25. Quotation from Honour, *New Golden Land*, p. 253.

26. Wilson "Declaration of War" in William A. Williams, ed., *The Shaping of American Diplomacy* (Chicago: Rand McNally, 1956), pp. 590-95.

24. Williams, *Tragedy*, p. 57.

28. Ibid., p. 93.

29. Honour, *New Golden Land*, pp. 259-60.

30. 1976 International Conference transcript.

31. Stearn, *Broken Image*, pp. 229-35.

32. Honour, *New Golden Land*,. p. 260.

33. Donald Fleming and Bernard Bailyn, eds., *The Intellectual Migration: Europe and America, 1930-1960* (Cambridge: Harvard University Press, 1969).

34. Henry Luce, *American Century* (New York: Farrar and Rinehart, 1941).

35. Cyril Connolly, "Introduction," *Horizon* (October 1947): 11.

36. Boorstin, *Democratic Experience*, p. 576.

37. Zbigniew Brzezinski, *Between Two Ages: America's Role in the Technetronic Era* (New York: Viking, 1970), p. 9.

38. Richard J. Barnet and Ronald E. Müller, eds., *Global Reach: The Power of the Multinational Corporations* (New York: Simon and Schuster, 1974), pp. 15, 143.

39. 1976 International Conference transcript.

40. Richard C. Longworth, "Lafayette, We Are Here—Good and Hard," *Saturday Review* (13 December 1975): 62.

41. The quotations in this and in the next several paragraphs come from the discussion at the 1976 International Conference and are taken from the transcript of that conference.

42. Jeremy Tunstall, *The Media Are American* (New York: Columbia University Press, 1977), p. 39 [summarizing Herbert I. Schiller, *Mass Communication and American Empire* (New York: A. M. Kelley, 1969)]. Tunstall concludes that the dominance of American media in the 1950s and 1960s is now waning.

43. Stearn, *Broken Image*, p. 269.

44. 1976 International Conference transcript.

45. Ibid.

46. Emmet John Hughes, "The Third Century, The Third Chance," *Saturday Review* (13 December 1975): 59.

47. Henry Steele Commager, "The Revolution as a Real Ideal," *Saturday Review* (13 December 1975): 110.

48. Jean-François Revel, *Without Marx or Jesus: The New American Revolution Has Begun* (New York: Doubleday & Co., 1971).

49. 1976 International Conference transcript.

50. Quoted in William Plaff, "Reflections," *New Yorker* (6 June 1977): 107.

51. Quoted in Nye, *Almost Chosen People*, p. 202.

PART 1
Culture, Media, and the Arts

INTRODUCTION

The Media Are American is the title of a recent book by Jeremy Tunstall.[1] The book jacket depicts Mickey Mouse devouring a globe made of Swiss cheese. Although the book itself suggests that American media do not dominate the non-Communist world to the extent that they did during the 1940s and 1950s, the cover and the title certainly reflect the common view of American cultural and media imperialism. Kojak and the Beverly Hillbillies, Spiderman and Dick Tracy, wire service stories, record albums, and feature films are all exported around the world, and together they carry American ideology, American products, and an American life style to other countries.

In some countries this tidal wave of American popular culture has overwhelmed native cultural production. Canada, a few years ago, in an effort to prevent being completely dominated by the United States, passed a law requiring that one-third of the records played on television and radio be Canadian. Other countries, such as Burma, go to great lengths to keep American and other foreign media from penetrating their borders. At the same time Indian, Japanese, Mexican, as well as Soviet films have developed their own spheres of influence, while many Asian and African countries control their own radio and televison programming. Still the appeal and impact of American popular culture remain overwhelming in many parts of the world.

The influence of American fine arts, classical music, architecture, and design are somewhat less obvious than the influence of popular culture. Charles Ives and Aaron Copeland are known in Europe and Asia, but they are not played as much as Duke Ellington and George Gershwin, or the music from popular musicals such as *My Fair Lady* and *Porgy and Bess*. American artists, especially since 1945, have had a wide impact on artists and collectors in other parts of the world. Jackson Pollock, Mark Rothko, Frank Stella and others are well known. In 1973 the Australian National Gallery paid two million dollars for Pollock's *Blue Poles*, which shocked and scandalized many in and out of the art world. But it also marked the coming of age of a modern American master. Yet American post-expressionist and pop art reach a small minority compared to the art of the Coca-Cola, Seven-Up, or Winston advertisements.

American architecture and design have also had an influence in many parts of the world. American skyscrapers and American-style hotels rise in many unlikely places. Sometimes those American buildings in foreign countries appear to be filled with Scandinavian furniture which had been imported into the United States, mass-produced, and then exported around the world. But there have been other influences. The American balloon-frame house finds its way, in one adaptation or another, to many parts of the globe. And American architects like Louis Sullivan, Frank Lloyd Wright and Louis Kahn have also had an influence on buildings around the world.

The following essays explore some specific areas of influence in arts, media, and culture.

In the first essay, Bruno Zevi, Italian art critic and architectural historian, looks at the influence of American architecture and urban planning on the rest of the world. He concentrates on American openness and democracy in urban planning, especially in the work of Frederick Law Olmsted, and on a new architectural language as developed by Frank Lloyd Wright. He also summarizes some recent trends from action architecture to advocacy planning. He concludes that in the matter of exporting and importing culture, the United States' balance of trade is positive "because it stands against the dictatorship of dogma, universal rules, styles, authoritarian principles."

The next essay by Dušan Makavéjev, a Yugoslavian filmmaker, is quite different in form and content. It is almost an autobiographical poem to America on her two hundredth birthday. He recounts the influence of Popeye, Mickey Mouse, Errol Flynn, Snow White, American food, chewing gum, instant coffee and the American Dream, which includes not just hope and freedom, but violence and instant death. "In order to comprehend the energy of American creativity," he writes, "one cannot just stand and stare dumbfounded at the Brooklyn

Bridge. . . . America is the Brooklyn Bridge *plus* the London Bridge transferred and installed in the Arizona desert."

The third essay by Maurice Horn, novelist, playwright, translator and expert on comic strips, describes the influence of American comics especially on France. American comics, he argues, "reached into nearly every home in the Western World and well beyond. . . . No other form (with the possible exception of the movies) holds such fascination and appeal for the general public, and none (with the possible exception of jazz music) is so overwhelmingly American in its expression."

The last essay by Charles Gillett, freelance journalist and expert on popular music, explains the influence of American popular music on British popular music, but he also shows how American music was influenced by many sources, and how the Beatles had a large impact on America. Cultural influence, as all these essays show, is never simple and never flows only in one direction.

NOTE

1. Jeremy Tunstall, *The Media Are American: Anglo-American Media in The World* (New York: Columbia University Press, 1977).

THE INFLUENCE OF AMERICAN ARCHITECTURE AND URBAN PLANNING IN THE WORLD _____

Bruno Zevi

In 1935 the Italian novelist, Mario Soldati, published an account on his two-years stay in the United States: *America Primo Amore*. Much later, in 1959, the book appeared in English with a different title. Instead of *America First Love*, it read *When Hope Was Named America*. The author explained the motive for the change: "Today we no longer go to America. It is America that comes to us."

Does this direction of trade, from the United States abroad, also hold true in architecture and urban planning? It does if we arbitrarily confine the American contribution to skyscrapers and superhighways, and note the spread of high-rise building and concrete ribbons all over Europe, Africa, and Asia. The most significant ideologies and achievements of the last two centuries were exported only partially and often in a distorted form. In fact, for a long time, the United States lacked an efficient foreign policy in urban planning and architecture. Its image undulated in an emotional gamut ranging from mythical dreams to bitter disillusion and resentment.

In recent years, it has been almost the fashion for American intellectuals, many architects included, to warn the rest of the world: please, be careful, do not repeat our mistakes. Such an attitude is generous but somehow abstract, because what the United States does with its cultural heritage is going to affect other countries in a radical way. That is why one cannot be detached and Olympian about the past two hundred years of American architecture. There is a rich patrimony here waiting for full recognition, for the proper vehicle to carry its powerful message. In architectural terms, one could even risk saying: "When hope *is* named America" or, more cautiously, "When hope *might* be named America." The final assessment of United States architecture, 1776-1976, obviously depends on what we are ready, here and abroad, to do with it.

This essay concentrates on three themes: 1) environmental planning versus academic city-planning, 2) the development of a new architectural language emancipated from the Beaux Arts, 3) contemporary research from pop and action-architecture to advocacy planning. Topics one and three mainly concern intentions, trends of thought, experiments and question marks. Topic two, on the contrary, is based on real accomplishments and could have a worldwide impact.

The conclusion may be anticipated by transposing to architecture what Alain Robbe-Grillet wrote a few years ago about literature. He compared the "fossil speech," continuous, unilinear, objective of the great French literature of the first half of the nineteenth century with the character of the nouveau roman, "discontinuous, mobile, aleatory, inclined to define itself as fictitious." He declared, "Bridge and chess have immutable rules. Our play is much freer. The point for us is to invent and destroy our rules with every game." It is not easy to embody such play in architecture and avoid chaos and self-destruction. Yet quite a few ingredients of American culture suggest new approaches toward this purpose. Otherwise, it could well be the end of the play.

ENVIRONMENTAL PLANNING VERSUS
ACADEMIC CITY-PLANNING

Everyone knows that the American attitude toward the traditional notion of "city" has been full of suspicion. The separation between town and country, as it grew from the territorial setup in Europe, was considered obsolete in the United States much earlier than in other countries. From Henry Thoreau to Lewis Mumford the urge for an alternative is clearly expressed, although a new, global option was not found, either here or elsewhere.

Americans felt that a democracy could not expand within the urban structures typical of despotic regimes. Something different had to be invented. Utopian communities from the seventeenth century to the present prove the existence and the resistance, despite many failures, of a counterculture in the field of the human habitat. Relevant factors in the same direction were the philosophies of men like Andrew Jackson Downing and Frederick Law Olmsted. It is not by chance that Olmsted's writings and the numerous books about him are now eagerly read everywhere. They are pregnant with hints that may help to give an answer to the urban crisis.

Landscape architects in the United States were not satisfied with the defense of the countryside beyond the city boundaries nor with saving portions of the city areas from being built on. They looked for a kind of growth that would fuse town and environmental planning. As S. B. Sutton states, Olmsted "tried, above all, to civilize the city; his parks simulated nature in response to the needs of an urban population. He recognized the necessity of extensive planning to provide for logical development of the city as an environment where a man could lead a meaningful life; and he saw the seeds of our contemporary problems and tried to prevent them from germinating. Obviously, the task was too large for one man." Indeed, the park was for him an instrument to free both the city and its architecture from the bondage of uniform, degrading patterns. A few quotations may testify to his vision. "We should undertake nothing in a park which involves the treating of the public as prisoners or wild beasts." Even more significant, "It is a common error to regard a park as something to be produced complete in itself, as a picture to be painted on canvas. It should rather be planned as one to be done in fresco, with constant consideration of exterior objects, some of them quite at a distance and even existing as yet only in the imagination of the painter." In other words, the park system as envisaged by Olmsted, at least in his most genial intuitions, would have been the means to overcome the schism between town and country, to avoid bureaucratic zoning and community segregation. It would have encouraged the birth of a free architecture along the lines inspired by his friendship with Henry H. Richardson. Olmsted said, "Openness is the one thing you cannot get in buildings. Picturesqueness you can get. Let your buildings be as picturesque as your artists can make them. This is the beauty of a town." Yet, probably his idea was that, in the integration of town and country, even buildings could achieve "openness." In any case, as Albert Fein writes, "The public park was one of those rare institutions embodying the spirit of a society: its utopian goals, specific social needs, and forms of expression. . . . The image of an organic whole remained constant in Olmsted's planning and design theory."

Opposed to the Renaissance geometry heavily employed in French gardens, Americans generally adopted English landscaping, but in a more aggressive key that could create a different territorial panorama of human settlements. They looked for a scheme of open spaces which would liberate the town, leave it "unfinished," and guarantee its democratic quality.

This was the "American alternative." It failed for many reasons, partly because it did not find an architecture capable of implementing it. The Chicago school of architecture was deficient in urban vision, and the marriage between its architecture and the landscaping movement did not occur. What is worse, a sensational divorce took place at the Columbian Exposition of 1893, when Olmsted's wonderful landscape was filled with classical and monumental buildings. At this point, landscaping became a subservient discipline, a corrective complement, though sometimes very important, to the traditional city. The environmental battle was largely lost.

Many historians now like to consider the Chicago Exposition of 1893 as a positive or, at least, as an inevitable event. This is not the place to discuss the objections to such an interpretation. No matter how beautiful the "City Beautiful" was, it denied the democratic option hypothesized by American culture at its most original.

The desire for an alternative, however, did not die. It keeps surging forth. It is enough to remember Frank Lloyd Wright's Broadacre City which, for a long time, was judged by the majority of us, historians and critics, as utopian, romantic, nineteenth-century. It came as a real shock when, a few years ago, in an article published in *Architectural Forum*, Jonathan Barnett, Richard Weinstein, and Jaquelin Robertson of the Urban Design Group of the New York Planning Department declared that Wright's thought was applicable even in tackling the problems of a great metropolitan area.

The point of the Broadacre City formulation is not whether you like it or not, but that this kind of development has actually happened, and that we have missed much of the opportunity to give it a rational, ordered form. . . . Jaquelin Robertson was on the American Institute of Architects' National Growth Policy Task Force, and he points out that there is much in their report which was anticipated by Wright more than forty years ago. Broadacre City's fundamental premise is that automobile-based settlement patterns require the total integration of the man-made and natural environment. . . . Wright does not look as impractically romantic today as the planners who expected Americans to put their cars away and settle in tightly organized communitties along the pattern of the English village. . . .Wright's ideas of 1932 are also timely in other ways. If you read *The Disappearing City*, you will be surprised by how much of it would sound very up to date if it appeared, say, in the Sunday magazine section of the *New York Times*. If there is such a thing as a "counter-culture," and if its denizens ever bothered to read anything, they would find Wright's outlook very congenial.

Identifying the impact of modern mass communications on urban decentralization and preaching the continuity of building and landscape, Wright also was seeking an American alternative to the European city and to suburban sprawl. As Norris Kelly Smith has shown in his excellent essay, *A Study in Architectural Content*, not even Wright was totally hostile to the city; otherwise he would not have designed a symbolic mile-high tripod for Chicago. In 1931 he had warned, "You must choose between the car and the elevator. I choose the car." Later he also tried the elevator, proposing that even a few megastructures of such gigantic dimensions would save the land, even if in a different, and in part contradictory, way than Broadacre. Both solutions aimed to avoid an urban catastrophe.

Among the many other contributions of American planners from the pioneers' time to the most recent research are examples of a rich and articulated philosophy as revealed in Los Angeles and Manhattan, in the greenbelts, in the preservation of historical sections of towns, and in the various theories on conurbation.

The outcome of this philosophy cannot be foreseen. However, the drive toward an "American alternative," a democratic human habitat on the land, is still strong and imaginative today, as many current experiments in United States cities and university investigations show. In Europe, too, we are striving for new processes in environmental design, for a new concept of "city-region" or "city-territory." In solving this enigma, American tradition is stimulating and inspiring.

THE DEVELOPMENT OF A NEW ARCHITECTURAL LANGUAGE

The essential fact about Frank Lloyd Wright is not that he was one of the greatest architectural geniuses of all times, but that he elaborated the instruments for a new democratic language to replace the Beaux Arts authoritarian precepts. This new language was not fully codified, however, and its effects consequently have been limited, failing to produce the general impact that it should have. It is almost a paradox: we possess a new language, ready to be used by everyone, to be "written" by architects and builders, to be "read" by art historians and critics, and to be "spoken" by the public. Yet, without a code, it does not achieve its full potential of communication.

The reason why Wright was able to create a new language is well known. He refused to have a Beaux Arts education, and thus he had no need to fight against it as his predecessors, Richardson and Sullivan, did with much effort and without complete success. Being free from academic slavery, he could adopt the valid parameters of the nineteenth-century architectural revolution: the new engineering; the arts-and-crafts movement of William Morris; Art Nouveau. He synthesized them in a different key (remember his famous lecture of 1902, "The Arts and Crafts of the Machine"), enriched by the merging of Western and Eastern cultures.

That Wright was the matrix of this new language is testified to by H. P. Berlage, Mies van der Rohe, J. J. P. Oud, Erich Mendelsohn and practically all leaders of modern architecture, with the obvious exception of Le Corbusier. The "De Stijl" group in Holland would be inconceivable without Wright and his passionate disciple, Robert van't Hoff. The same is true for much of the German cycle up to 1933, notably such personalities as Hugo Häring and Hans Scharoun. It is particularly significant that openly contrasting currents had a common inspiration in Wright: the "Amsterdam School": its antagonist, "De Stijl"; Expressionists; Functionalists. So vast was the range of Wright's language that each one could delve into it or refer to it. Even Le Corbusier, without admitting it, followed a "Wrightian" path in the Chapelle de Ronchamp and subsequent works, when he understood that architecture is not only *le jeu savant des volumes assemblés sous la lumière* but, above all, the creation of spaces.

Why is it that a language was not derived from Wright, while we had so many Mannerist trends based on Le Corbusier, Gropius, and Mies? Mannerism implies the mistrust of stylistic rules and usually needs models to betray, "orders" to scorn. Wright is the antirule. He cannot be imitated, and he does not allow "exceptions" to the rules, simply because they are not there. Such a phenomenon is not unique in history. In some measure, Michelangelo as architect and Borromini—who were figures similar to Wright—created new languages which were not codified. Their influence, too, was very limited. Both were considered geniuses, almost superhuman artists, to be dutifully celebrated for a time, but to be shelved in the Valhalla of heroes and forgotten as soon as feasible. Classicism prevailed again and, being the language of power, accepted only a few signs from Michelangelo's and Borromini's architecture, for use in a grotesque or decorative sense. Something analogous seems to be happening to Wright. So the greatest contribution of American architecture to the world runs the risk of becoming unfruitful.

This problem was discussed in a symposium organized by Frederick Gutheim in 1975 for an *Architectural Record* publication. A summary follows of the seven basic "invariants" or constant antirules stemming from Wright's most original messages.

The first invariant could be called a "list or inventory of contents and functions." It means "no" to all conventions, habits, and readymade phrases; to all esthetic taboos such as classical proportion, rhythm, balance; to all preconceived grammars and syntaxes; to all dogmas about modular repetition. This is the fundamental principle that Wright derived from the preaching of Morris and from American vernaculars: an architecture descriptive of its human requirements, without any concern for a synthesis either a priori or a posteriori. It implies "zero degree" in architectural writing, de-structuring of all the Greek, Roman, Medieval, Renaissance, Baroque, and Enlightenment canons. De-structuring—in order to rediscover what is specific in every element, be it a window, a door, a room, a community, and in order to disregard the notion of "series" of windows, of equilibrium between planes and voids, of symmetry. Even for Wright it took a lot of time to arrive at this "zero degree," but he achieved it on every scale, from the small Prairie house to Falling Water. This approach is perhaps the only one that can save architecture from perpetual oscillation between classicism and Mannerism, between rules and exceptions to the rules. It is a language which reinvents its own rules at every phase.

Dissonance is the second invariant, fully instrumental in expressing the diversity of contents categorized by the list or inventory. Classicism is based on uniformity, assonance, repetition, symmetry. It cannot admit that each opening, each room, each house may be radically different from all others. because lights, shapes, and spaces have to be different. The modern language, on the contrary, exalts dissonances. It appropriates the musical lesson of Arnold Schönberg, who stated clearly that the problem was not to admit a few derogations from academic rules, but to establish the exception as a rule. From Art Nouveau to the Bauhaus, dissonances offered the method to avoid falling back on classicism. Yet, whereas in Europe and generally in the so-called "International Style" they were often used for their own sake, producing new formalisms (more vital, however, than the old ones), in Wright dissonances are always strictly bound to a creative interpretation of contents and functions.

Antiperspective tridimensionality is the third invariant. Meaning the elimination of a privileged viewpoint, the moving of the observer around, above, under, and inside the architectural object, the vanishing of facades and especially of the hierarchy of facades, tridimensionality is attributed to Cubism's influence on architecture. However, while Cubism to achieve this objective destroyed the building mass, Expressionism obtained an anti-perspective, anti-Renaissance tridimensionality without renouncing the dynamic impulses provided by materials. Wright, as we have seen, inspired both the cubist and the expressionist architects, yet never reduced the building envelope to cardboard and never accepted the hysterical laceration of materials as if they were in a permanent state of incandescence. Now, many contemporary architects are tired of Cubism, and many of Expressionism, yet some are going back to Expressionism and others to Cubism. Only a very few, in their best works, seem to have grasped the complex operation conducted by Wright.

Four-dimensional decomposition is the invariant that the "De Stijl" group took from Wright, and forms the substratum of Mies van der Rohe's European work. Though being the most serious attempt to give modern architecture a grammar and a syntax, again it was an intellectual reduction of Wright's language. It argued that, in order to negate Renaissance tridimensionality, there was no better escape than to go back to the two-dimensional, by breaking the building mass into slabs and reassembling them in such a way that they could never reproduce the box. A code of mere slabs, however, is the denial of the structure and the tactile nature of materials. It is a unilateral interpretation of Wright's comprehensive approach, which could destroy the box four-dimensionally without giving up the third dimension.

Cantilever, shell, and membrane structures. This is the engineering invariant acknowledged by every architect, but rarely integrated into architecture, at least not in normal building. The schism between structure and envelope, a dichotomy between bones and skin, is largely persistent. Wright's effort was directed at involving all architectural elements in the structural fabric, preventing the tremendous waste usually seen in construction. He did not always succeed, but this was his aim that later technologies were to implement and enrich.

Temporalizing space. Of the seven invariants, this is the most typically "Wrightian." The Taliesin master worked with space from the very start. Space not to be contemplated as an abstraction, but to be lived in; space as the real receptacle of contents and functions, therefore a dynamic space; cavities which are no longer the void boxed in, where man feels extraneous, but shaped to his movements and his repose, made for work and recreation, for existential light and shadow. As Norris Kelly Smith saw, Wright rejected not only the static space of classicism, but also the compromise between the Biblical conception of time and the Greco-Roman spatial concept. He adopted the spiral in the Guggenheim Museum as Borromini had in Sant'Ivo alla Sapienza, but again on a human, not only on a symbolic, level.

The last invariant concerns building/town/landscape/territory reintegration or continuity. It means open scenery, ready to absorb and be contaminated by its surroundings, rather than isolated objects. It is related to Einstein's theory of "field."

The object of the *Architectural Record* symposium was to submit the viability of transforming Wright's language into a popular idiom. His work has been a turning point, the major contribution to architecture produced in American history. This, however, is not enough. If we relegate his genius to a pedestal, removed from the daily life of common man, if we consider him like a god to be worshipped by a small minority and set aside by the rest of us, we would do a disservice to the progress of architecture. One may detest Wright as a personality, find him egotistical, self-centered, narcissistic, or whatever you want. One may dislike many of his buildings and judge the Guggenheim awful. That is not the issue. If we want to develop a free mode of architectural communication, a language is indispensable. Wright's code is not the final word, based as it is on antirules and not on "orders," on seven "noes" to all kinds of imposition. It is a starting point, like Schönberg's dodecaphony, a springboard with an even greater potential of liberation for new adventures. Yet, if we ignore it, the risk is regression, almost a hara-kiri. This, too, may be fun, but why?

CONTEMPORARY RESEARCH, FROM POP AND ACTION-
ARCHECTURE TO ADVOCACY PLANNING

Since the end of World War II, American art has become a dominant factor in international culture. In architecture, as we have seen, it was a fundamental guideline at least from 1910 on, but great stimuli have sprung from the United States in recent years, often reorienting architectural trends abroad. Louis Kahn was "a hero" in Italy, just as in India and Japan, although the classical interpretation that many critics give his work—static spaces instead of fluidity, monumental accents, Beaux Arts connotations—arouses doubts and suspicions, making his hypnotic prophecies more illuminating than some of his later buildings.

The most significant artistic messages from the United States in the recent decades can be briefly indicated, keeping in mind that no list could be complete:

• Jackson Pollock. His paintings may be seen as a sort of landscape/townscape, quite different from the geometric methods and procedures of Mondrian, Léger and other abstract artists. His "dripping" technique seems to suggest a flowing urbanization. For what we are seeking in the way of a new habitat, isn't there a metaphor in his "aerial views"?

• Pop-art. This was perhaps the most provocative of the various pronouncements. It really changed our perception of urban and rural scenery, revealing the esthetic value of the ugly, of the derelict, of the functionally useless, thereby determining a radical turn in the attitudes of planners and architects in regard to the polyphonic cacophony that is beyond their control. Many felt, with Robert Rauschenberg, that "art is not enough and life is not enough"; our real task is not to compensate life with art, but to "fill the gap" between the two. All that had been excluded from architecture—barriadas and favelas, bidonvilles, barracks, slums and so on—became essential subjects to be studied. The "architecture of democracy" was sometimes identified with what, up to that time, had not been considered architecture at all. In the Vancouver Conference on Habitat, promoted by the United Nations, the competition for squatters was perhaps the preeminent initiative.

• Anonymous building. Many events preceded, accompanied, and followed the pop-art currents. Notable among them was Douglas Haskel's *Architecture and Popular Taste* of 1958, in which he attacked the critics' position on the so-called dreary, corrupt, hopeless environment that he saw as the symptom of a new "era of mass consumption," the triumph of the common man and of "democratic wilderness." Then there was Robert Venturi's and Denise Scott Brown's passionate and extremely acute revaluation of the signs and symbols of commercial vernacular and ordinary building. The slogan "Las Vegas is to the strip what Rome was to the piazza" had a tremendous reverberation in countries like Italy, since Rome itself is made up not only of piazzas, but mainly of magmatic suburbs whose existential value can be grasped better through Las Vegas's binoculars than through the telescope of Renaissance and Baroque ideologies. Of course, Bernard Rudofsky was decisive in a parallel line, with his *Architecture Without Architects* and other books. This kind of research did not always originate in the United States. It imported elements from abroad, especially from Great Britain, but here it reached an intensity unknown elsewhere. Moreover, intellectual issues suddenly became a challenge for action. Jane Jacobs' *The Death and Life of Great American Cities* should not be forgotten even in such a rapid inventory. Indeed, the Architectural Heritage Year of 1975 in Europe could be interpreted as a version of the crusade conducted in the United States; and in our countries we have the obstacle of conservative groups always ready to defend a monument or a medieval hill town, but not to recognize the meaning of a slum or of a squatter village.

• Advocacy planning, in all its heterogeneous manifestations, was an explosive incentive in the discovery of "subcultures," in the struggle for assuring the freedom of the user to manipulate his own environment, against "professional imperialism." This populist movement had the effect of an earthquake on architects and students. The United States has exported the ever-expanding idea of a behavioral revolution in the relationship between architects and people. Despite the limits and exaggerations of its methodology, advocacy planning has infused new blood into a culture that was progressively becoming elitist and sterile.

There can be one reservation about these messages. Too often they present themselves not as natural prolongations and enrichments of the modern movement, but in opposition to its so-called "functionalist dogmas" and "universal norms." They indict the whole modern movement instead of the Esperanto-like, classical, pseudomodern, boxy character of most contemporary building, which is in fact the antithesis of what the masters, from Wright and Mendelsohn to Le Corbusier and Aalto, stood for. The populists tend to deny the past on which their own conquests rest, in order to start all over again, rejecting the new architectural language, our only medium of communication. This risk should perhaps be mentioned: some avant-garde architects, instead of exploring and popularizing the modern language, are sometimes going back to reactionary idioms.

That is why it is essential to evaluate the pertinence of American-built architecture, now excessively overshadowed by the sparkling hypotheses of the counterculture movements.

Most of the American quality production which influenced the world during the last decades may perhaps be defined as Mannerist, in the most positive sense of this term. The continuity of the modern movement and its developments from the 1930s, 1940s, and 1950s has been due to the Mannerists who sought a meeting ground among Wright, Le Corbusier, Mies, and Aalto, though it is rather melancholy that Wright did not receive the attention deserved by his stature. In general, three Mannerist streams may be distinguished:

• The first is similar to the historical Mannerism of the sixteenth century: a conceptual reflection on the work of the masters and of their initial progeny, like Giuseppe Terragni or Rudolf Michael Schindler. The "five architects" of New York have given the most coherent expression of this approach, and their resonance needs no comment. Their virtue rests on the fact that they defend architecture as a discipline and continue to refine the new language, even without trying to make it popular. They are not ready to abdicate and to abandon our modern heritage.

• The second, which frequently uses Louis Kahn as an alibi, is less clear in its intentions, because apparently it seems willing to rebuild a sort of classicism in order to have something solid to rebel against. Such a process is obviously dangerous since the modern movement is essentially anti-classical and to force it into academic schemata is an equivocal operation. In this context, the exhibition of the Ecole des Beaux Arts at the Museum of Modern Art in New York had consequences remote from the aims of its promoters, if not opposite to their goals. Many architects and critics interpreted this show as a declaration of bankruptcy of the modern movement and as an invitation to go back to classical architecture, emblematic of political and social authoritarianism. Fortunately, this attempt at revivalism has been dismissed also by the best followers of the Philadelphia school.

• The third Mannerist stream is active and expansive. It is not satisfied to reflect on the lessons of the masters and, in general, rejects any deal with classical theories. It wants to go forward. From the late Eero Saarinen to Paul Rudolph and Charles Moore, to mention a few of the dozens if not hundreds of names one could cite, this kind of Mannerism has been fertile, extrovert, pragmatic, unworried about making mistakes, and thus able to correct them. From California to New England, it has been experimenting with new ways, demonstrating that the modern movement may be going through a neurotic and perhaps even a psychotic period, but this is because it is alive and conscious of the many problems we have to face.

"Action-architecture" is probably still the most comprehensive statement of the United States message today. As G. M. Kallmann stated, "The revolt is directed not so much against the fundamentals of the modern movement as against more recent shallowness and abuses." The search is for "a harsher esthetic than that of the present modish eclecticism," for "transcending the single finite form, self-enclosed and raised to universal significance," for interrelating buildings "in a complex scene" so that they appear "as mere passages in the unending game of space around them"; for fluid images which revive "the aspirations of the early expressionists and futurists" (and one might add also of the Russian constructivists) "now reinforced by the acquisition of mathematical and topological mastery;" for a radical architecture with gestures "which are permitted to develop maximum impact without censoring limitations"; for "shock therapy in galvanizing architecture out of its lethargy"—a striving "for confirmation of identity and existence to counter the modern fear of nothingness."

Many of the impulses of "action-architecture" were nurtured by foreign experiences, British Brutalism in particular, or by the visual arts. In the United States, however, they maintain in spite of their ups and downs a permanent vitality. Another architect worth quoting is John Johansen, especially for his philosophy as it is incarnated in the Mummers Theater of Oklahoma City, one of the buildings most discussed by architectural students abroad. "The Beaux Arts is still very much with us, whether classically geometric or romantically amorphous," he complains; "formalism, centrality, ordered sequence and individuation of building design cannot deal with the demands that urban problems are now making upon the profession." Pleading for "permutational and open-ended programming, indeterminacy in which structures may not look the same from year to year, life-generated assemblages, components with subcomponents attached and then connected by circuiting systems," Johansen stands for "surprise, unexpected juxtaposition, superimposition, crowding, segregation and confrontation of elements which accommodate the human movement patterns." In his opinion, "the concern is that of reality, immediacy" with unpredictable final appearance. "Facets, not facades result in bombardment of composite images," because "multiple simultaneous station-points" are outmoding "not only the axially fixed station-point of the Renaissance," but also "the moving station-point of Siegfried Giedion's space-time." Hence, "the relationship is organizational, not formal. Slang, not eloquence, is foremost."

The analogy between this kind of architecture and the new literature proposed by Robbe-Grillet is quite evident. The players' rules cannot be static, they have to change with every game. Isn't this the most profound and ironic lesson to be derived from two hundred years of American architecture?

Many items of equal if not greater importance have been omitted here. The impact of America's architectural history cannot be summarized in a few pages. Yet, from selecting three subjects—environmental planning versus city planning, the new architectural language, and contemporary research, from pop and action-architecture to advocacy planning—one conclusion emerges. The United States imported all the goods that could be brought in from the West and the East, but its balance of trade is positive, because it stands against the dictatorship of dogmas, universal rules, styles, and authoritarian principles.

We are now living in the era of "de-": de-planning, de-technology, de-architecturization, de-nigration of the modern movement. It is a chaotic, amusing experience, profitable even in its masochistic aspects. When the epoch of "re-" surfaces again, urging for a new re-integration, we will be able to rely upon a consistent American culture, centered on Frank Lloyd Wright. The leap will then appear even greater. How many nations have made more of a difference in the last two centuries? Truly, we might go back to the Italian account of 1935 and say, even about United States architecture today: *America primo amore.*

NIKOLA TESLA RADIATED A BLUE LIGHT _____

Dušan Makavéjev

APPLIED OPTIMISM

Mobil's series of TV commercials on the theme "The Spirit of America Is the Spirit of Achievement" (excellent both in concept and realization) is an example of Applied Optimism in the best tradition of Steichen's *Family of Man*.

I am suspicious toward the subjects of Optimism, Health, and Patriotism. Happy Birthday.

But this hag is two hundred years old, and still so lovely.

Eternal youth.

It's good you squeezed out those boils. The clean face *is* important. Scars are less ugly than those red greenish carbuncles.

Here's mud in your eye.

The Chinese are said to count years backwards: you always have the number of years *remaining* to you, not the number of years you have *spent*. At birth, you are seventy-five; afterwards your years diminish. After seventy-five you show clear profit.

In big Japanese department stores one can buy one's own gravestone and the complete funeral ceremony—on the installment plan.

In the Soviet Union, great importance is attached to the place one is going to be buried in: in the walls of the Kremlin or in some ordinary cemetery.

Is the burial in the ground ecologically healthier than the cremation?

I'd like to be useful to the end. If you wish to be active even after death, donate your blood and organs to appropriate banks. Bequeath your skeleton to a university. Your heart will tick on in someone's chest. Your eyes will watch movies. Your kidneys will produce someone's urine.

Ah, these birthdays, they always inspire melancholy thoughts!

How did you achieve this freshness? A Triumph of Will? Don't be indecent.

Things are not what they seem to you. Not by a long shot.

Everything's much worse and much better than it seems.

I like what you said about eyes. Is it really feasible? I don't mind dying if I'll be able to go on watching movies.

Isn't it dangerous to allow great nations to think about themselves constructively and positively, without self-irony?

But, anyhow, they have no intention of asking for anyone's permission.

The story about the elephant in the china shop. Who cares about china anymore? It's pure Buster Keaton, a merry chaos.

Ask children: do they want small porcelain figurines forever or a five-minute ride on the elephant's back?

The elephant who wanted to stamp out a mosquito eventually came out as that mouse who wanted to fuck a cow.

The Principle of Socialist Realism: speak about Positive Hero, Reflect Reality (but recognizing the elements of Future in it).

Comparing most popular Russian and American films we shall easily ascertain that Hollywood is much better at understanding and realizing the Principles of Socialist Realism.

Popeye the Sailor influenced me positively, and, already in my fourth decade, I still inordinately love spinach.

Among the animals, I like mice best. In every mouse hides the Spirit of Mickey Mouse.

AMBIVALENT MEMORIES

I was five years old. My uncle Steva took me to the movies. Mickey, Goofy, Horatio, Clarabelle and Company formed an orchestra. They started playing and then a terrible wind, a storm, came. They flew in all directions, still playing. That was irresistible.

The audience giggled and I was choking with laughter. Then horror began. Something was leaking down my leg, wet and warm, a puddle was spreading. Luckily, it was noisy in the cinema and people around me didn't notice anything.

Out of the enthusiasm I have wet myself. Oh, shame! Uncle Steva took me out in a hurry.

My mother is seventy-two and she still likes telling how I was as curly as Shirley Temple—forty years ago.

Around my eighth year, after seeing *Robin Hood*, I believed I was in love with Olivia de Haviland. In fact, I wanted to be like Errol Flynn. That is to say, I wanted to be like Robin Hood.

Then *Young Tom Edison* came and I wanted to publish my own newspaper; that is, I wanted to be like Mickey Rooney; that is, like Tom Edison; that is, like Andy Hardy.

A novel entitled *Chicago* was coming out in the form of Tuesday and Friday booklets. In it, a mad scientist had invented a matter called "crystalopyr," which reflected sun rays in such a way that, on one side, everything turned into ice, while everything burned on the other. A crystalopyr plane was in production; the destruction of the world was in preparation.

A year later, at 6:00 A.M. on 6 April 1941, German incendiary bombs made the prophecy of *Chicago* come true and burned 30 percent of Belgrade. Twenty thousand inhabitants of Belgrade died on that day, before breakfast, as Fodor's *Guide* puts it. The town was turned into congeries of dolls' houses—houses without fronts disclosed intact apartments, dining rooms with chandeliers, dentists' offices.

German occupation began. My school was taken to see *Snow White and the Seven Dwarfs.* Snow White and the dwarfs spoke German. According to German custom, the film was dubbed in their language. We were offended.

Easter of 1944 was a beautiful, sunny day. Humming came from the sky, the squadrons of Liberators sparkled. People waved at them, happy with the near end of the war. Bombs started to thunder and raise dust. A maternity clinic in our neighborhood was hit. Babies were found in the treetops. There were thousands of dead civilians, but everybody was still glad to see the Allied planes.

The liberation came, Tito's partisans and the Red Army. Roosevelt died. New People's Power proclaimed a three-day national mourning. Cinemas were closed. There was no music in restaurants. For three days flags fluttered at half-mast. I wondered: have they buried him in his wheelchair?

People were overjoyed with American food packages (we had not seen chocolate for four years). However, one item caused consternation and general mockery—pork in the apple sauce. If you are truly interested in "the absence of the United States influence," here it is: my people will *never* taste such muck as pork in the apple sauce.

What is the magic of chewing gum?

For months on end we ate powdered eggs (there were barrels and barrels of them). Everybody called this food "Truman's balls" (in our language we have the same word for "balls" and "eggs").

Twenty years later a Belgrade youth weekly, *Mladost*, conducted polls trying to find out who were heroes of contemporary youth. At the top of the list: Ché Guevara and John F. Kennedy.

Late sixties. The policy of open frontiers. With a Yugoslavian passport you can travel to over fifty countries—without a visa.

The foreign influences become more complex every day.

Young playboy and criminal Milan Milosević (one of the legion of adventurers who went into the world after running around with American crews making films in Belgrade) was found dead in the bathroom of Mickey Rooney's Hollywood house.

In a nice casket his body reaches Belgrade airport, expenses paid by Alain
Delon. It is met by dozens of hysterical teenage girls.

Milosević's mother tells all about her son, in a weekly magazine series.

Among other things, she produces a morbid detail: a few months later
("around Christmas," says Mom), Delon sent his friend's mother a plastic
bag with Milan's intestines, taken out during the embalming.

I live in Belgrade, at the corner of Lenin Boulevard and John F. Kennedy
Street.

My mother-in-law lives on Charlie Chaplin Street.

Late sixties. Godard uses the following metaphors: "Walt Disney and
blood," "the children of Marx and Coca-Cola."

In my last film, *Sweet Movie*, lovers make love in sugar; it ends in
murder. Blood mixes with sugar (during the shooting we called this scene
"jam session"). I had in mind a scene from Resnais's *Hiroshima, Mon
Amour* with lovers plastered with sand. The effect was very sensual—and
unpleasant. I strived to make it pleasant.

Has this scene also been fathered by a need to "surpass" (or interpret) the
ambivalence of the image-concept "Disney-blood"?

"DRANG NACH WESTERN" AND DANGERS
OF LINEAR THINKING

"To catch up and overtake America"—Stalin. In early and innocent
days of my school activism, we read in Stalin what a Communist should be.
He should display, says Uncle Joe, the combination of Bolshevik persistency
and American practicability.

America served as a model both to Russian futurists and Lenin.

"To catch up and overtake America" is a fatal slogan. We already know
from the ancient Greeks that even a rabbit cannot overtake a turtle. I know
that many of my American friends do not enjoy having to run so much. I
guess they were told as children: "Run so that nobody can overtake us."

I like Instant Coffee and Instant Soup.

When Instant Death was introduced, in 1945, as applied in Hiroshima
and Nagasaki, I caught myself, a thirteen-year-old boy, in a dilemma: I liked
it very much, although I knew it wasn't nice that I liked it. Then everybody
got Instant Excuse: Instant Death has brought Instant End of War.

Instant Beginning and Instant End.

The production of Absolute Happiness comes next. It is curious that this
concept (the guided creation of generations of completely happy human be-
ings) did not appear in Pavlov-oriented Soviet psychology, but at Harvard,
with B. F. Skinner.

Where does it come from, this striving of America to make other nations
happy—against their will?

The last three big wars were conducted by the United States of America in Asia: Japan, Korea, Vietnam. Did the first really bring the absolute victory? Did the second really secure the status quo? Why does America—with so much pain and confusion—refuse to recognize traces of the American Revolution and the Declaration of Independence in the establishment of the national identities of Vietnam and Cuba?

For years, the humiliated and offended, the heretics and dreamers, the hungry and those who "think differently" thronged to the West, to America. From the East Coast to the Rockies and beyond, there was always—more West. After World War II, this "Dang nach Western" has brought the Americans to the Far East.

We are scared by the discovery that the Far Westerners are identical with the Far Easterners and that they reject, "against their best interest," our concepts of time, history, nature, civilization, as well as our sadomasochistic-Christian concept of life, the best (and only) in the world.

Czech humorist Jaroslav Hasek has a group of people meeting every day in a beerhouse somewhere.

There, in the beerhouse, they found "The Party of the Moderate Progress Within the Law."

The American could be considered members of "The Party of Immoderate Progress Outside Any Law."

THE FACTORY OF UNIVERSAL DREAMS

Hollywood.

The national pride of Yugoslavs: Slavko Vorkapick, Carl Malden, Peter Bogdanovich.

Another contribution of our national genius to Hollywood: *Vampir*, the only Serbian word that has entered all the languages of the world.

Vampire (F, fr. G *vampir*, of Slav origin; akin to Serb. *vampir* vampire, Russ. *upyr*) 1: a bloodsucking ghost or reanimated body of a dead person believed to come from the grave and wander about by night sucking the blood of persons asleep, causing their death. [*Webster's Third New International Dictionary*]

A real vampire: the biggest living World War II war criminal, Andrija Artuković, the creator of the well-known extermination camp Jasenovac (Croatia, Yugoslavia), personally responsible for the execution of 500,000 Serbians, Jews, and Gypsies, lives scot-free, in Los Angeles.

On the occasion of America's two-hundredth birthday, David Robinson writes about the American Cinema as the Universal Dream.

In fact, the everyday life of America—in its paradisaical aspects of Freedom and Affluence, in its infernal aspects of Freedom of Sin, Greed and Lust, with its bursting of all dams preventing Orgy of Desires— represents the wide-open playground of the Universal Dream. All practical operations (economic, social, cultural, and private) are performed in the oil of the Universal Dream, providing everything with dampening and acceleration.

A fascinating situation: a TV commentator blows out his brains on camera. After this, I cannot watch TV news in America, without hoping, in some dark corner of my soul, that maybe now this commentator I am seeing and hearing . . .

In America there is no shame of desires. Already a half-a-century ago, Europe had scientifically ascertained the immorality of desires, but it still retains the repression of desires. Legitimacy of desires in America makes it possible to use them as fuel.

ENERGY

Does America know certain secrets of mobilizing human energies which are unfathomable to the rest of the world?

Discontinuity?

A self-mocking Serbian story from World War I. At the time of the Saloniki front, a child is drowning in the harbor of Saloniki.

A crowd watches from the shore.

Suddenly, a heroic Serbian soldier is in the water. He saves the child and reaps the applause of the spectators.

Afterwards, on the shore, someone overhears him, swearing: "If I get my hands on the motherfucker who pushed me in!"

Has not the whole of America come into being by a sort of voluntary "Who-Pushed-Me-In" technique? Millions swam across the ocean and, once on the other shore, went on living as best as they could.

They were applauded from the ancient shore.

To bring oneself to the point of no return.

Starting from zero.

The national income of Bangladesh is $70 a year per inhabitant; of Yugoslavia—$1,060; of the United States of America—$7,020.

But still everybody behaves as if starting from zero. Although American "zero" is $7,020.

The childhood dream of Nikola Tesla, in a deep province of the Austro-Hungarian Empire (today: Lika, Croatia, Yugoslavia), was to go to America and install a gigantic wheel at Niagara Falls which would produce unheard-of quantities of energy.

In 1884 Nikola Tesla, at twenty-eight, comes out from the immigration office in Castle Garden, Manhattan, with four cents in his pocket. He works as an electrician, digs holes for two dollars a day, founds Tesla Electric Company, and creates the polyphase system of alternating current.

At the same time, Edison and John Pierpont Morgan work steadfastly on the development of the direct-current system. Edison's direct current has a maximum reach of a one-mile distance from the power station.

According to some stories, Edison and Morgan go around New York killing chickens with the alternating current in order to prove how dangerous it is. In 1888, with a million dollar check, George Westinghouse buys forty patents from Tesla—the complete system. Using the alternating-current system, Tesla illuminates, on Westinghouse's behalf, the whole 1893 World Columbian Exposition in Chicago. Westinghouse obtains the contract to build the Niagara power station. In 1896 Buffalo is illuminated by the alternating current, coming from Niagara, twenty-two miles away.

Soon the whole of America is covered with pylons—the cheap energy can be obtained, like water, out of the wall, in every house.

Teslsa's ultimate dreams were wireless transmission of the electric energy, a system of interplanetary communication, and radio contact with the cosmos. In 1899, in Colorado Springs, he lit two hundred bulbs, without the use of wires, from a twenty-five mile distance. He also produced man-made lightning flashes.

It was a poor eighty-year-old man who, in the early 1940s, fed pigeons every day in front of the New York Plaza Hotel and led a lonely life with a female pigeon at the Waldorf Astoria.

Seventy years earlier, he was a young man who had visions and nightmares, who got attacks of nausea at the sight of a peach, who went beserk at the sight of pearls, and became ecstatic when faced with even, smooth surfaces or sparkling crystals, and who could not work with numbers not divisible by three.

He claimed that in moments of heightened creativity he was radiating a blue light.

In 1968 *Life* magazine published a cover photo of an astronaut on the moon. Gary Burnstein (Ph.D. in psychology, a passionate researcher of Nikola Tesla and Wilhelm Reich) drew my attention to the blue halo around the astronaut in the atmosphereless moonscape.

The experts convinced themselves that this blue halo was caused by some fault in the film's negative.

Already, back in 1934, Reich had explained to Erik Erikson that all living creatures radiate a blue light. Erikson did not believe him. Reich invited Erikson—it was in Denmark, during the summer vacation—to observe with him couples making love on the beach, in darkness. He asserted that the blue radiation, which becomes more intense during the sexual act, can be observed by the naked eye. Since then, Erikson considered Reich mad.

Many others considered Reich mad at the time of his death in Lewisburg Prison, Pennsylvania, in 1956.

In the early 1950s Reich was trying to draw public attention to poisonous masses of static air hovering over cities, like black clouds. A few years after his death, people started talking about the struggle against the pollution of the atmosphere and about black masses of static air.

It is quite superfluous to speak about the freedom in America in Old European terms of freedom as democracy.

In regard to freedom of information—"free circulation of men and ideas," and legal security of the individual—America is a few shades freer than the most progressive European democracies. This freedom, however, represents just a tiny part of American freedom, if we speak of Freedom being understood as the radiation and chain reaction of Human Energy.

The Old Europe spends enormous energies defending itself from the "abuses of freedom": "public disorder," "chaos," "bad taste," "immorality," "nonsense," "stupidity."

Public and private life of the people in the European democracies is cut by a series of gashes of invisible censorships.

In order to comprehend the energy of American creativity one cannot just stand and stare dumbfounded at the Brooklyn Bridge, as did Mayakovsky, who wrote an ode to the Brooklyn Bridge as a marvel of modern technology. America is the Brooklyn Bridge *plus* the London Bridge transferred and installed in the Arizona desert.

The freedom of physical and spiritual risk should be measured on the frontiers where that risk turns into failure, self-destruction, madness, nonsense, game. These are the Open Frontiers of America.

If the elegance and functionalism of the Hoover Dam are America's response to the perfection of Mona Lisa's smile, let us talk then about the end of Western Civilization.

The monstrous beauty and uselessness of San Simeon represent the moment in which the stupidity of shameless richness explodes into a new formula, according to which it is allowed to turn everything upside down in order to start from scratch.

The secret of the fascinating and "inhuman" qualities of Manhattan, which are stubbornly conserved and regenerated, consists in the chaos which *stubbornly refuses to be ordered* and thereby keeps open all roads towards the permanent creation of new beginnings.

The freedom of risk is paid in blood and enjoyment of life, which is nothing else but a healthy nonsense.

Perhaps we are dealing with a machinery that has a built-in acceleration mechanism, while someone forgot to install a brake?

That remains to be seen.

During the past two hundred years, greedy pioneer-America brought over from Black Africa a multimillion Gulag of unpaid slaves. Now, at the center of the beginning of America's new identity, there is a living reservoir of beautiful and dangerous Black energy which will bring new beginnings. Or new ends.

Like so many other centers, radiating still-invisible blue rays.

DISCOVERY OF MAN ON THE MOON

It was the night between 20 and 21 August 1969 on the open Atlantic.

Bojana and I were on our way back from America to Europe, on the Italian ocean liner *Rafaele*.

Two days earlier, apart from the sea, there was nothing around us. I was waiting for the Azores to appear, on account of Mayakovsky.

The Azores duly appeared and stately sailed past us, on their way to America.

"And life will pass by, like the Azores did."

It seemed as if we were sailing through the lines of Great Vladimir. He did not sail out of this life like a tame, lazy island; he blew out his brain with a revolver bullet. But that's another story.

That evening in the ship's cinema we saw Toshiro Mifune and Lee Marvin in Boorman's *Hell in the Pacific*. It was strange, it was a good prelude to what was going to happen to us that night.

In the middle of the ocean—a ship, a cinema in the ship, in the cinema—was an ocean, but not this ocean, the *other* ocean, at the antipodes.

Nobody slept that night.

All of the ship's drawing rooms were full of people, in semidarkness and silence. Everybody was watching Armstrong and Aldrin, the first steps of the men on the Moon.

It all came in poetically smudged video-images, like Norman MacLaren's *Pas de deux*. Our compatriots, the earthlings, did not walk. It was more like hopping and floating in the no-atmosphere of the Moon. It was more like that time when we were fish, than when we ventured on our first steps, being a one year old.

It was very solemn, that TV watching, and it went on for hours. This was not watching, but *being present*, accompanied by the awareness that at the same moment hundreds of millions of other men, maybe even a billion of them, were doing the same thing.

In that act of mass baptism, we were becoming, all together, compatriots—earthlings, soaked in the highly primitive emotion, the feeling that we, the men of the Earth, have set out on a new journey. Sitting by a TV set on that night meant the approval of that risk, acceptance of all new worries and perils, readiness to be surprised: we were off, come what may.

State and national frontiers were ajar, slackened. All together, we were following the Earth Team, not the American Team. (The term "Race with Russians" retains a sense only in the dumb linear logic of people still believing that the earth is flat, still seeing the world from "here" to "there." What "race" is possible, once you start *in all directions*?).

Later, the coming-out of the astronauts from the spacecraft and their walking-floating in Space showed even more obviously—with that so-prominent umbilical cord—that we were faced with a *dramatization of the act of birth*, that the whole fantastic science-fiction theater performance was, in fact, a *celebration of human birth*.

In that way the *discovery of man* was performed on the Moon.

The ship was sailing silently over the ocean, there were people in the drawing rooms in the ship, TV sets in the drawing rooms, and the Moon on TV screens. I was coming into these drawing rooms full of silent people, and I was going out to watch the moon from the deck.

Jules Verne.

We have descended twenty thousand leagues under the sea and we have stepped on the Moon. We went to the center of the Earth and we have entered the human brain.

Far, far, away, Jules Verne floated in the dark sky, disguised as the moon and very lonely.

AMERICAN COMICS IN FRANCE: A CULTURAL EVALUATION _____

Maurice C. Horn

The comics—and especially the American comics—reach daily into nearly every home in the Western world, and well beyond. They constitute a genuine sociological and cultural phenomenon that has already spanned over eighty years. No other form of art (with the possible exception of the movies) holds such fascination and appeal for the general public, and none (with the exception of jazz music) is so overwhelmingly American in its expression. Yet the comics have until recently suffered only scorn, neglect, and ignorance in the country of their birth. Scores of articles and publications have been devoted to the real or supposed influence of minor American novelists or painters in countries near or far, but the contributions made by American comic strip artists have gone largely unnoticed. It is, of course, the fate of all new art forms to be greeted with derision. Against the comics, the laughter has been longest and loudest. Yet is it reasonable to assume that the reading, day after day, week after week, of American comics by foreigners could have gone on without perceptible impact? And is it reasonable to assume that the reading of American comics would not affect foreigners' perceptions of the American people, their institutions, and their culture?

This case study of the influence of American comics in France (and, by extension, in other French-speaking countries) is an attempt to answer these questions.

AMERICAN COMICS IN FRANCE: A SHORT HISTORY

The first American comics appeared in France shortly after the beginning of this century. These were direct translations of American Sunday comics. Unlike comics in the United States, however, which were part and parcel of the newspaper and aimed at adults, these stories were, in France, either collected in picture books for children, or published in children's magazines. Thus the French had their first taste of American comics: R. F. Outcault's *Buster Brown*, Rudolph Dirk's *The Katzenjammer Kids*, F. B. Opper's *Happy Hooligan*, Winsor McCay's *Little Sammy Sneeze* and *Little Nemo*, George McManus's *The Newlyweds and Their Baby* were all translated into French, well before World War I. The characters, however were given French names (*The Newlyweds*, for instance, became *M. et Mme. Nouvomarié*) and it is unlikely that the young readers (or most of their parents) had any inkling that these stories were, in fact, imported from the United States.

This situation was to change after World War I. Europeans in general (and the French in particular) had become much more conscious of things American. The custom of nationalizing American characters had not changed (*The Gumps* had become *La Famille Mirliton* for instance) but these stories were now presented as being of American origin. Also, for the first time, comic strips started appearing in French newspapers (*Felix the Cat* in the 1920s and later *Tarzan* and *Mickey Mouse*). However, they still remained a novelty and contributed only a small percentage of the comic stories published in France.

A drastic change occurred with the publication on 21 October 1934 of the first issue of *Le Journal de Mickey* ("Mickey's Journal"), a children's newspaper of an entirely new type. Not only was *Mickey's* format almost twice as large as that of the traditional children's paper (roughly corresponding to American tabloid size), but its contents were almost exclusively made up of comic strips, most of them American. It contained not only *Mickey Mouse* which gave it its title, but also *Jungle Jim* and *The Katzenjammer Kids*, among others.

The success of *Le Journal de Mickey* among its young readers was immediate and overwhelming. In the years following, no fewer than fifteen new illustrated newspapers were printed in France as well as Belgium. They all made predominant, and sometimes exclusive, use of American material. This material was more colorful, more varied in tone and in themes, than anything the French cartoonists had then to offer. Soon Flash Gordon (alias Guy l'Eclair), the Phantom, Popeye, Superman, and countless other comic page heroes were as well known on the European side of the Atlantic as they were in the United States. The traditional French "illustrés," which had been stubbornly clinging to their outmoded outlook, tried tardily to adapt, but their production was no match for the more suspenseful and jazzier American comics. Had it not been for the coming of World War II and the ensuing German occupation, when American comics were banned, the French comics industry would most likely have gone under.

Paradoxically, this ban which was nearly total by 1942 only increased the American comics' hold on their young readers. The collection and preservation of the prewar "illustrés" began around this time. More importantly, these stories for the first time were seen as representative of the best values America had to offer—freedom, individuality, democracy—and they stood out as so many beacons in the dark night of Nazi oppression.

With the end of the war, the American comics made a massive comeback. The American syndicates and comic book publishers simply poured their backlogged production into new or revived publications. Organized political opposition, however, sprang up, both from the Left and from the Right. The Communists were opposed to the American comics because they exalted values that ran counter to Marxist ideology, and the Conservatives were against them because they were foreign and contrary to the nationalistic spirit. In July 1949 after several unsuccessful attempts, a law was passed that established an oversight committee to watch over children's publications, but whose main goal actually was to discourage publication of American comics in French publications.

The law of July 1949, as it became known, worked. The votes of the committee members were heavily weighted against American comics. One by one, French publishers became targets of the committee, and rather than face lengthy and costly court fights, some of them dropped American material altogether. The committee's zeal was fiercest against the French versions of American comic books (*Superman, Batman*) which their publishers ultimately had to give up, after a series of court decisions ruled that the characters were "harmful to youth."

By the 1960s, only the more innocuous American series (such as *Blondie* and the Walt Disney creations) survived in children's newspapers. French adult newspapers continued to publish a greater range of American material, but in far reduced numbers. However, for reasons that will be examined in greater detail later, the last fifteen years have seen a resurgence of interest in American comics that soon translated into a boom. Daily newspapers are again prominently displaying American comic strips (*France-Soir*, France's most widely circulated daily, for instance, for a long time featured *Peanuts* on its front page). American comics again find their way into French (and Belgian) magazines for children. And American comic books, including the so-called underground "comix," are now being translated into French in ever-increasing numbers.

At the same time, new generations of Frenchmen are discovering the titles that had enchanted French children and their elders before the war. Now regarded as classics, *Little Nemo, Flash Gordon, Tarzan, Prince Valiant,* and *Winnie Winkle* have been reprinted in lavish hardbound editions which are enjoying a tremendous artistic, as well as popular, success.

THE AESTHETIC AND CULTURAL INFLUENCE
OF AMERICAN COMICS

The French have always claimed that they introduced the first long-running comic strip, Christopher's *La Famille Fenouillard*, in 1889. The objection that this picture-story never made use of the balloon—a cloud-shaped form issuing from the lips of the characters and containing dialogue, and regarded as one of the prerequisites of a bona fide comic strip—never fazed them. Be it as it may, American cartoonists have influenced their French counterparts from the start (and not vice versa). As we have seen, American comics were translated into French as early as the turn of the century, but there can be found no evidence of the reverse process. In fact, only in recent times have French-language comics reached the United States in any sizeable number.

There is also evidence that at least some of the French cartoonists were receptive to the innovations of the early American comic artists. Louis Forton, generally regarded as one of the pioneers of the French comic strip, was especially fascinated by the work of American cartoonists and by America in general. One of the longest sequences of his fabled *Les Pieds-Nickelés* was to take place in the United States. Not only did he borrow characters and situations from such luminaries as F. B. Opper and Richard Outcault (a universal and long-standing practice known in cartooning circles as "the swipe"), but he was the first French cartoonist to regularly introduce balloons in his pictures, along with the traditional text-narrative under the panels.

The use of a lengthy narrative instead of balloons was one of the hallmarks of the French comics. Because of literary shibboleths, publishers and educators frowned on the balloon as being nonliterate. In the 1920s, however, French supplements for children made increasing use of imported American material (*The Gumps, Winnie Winkle, Reg'lar Fellers*, among others) which employed balloons in preference to text. Because of the greater ease in reading, not to mention more dynamic story-telling resulting from the use of the device, the American series soon outstripped the French products in popularity. This success can be seen as the primary cause of the creation, in 1925 only, of the first French comic strip to make use of the balloon exclusively, Alain Saint-Ogan's classic *Zig et Puce*. Significantly, the first episode of the series was titled *Zig et Puce veulent aller en Amérique*—"Zig and Puce want to go to America."

In the following years, French cartoonists increasingly turned to their American colleagues for inspiration (notably in the choice of more suspenseful story-lines) and technique (the more skillful use of framing their panels, for instance, or a more spacious page layout). However, American influence was progressing slowly among many cartoonists who clung to out-moded techniques, either because of pressure from tradition-bound publishers, or simply because they lacked the necessary talent or imagination.

Their chosen medium was also an advantage to the routine cartoonists at the expense of the innovators. In France, most illustrated stories appeared in newspapers for children, such as the weekly *journaux illustrés* ("il-lustrated newspapers") which carried short stories, tales, articles and pearls of wisdom in addition to comics. This format had hardly varied since the nineteenth century. It is, therefore, no surprise that *Le Journal de Mickey* created such a sensation when it first appeared. This newspaper and its later imitators (*Hurrah, Adventures, Jumbo*, among others) caused a veritable revolution in the reading habits of young Frenchmen. No study has been made of the impact of American comics on their readers, as was done with American movies. But at least among schoolchildren, the impact was con-siderable, and certainly outstripped that of the movies. I grew up during the late 1930s in Paris, and I can testify that every Frenchman of school age was fascinated by the American comic heroes. We especially devoured the adventure strips, thrilling at the perils of Flash Gordon (renamed Guy l'Eclair), applauding the exploits of Mandrake the Magician, or sharing Tarzan's adventures in darkest Africa. The enthusiastic response evoked by American comics in the minds of their juvenile readers would show up in unexpected quarters a generation later.

This period, the middle and late 1930s, probably marked the entrance of the American comics, though often under assumed names, into the mass consciousness of the French. Certainly Blondie, Maggie and Jiggs (known as "la famille Illico"), Popeye, Mickey Mouse, the Katzenjammer Kids ("Pim, Pam, Poum"), or Superman ("Yordi") were as widely known in France as they were in the United States. There can be no doubt that they also introduced, along with American movies, new notions and new at-titudes among Frenchmen. In the absence of any valid study, this conclu-sion cannot be irrefutably demonstrated, but it can be inferred from one in-stance among many—that is, the fact that French mothers often coaxed their resisting children into eating their spinach with the argument that it would make them "as strong as Popeye."

The French cartoonists, underpaid and unappreciated, reacted against the American invasion first with anger, then with resignation. The more talented tried to adapt, and some went on to develop their own distinctive style along the lines set down by American artists. Others, less talented or lazier, resorted to imitation, or even downright plagiarism. Stories imitating *Brick Bradford, Terry and the Pirates*, or *Superman* abounded, as did strips with an American locale. New York and the Far West were the most popular, because they were the easiest to recognize. Extreme confusion reigned. Some artists took on Anglo-Saxon pseudonyms and worked in close mimicry of Alex Raymond or Milton Caniff, while others went on to continue, as best they could, the American series whose flow was being progressively cut off by the outbreak of World War II. It is not exaggerated to say that all through the 1930s and 1940s, French cartoonists lived in the awesome shadow of their American counterparts.

Perhaps even more important were the changes that American comics brought to the traditional children's newspapers. All of a sudden, primacy was to be given the image in preference to the usually ponderous text the editors had been foisting on their young readers. The changes were drastic and, for some, traumatic. With the surge of all-pictorial newspapers for children, pedagogues were soon up in arms, claiming that the publications only helped to raise a nation of illiterates—a fact that has long since been disproved. However, their protests were of no great avail. Despite the enactment of a law prescribing a minimum of 25 percent of textual content (an edict more honored in the breach than in the observance) French-language illustrated newspapers from *Le Journal de Mickey* (new format) to *Pilote* devoted an overwhelming amount of space to comic strips. The American comics also helped to raise the readership age of these papers. Many stories are now aimed at young adults, even mature readers. While *Le Journal de Mickey* is still predominantly designed for children of school age, the readers of *Pilote* and, to a lesser extent, those of *Tintin*, are much older on the average.

Another innovation wrought by the invasion of American comics in the 1930s was the introduction of the comic book format, characterized by a monthly rather than a weekly periodical, a smaller format, and contents devoted to a single character. While they present some variations from their American models (using, for instance, only black and white, instead of color on the inside pages), the French comic books have by and large adopted the themes and approach of their American counterparts to such an extent that they were, and sometimes still are, a favorite target for censorship authorities.

While the direct influence of the American comics is no longer as overwhelming or even preponderant as it once was, its presence still continues to be felt at all levels of comics publishing. The French comics production has certainly come of age, but all of the people involved know how much they owe to the American comics and the trails they were the first to blaze. If the American series had not established both the existence of a definite need and the means to fill it, the Europeans, including the French, would not have been able to develop, or at least not to the same extent, a viable comics industry. Even Hergé's *Tintin* and Goscinny and Uderzo's *Astérix* owe a large debt to American inspiration. Hergé has admitted that he learned his story-telling technique from his American colleagues (Caniff being chief among them), while the premise and theme of *Astérix* are so similar to those of *Popeye* that some French critics have accused Goscinny of outright plagiarism.

There is one field of comic art in which America still remains supreme: that of the avant-garde comics. The American "undergrounders" are literally worshipped in France, as well as in other parts of Europe, and none is more widely admired than Robert Crumb. (A 160-page monograph on the man and his work has recently been published in Paris.) The influence of Crumb and his companions, such as Gilbert Shelton and "Spain" Rodríguez, is readily apparent in the cartoon series published in such radical magazines as *Hara-Kiri*, *Charlie*, and the now-defunct *Actuel*, as well as in the works of the most aspiring French cartoonists.

American comics have also played a role, albeit an understandably more limited one, in other visual art fields. Some early French filmmakers like Jean Cocteau and René Clair, who have both written lucid essays on the comics, had occasionally indulged in some borrowings from cartoon techniques (notably Clair's *Entr'acte*). It was with the advent of the so-called *nouvelle vague*, however, that comic strip effects took their legitimate place in the cinematic language. In the forefront of this trend is Alain Resnais, himself an avid reader, collector, and admirer of American comics who, out of his love for the medium, smuggled a copy of a *Mandrake* comic book into a sequence of his world-acclaimed documentary on the French Biblio-thèque Nationale, *Toute la Mémoire du Monde*. In *Muriel*, under the influence of Burne Hogarth, Resnais often resorted to whitened-out backgrounds which would throw the characters in the forefront into sharper relief.

Claude Chabrol, François Truffaut, Roger Vadim, and Alain Jessua have also shown traces of American comic strip influence in their films. Most interesting of all in this respect is Jean-Luc Godard's *Alphaville*, in which the use of shallow space, bleached-out backgrounds, and violently contrasted lighting are all clearly derived from Chester Gould's *Dick Tracy*. Even Eddie Constantine, the film's lead character, was made to look like Tracy, with his snap-brimmed fedora and beat-up trench coat.[1]

The American comics have also been influential among fine artists. The surrealist painters admired the American strips for their oneiric qualities, while Picasso had the comics read to him every week by his friend Gertrude Stein. Some of his drawings, especially *Sueño y Mentira de Franco*, come very close to being comic strips themselves. When a group of French and European painters decided in the late 1950s and early 1960s to liberate themselves from what they saw as the suffocating yoke of Abstract Expressionism, they naturally turned to the comics, and more precisely to the American comics, for inspiration. The school known as "Figuration Narrative" introduced universally known comic figures in their canvases as

easily understood iconographic symbols. Both Bernard Rancillac and Hervé
Télémaque explored the mythopoetic implications of Mickey Mouse and
other Disney characters, while Tarzan and Superman have been incorporated with persistent regularity into the works of Jean-Louis Brau. These
do not appear as sociological objects, as is the case in the paintings of
Lichtenstein, but rather they reflect the preeminent position occupied by
American comic strip figures in the cultural heritage of Western man.

The influence, explicit or subliminal, of American comics can be detected
in virtually every form of visual expression in France, from advertising
(with Blondie helping sell a new kind of can opener, or Wimpy lending his
name to a fast-food chain), to editorial cartooning (with the United States
variously depicted as a triumphant or battered Superman, according to the
situation), and to book illustration (Hogarth's *Tarzan* has recently been
utilized to teach young Frenchmen the principles of the New Math). Thus
the position that American comics occupy in the minds and in the collective
consciousness of Frenchmen seems secure.

THE SOCIAL IMPACT OF AMERICAN COMICS IN FRANCE

In conjunction with Hollywood movies, the American comics have been
the medium most instrumental in forging Frenchmen's perceptions, ap-
prehensions, and misconceptions of American society, institutions, and
mores. As the French sociologist Evelyne Sullerot observes, "one cannot
study American society . . . without reference to Blondie, Popeye, Dick
Tracy, or Maggie and Jiggs."[2] For a majority of Frenchmen, the United
States has for a long time been perceived as a vast continent, somewhat
equally divided between a wilderness inhabited by cowboys and Indians,
and towering, inhuman cities peopled chiefly by gangsters. This simplifica-
tion, which I have hardly caricatured, was borne out by opinion surveys
taken as late as the 1950s. Moreover, certain myths can be directly traced to
a misreading of American comic strips. The commonly held belief among
Frenchmen that the United States is a matriarchal society derives, in no small
measure, from such domestic features as *Bringing Up Father* and *Blondie*,
where the husband is either bullied or hoodwinked by his wife. This view
has received considerable reinforcement in recent times from the host of
American situation comedies which are regularly flooding French television
screens. Another myth fostered by American comic strips is that of an impersonal society where the family survives only as an institution of conve-
nience which would fall apart were it not for the existence of innumerable
laborsaving gadgets like the refrigerator, the electric dishwasher, and even
electric toothbrushes.

Along with the negative views often associated with the reading of American comics, more positive perceptions have also emerged. From the underlying themes of the American series, the French have been able to gain insight into the openness, vitality, and informality characteristic of American society, in contrast with their own, more rigidly structured society. The French also admire the American ability to laugh at themselves, to publicly air their faults and shortcomings in such iconoclastic strips as *Li'l Abner*, *Pogo*, and *Doonesbury*. But what becomes clearer to the French from the reading of American comics is their advocacy of unfettered individual freedom. As Pierre Couperie noted, after observing that American comics had been banned in Hitler's Germany, Mussolini's Italy, and Stalin's Russia: "It is certain, on the other hand, that [the American comics] preach individualism: for this reason they have had the honor of being persecuted by all the totalitarian regimes."[3]

Because, as we have seen, the recently imported American comics had such a tremendous impact on their young readers, attacks upon them were started from all sides. As the comics grew more and more popular, the attacks grew louder and louder. Some of the objections came from legitimately concerned educators; others were the product of embittered competitors; yet others were politically motivated. The Communist party was especially vociferous against the American strips in which they alleged to see a concerted effort to subvert the minds of their unsuspecting readers. Thus the noted critic and polemicist, Georges Sadoul, wrote in a study significantly entitled *Ce Que Lisent Vos Enfants* ("What Your Children Are Reading"): "These newspapers [publishing American comics] are pouring into the impressionable brains of children the lowest type of pornography, and a taste for murder and the exploits of gangsters . . . the wish to become a spy . . . the wish to participate in a civil war designed to reinstate some kings on their thrones."[4] These intemperate pronouncements, which their author tried to retract some twenty-five years later, may have been caused in part by Sadoul's disappointment at seeing French children (including his own, as it later turned out) devour the American series, while shunning the culturally "correct" children's newspaper, *Mon Camarade*, which he was then editing.

These attacks culminated in the creation, by the law of July 1949, of the Commission for Oversight and Control of Publications for Children and Adolescents. This commission, made up of a total of twenty-eight members (including a husband and a wife supposedly representing all of France's fathers and mothers!) could not ban publications outright, but could "discourage" publishers from running certain strips which they judged objectionable and, if necessary, recommend prosecution of the offending publishers to the Attorney General. (While the commission's members have always denied that they were systematically anti-American, it is of interest to note that their deliberations—conducted in secret—have led to a number of prosecutions, over 90 percent of which have been aimed against American features.) As comics' historian, Edouard François, has noted: "The result of such policy . . . the American sources have dried up [was to bring about] . . . an unseemly hodgepodge of which hardly one-third . . . was acceptable or any good. . . ."[5]

In reaction to all these discriminatory measures, there developed in the 1960s a number of organizations whose aim was to defend the comics, particularly the American comics, against the accusations of their detractors. The original membership of these organizations was made up almost exclusively of former readers of American strips who had surprisingly grown up to become quite articulate, in spite of all the dire predictions of the doomsayers. The first such organization, the Club des Bandes Dessineés, boasted a roster which included the filmmakers Alain Resnais and Chris Marker, the sociologists Edgar Morin and Evelyne Sullerot, the writers and critics Francis Lacassin, Claude Beylie, Pierre Couperie, Hubert Juin and others, as well as Jean Adhémar, the curator of the Bibliothèque Nationale, and Pierre Lazareff, the publisher of *France-Soir*. The fact that many of those leading the parade in defense of American comics were Left-leaning was an indication of how far the social climate had swung, from total and unmitigated condemnation, to wholehearted acceptance. To the traditional objections raised against the American comics, Lacassin, for instance, was to peremptorily declare: "Those leftists who despise the comics are only . . . the *watchdogs* of a middle-class culture whose prejudices and taboos they have espoused."[6]

The most extreme case of all is probably that of Jacques Sadoul, son of the aforementioned Georges Sadoul, and grandson of his namesake Jacques Sadoul, who was the delegate of the French Communist party to the first Comintern meeting in Moscow in 1919. Not only is Sadoul one of the staunchest defenders of the American comics, but he has also written a number of cogent articles and books on many aspects of contemporary American culture, including comics, films, science-fiction, and so on.

The efforts displayed by these enthusiastic lovers of the medium have resulted in a renewal of appreciation for American comics among large segments of the French public, especially among the intellectuals and the young which represents a good omen for the future. Tarzan, Superman, and Flash Gordon, not to mention Popeye and the Katzenjammer Kids, are now well-rehabilitated in the eyes of the public, and even in those of educators. Now comics are studied in French universities. There is even a credit course at the Sorbonne on "History and Aesthetics of the Comics." A great many exhibitions of comic art have taken place all around the French country, and there is a yearly International Comics Conference at

Angoulême in southwestern France. Granted that all these manifestations include comics of all nationalities, the lion's share still goes to the American variety which still holds the greatest fascination, despite a grave decline in quality. For example, at the 1967 exhibition, "Bande Dessinée et Figuration Narrative," at the Louvre, almost 90 percent of the wall space was given over to American comics, and the first two one-man shows organized by the French organization, Socerlid, were devoted respectively to Burne Hogarth and Milton Caniff. It is, therefore, not an exaggeration to state that American comics play an important and growing role on the French cultural scene, and that they help promote a better understanding of American culture among Frenchmen. In recognition of that fact, the American Cultural Center in Paris has recently organized a traveling exhibition of the best in American comic art.

The respectful attention given to American comics in France is further evidenced by the number of critical essays, aesthetic evaluations, and political glosses concerned with American comics. A few years ago, Lee Falk, creator of *Mandrake* and *The Phantom*, found himself in Paris, where he was quickly drawn into a then raging debate over the Phantom's alleged racism and imperialism. As a general rule, American cartoonists who come to France for lectures or conventions are likely to be mobbed by French journalists as well as by admirers, and are invariably asked to present their views and expound their ideas on French television—a sure sign of the exalted status that is currently attributed to them.

The influence of American comics has even filtered down to the routine of everyday life. The French can be caught using basically American onomatopoeias, derived from the comics (such as zing, gasp, zip and argh) in their conversation. This fact so struck stand-up comedian Guy Bedos that he built an entire monologue around it. One last cheering note: in many parts of France, uncommonly bright children are now called "les pineutes," in homage to Charles Schulz's precocious band of intellectual tots.

CONCLUSION

In his celebrated collection of essays on popular culture entitled *The Mechanical Bride*, Marshall McLuhan predicted that American comics would be discovered by the French as a serious art form ten years hence. This was in 1954, and McLuhan's prediction has been proved uncannily accurate. Of course the French have always prided themselves on being cultural discoverers. They point out that they were first to discover the merits of, among others, Edgar Allan Poe, jazz, William Faulkner, and gangster movies.

However, the case of the comics is markedly different. The French are not merely pointing out some important and long-neglected contribution made by the United States within the framework of an already established cultural form. In the French view, the comics constitute an original and distinctive twentieth-century art form that can only be compared in importance to the cinema. The preponderant role played by American artists and editors in the pioneering and development of this form is to them testimony of the vitality, imagination and preeminence of the American culture in the modern world. In France, at least, it is not exaggerated to say that the American comics are regarded as one of the great cultural achievements of the United States, one of its foremost contributions to Western culture and eventually to world culture as well. This view can be best summed up by quoting from the foreword to the catalogue of the exhibition, *Bande Dessinée et Figuration Narrative* (translated in the United States under the title *A History of the Comic Strip*):

The comic strip, and particularly the American comic strip, which has produced from eight to twelve million pictures since its birth, has created the largest and most abundant iconographical field in history. Far from being simple, its content is the product of an incredible network of influences and traditions, both conscious and unconscious, all of which belong to the ensemble of a civilization and its past.[7]

As the French say, *Une mode qui dure n'est plus une mode.* A fad that lasts is no longer a fad, and adulation of American comics, once regarded by the skeptics as a passing fad, is now part of the French cultural worldview.

NOTES

1. The French critic Michel Caen has written a very enlightening study of the influence of Dick Tracy on the works of both Godard and Resnais in a special issue of the library magazine devoted to the comics. *See* "Comic-Strip et Celluloïd," *Les Lettres Françaises* (30 June 1966): 17-18.

2. Claude Couffon, "Entretien avec Evelyne Sullerot," *Les Lettres Françaises* (30 June 1966): 17-18.

3. Pierre Couperie, *Bande Dessinée et Figuration Narrative* (Paris: Société Civile d'Études et de Recherches des Littératures Dessinées, 1967), p. 177.

4. Georges Sadoul, *Ce Que Lisent Vos Enfants* (Paris: Denoel, 1938), p. 3.

5. Edouard François, "Histoire de la Bande Dessinée," *Française* (Paris, 1972): 31.

6. Francis Lacassin, "Le Droit de Rever," *Les Lettres Françaises* 30 (June 1966): 5. Italics in original.

7. Pierre Couperie and Maurice C. Horn, *A History of the Comic Strip* (New York: Crown Publishers, 1967), p. 4.

BIG NOISE FROM ACROSS THE WATER: THE AMERICAN INFLUENCE ON BRITISH POPULAR MUSIC _____

Charlie Gillett

Until 1964 most Americans were unaware of whether or how their music was heard by the rest of the world. Tourists noticed familiar songs on European jukeboxes, and draftees serving time overseas could find American music on the radio. But back home in Indiana, pop music was just a part of the American way of life, along with baseball and hamburgers. Who knew or cared that Elvis Presley was more famous in Europe than any local soccer star or prime minister?

The Beatles shook that insularity for good when their records took American radio by storm in the early part of 1964, raising the questions, inside and outside the record business, where did they come from, and who else is there like that?

TRANSATLANTIC ECHOES

Ever since America began developing its own derivatives of the British folktunes taken across the Atlantic by emigrant settlers, Britain has become a reverse outpost of the American musical empire. Diligent researchers, notably Cecil Sharp in the early years of this century, successfully traced and identified surviving relics of traditional British songs and melodies in the repertoire of Appalachian musicians. But the main body of American popular music has moved far from those sources, under the influence of African-based rhythms and harmonies introduced by slaves and their descendants.

Britain, while allowing its own musical heritage to wither and die, has acted as a musicological hothouse for the diverse innovations of black American musicians and entertainers: Minstrelsy, Ragtime, Dixieland, Charleston, Swing, Boogie-Woogie, Rock 'n' Roll, Twist, Blues, Motown, and Funk have all conquered Britain as thoroughly as they took America itself, sometimes even more completely.

While America has tended to drop one style as another was established, in Britain they can overlap and coexist. This creates a bewildering battleground where American styles from various periods of the century fight for space in the media with current American hits and the few records which owe relatively little to American influence. For example: in May 1976 the British Top 10 Hits chart included "Jungle Rock," a rockabilly record made in 1957 by the obscure Hank Mizell; reissued hits by Fats Domino ("Blueberry Hill" from 1956) and Dion ("The Wanderer" from 1961); and British reworkings of the recent truck-driving monologue "Convoy" and the 1927 boogie-woogie classic "Honky-Tonk Train Blues." A Glenn Miller single, first issued in 1943, had just dropped off the chart.

This British fascination with Americana is not limited to music. The American influence spreads through most of popular culture: fiction, comic books, TV, and most of all, the movies, where the image of America offers an exciting alternative to the reality of Britain outside the cinemas.

Britain's own culture is stultified by class division and prejudices, fostered by an upper-middle-class media elite which too often reinforces class structures and stereotypes in its drama and entertainment presentations. If America is not exactly a paragon of social equality and racial harmony, it still offers an image of itself on TV and movie screens which is more open, where the audience can find space to move and hope for change.

There are limits to American imperialism. While British firms surrender to the creeping power of multinational corporations, the British public remains doggedly faithful to its own sports. Soccer, rugby football, and cricket hold out against tentative inroads being made by basketball, softball, and volleyball, both as participant and as spectator sports.

In the world of music, there has even been an apparent reversal as British musicians take a firmer hold on American ears. But is that real, or just a rebound of the big noise from across the water?

THE FIFTIES

In the twenty-year period before the Beatles, the British music business was a backwater, content to fend off the American challenge with halfhearted cover versions of American hits. The British-made records enjoyed every advantage. Paying lower royalties to the artists than to American licensees, the record companies promoted the British records more enthusiastically because their profits would be higher. Available for radio, TV, and national package-tour stage shows, the British artists were better known. Locally written songs followed the American formulas, the same chord changes, the same Americanized rhymes (maybe/baby, funny/honey, cruel/fool, madly/badly/sadly/gladly), and had extra promotional support from the publishers who made more money from British compositions than from the American songs they represented.

Still, in the five years between 1955 to 1959, more than half the records in the British Top 10 Hits were made in America (see Table 1). There was a flair, a professional finish, a feeling of higher quality, an *authenticity* in American records which the British copies could rarely achieve.

Table 1 **Ten Top Hits in the United Kingdom and the United States: 1955–1975**

Year	Number of Hits			Percentage of Hits	
	U.K.	U.S.	Total	U.K.	U.S.
1955	39	41	80	48.8	51.2
1956	27	49	76	35.5	64.5
1957	26	45	71	36.6	63.4
1958	26	47	73	35.6	64.4
1959	32	42	74	43.2	56.8
1960	46	39	85	54.1	45.9
1961	51	39	90	56.7	43.3
1962	44	41	85	51.8	48.2
1963	57	36	93	61.3	38.7
1964	83	21	104	79.9	20.1
1965	78	32	110	70.9	29.1
1966	70	36	106	66.0	34.0
1967	78	26	104	75.0	25.0
1968	66	31	97	68.0	32.0
1969	58	42	100	58.0	42.0
1970	58	53	111	52.2	47.8
1971	64	41	105	61.0	39.0
1972	64	45	109	58.7	41.3
1973	83	37	120	69.2	30.8
1974	90	37	127	70.9	29.1
1975	93	44	137	67.9	32.1

So Britain worshipped the same stars as the Americans, sometimes more fervently. Johnnie Ray and Frankie Laine in particular were enormously popular during the early 1950s, causing scenes of abandoned hysteria at airports and stage doors which anticipated most of the frenzy attached to rock 'n' roll a few years later.

Rock 'n' roll was everything in Britain it has been in the States, and more. Americans experienced rock 'n' roll as the final and inevitable eruption of a musical groundswell which had been building for ten years. If Louis Jordan was not exactly a household name, he sold millions of records for Decca during the late forties, and the sound of his lively boogie shuffles and sharp little sax solos was part of the background noise of American city life. Bill Haley and His Comets simplified and accented the boogie beat, making it more accessible to the pop audience.

British teenagers in the 1940s and 1950s had no chance of hiring a rhythm and blues combo to play at their school dance, but had to settle for a homegrown variant of the Les Brown band—smooching sax section, droning crooner, and strict tempo rhythms: foxtrots, quicksteps, and the last waltz.

It didn't take many plays of Bill Haley's "Shake, Rattle and Roll" and "Rock Around the Clock" to find that this was great stuff to dance to, and the papers called it "rock 'n' roll." Even the bands in the Palais and the Maison de Dance had to learn the new numbers. But no guitar player could come close to the feel of Carl Perkins on "Blue Suede Shoes," Buddy Holly on "That'll Be the Day," or Chuck Berry on "Roll Over Beethoven." No band had a piano player who could reproduce the feel of Jerry Lee Lewis's "Whole Lotta Shakin' Going On" (how do you *relax*, while playing a fast boogie?), or even the sax-section parts of Fats Domino's "I'm in Love Again," and Little Richard's "Long Tall Sally." In Britain, rock 'n' roll was *recorded* music, and definitely *American*.

But despite all the thrills and the impact, rock 'n' roll never took over Britain to the extent that legend would now have it. Apart from anything else, there was always a large section of the audience, especially the girls, who preferred softer stuff—Pat Boone and Elvis doing ballads. And the BBC radio programmers of the time preferred to please that audience, fearful of alienating adults with raucous nonsense.

The BBC (British Broadcasting Corporation) is a government-owned "public service" organization whose attitude towards pop music at that time veered from disinterest to disdain. Apart from an easy listening breakfast-time record show, all too tellingly titled "Housewives' Choice," the BBC Light Programme's music policy was to broadcast live versions of Tin Pan Alley standards (and their current equivalent) played by dance bands and Palm Court quartets. Only on weekends was some concession made to the teenage music audience with the Saturday morning "Saturday Club," whose policy of featuring live groups provided the only outlet for the coffee-bar/cellar-club music scene which developed during the late 1950s.

Oddly, but typically in the recent history of British pop, rock 'n' roll did not have a strong effect on British live music. A few singers and guitarists tried to copy the American records, and a cockney entertainer called Tommy Steele was incongruously launched as Britain's "answer to Elvis." But he wisely settled for a career in musicals which better suited his music hall instincts.

Meanwhile, the strongest live musical alternative to dance bands was dixieland jazz. Among the leaders here were cornet player Ken Colyer, a purist fan of New Orleans jazz who refused to stray far from the arrangements of records made in the early years of recording, and trombonist Chris Barber, who left Colyer to lead a more adventurous, but still traditionally based outfit. Whereas any British live versions of current American material invariably sounded limp and inadequate compared to the familiar "original version," few people had models to compare the British traditional jazz with. It sounded fresh, different, and infinitely better than other available live music in Britain.

Without deliberately cultivating widespread popularity, the jazz bands became increasingly popular, culminating in international hits for Chris Barber in 1959 with "Petite Fleur" (featuring clarinettist Monty Sunshine on an old Sidney Bechet tune); Acker Bilk in 1961 with another clarinet instrumental, "Stranger on the Shore"; and Kenny Ball the same year with "Midnight in Moscow."

But even more popular than the trade jazz movement was its offshoot, skiffle. Introduced between the sets of Chris Barber's gigs by the band's banjo player, Lonnie Donegan, skiffle emerged first as a novelty when "Rock Island Line," a monologue by Donegan recorded for a Barber album, was issued as a single in 1956 and made both the British and American Top 10. Lonnie left to pursue a solo career, putting drum and bass behind two-and-three-chord story-songs adapted from the repertoire of 1940s folksingers Woody Guthrie and Leadbelly.

Alternating frantic stories about American race horses, gambling men, and geographical landmarks with jaunty midtempo numbers about sheriffs, gamblers, and Confederate battles, Lonnie Donegan outsold every other British recording artist during the years 1956 to 1960. Only toward the end did he introduce British-based material. Recorded in primitive conditions by current standards, and with musicians of modest technical ability, Lonnie Donegan's records have a homemade sound which makes his popularity difficult to understand twenty years later. But in his time, Donegan was recognized as an adventurous innovator who ignored most of the conventions of pop music at the time, above all choosing interesting "real" subjects to sing about. No soppy love songs. The enormous success of his rudimentary style inspired more imitators than any other contemporary artist, and although no other skiffle performer had more than fleeting success, most of the British stars of the 1960s had made their debuts in skiffle groups.

Meanwhile, British record producers grappled with the magical mysteries of rock 'n' roll, and after three years of playing it too fast and frantically, in 1958 they came up with a minor classic of the genre: "Move It," by Cliff Richard and the Drifters. A hurriedly recorded B-side, "Move It" had a confidence and originality that had eluded earlier efforts. The singer kept up the pace without losing pitch or tune, the guitar was clean and rich, the arrangement ingenious. It made number two in the chart, and set Cliff Richard off on a career of more than fifty hit records in Britain, and success in most other countries of the world (including, late in 1976, the United States).

In Cliff Richard, Britain for the first time had a singer who could match the Americans, not only on record but on stage and TV too. Previously, there had been no British rock 'n' roll artist who could credibly top a package-tour bill. Rock 'n' roll had been delivered to Britain in the authentic forms of Frankie Lymon and the Teenagers, the Platters, Bill Haley and His Comets, The Crickets, featuring Buddy Holly, Jerry Lee Lewis, and others. Most of these artists were also squeezed onto a TV variety show somewhere, and from 1957 onwards the teen-oriented "Oh Boy," produced by Jack Good, generated as much excitement as the local scene could generate, with injections from stateside visitors.

In contrast to most people working in the media at the time, Jack Good was personally excited by rock 'n' roll, and was more conscious of its "image" possibilities than many of the artists themselves. Using theatrical props and dramatic lighting, he presented "Oh Boy" with missionary conviction and enthusiasm, and successively introduced Marty Wilde, Cliff Richard, Billy Fury, Adam Faith, and Johnny Kidd and The Pirates to the nation in the years 1958 to 1960.

During these years the American record business had itself come to terms with rock 'n' roll, replacing most of the originators with artists who "looked better" on TV, and adapting the rhythms to suit teen-oriented lyrics with fully orchestrated arrangements. Paul Anka, Ricky Nelson, the Everly Brothers, Connie Francis, and Bobby Darin became the dominant figures, and Britain could more easily match them with equivalent doleful crooners, backed by musicians and arrangers who had been worried for a while that the spontaneous improvisations of rock 'n' roll would end their careers prematurely.

Some of the new American singers came over to tour in package shows, but while some thrilled the audiences—Sam Cooke, Duane Eddy, Johnny Burnette—more of them lacked impact on stage without the helpful studio devices of echo chambers and double tracking. The audiences were more struck by the last great rock 'n' roll package, featuring Gene Vincent and Eddie Cochran, supported by young British hopefuls including Billy Fury.

Gene Vincent, a gentle introvert from Virginia, was encouraged by Jack Good to dress up in black leather from top-to-toe, which suitably impressed the crowds. But it was Cochran who had the longer-lasting effect through his tips on how to play various styles of rock-'n'-roll guitar which he passed onto Jim Sullivan, already a session musician on records by Marty Wilde and others, and subsequently tutor and advisor to many of the leading British guitar players of the modern era, including Led Zeppelin's Jimmy Page and Deep Purple's Ritchie Blackmore.

But although these package shows were the visible surface of the music scene, radio was the dominant outlet—how most people heard music. The only rival to the BBC's Light Programme was a commercial radio station based across the English Channel in Luxembourg, which broadcast in English every evening and sold most of its air time in blocks to the British record companies. Four companies, Decca, EMI, Philips, and Pye, virtually monopolized the British Top 10 Hits through 1966 (see Table 2). The Luxembourg shows gave the big four a guaranteed outlet to a captive audience which had virtually no alternative source of pop music after six o'clock in the evening.

THE SIXTIES, BEFORE THE BEATLES

The growth of British pop music during the early 1960s was static, at least on the surface. The balance of Top 10 hits tripped towards British productions for the years 1960 to 1963 (see Table 1), consolidating the hold on the market of the four major companies whose A and R staff invariably supervised the majority of recordings.

Among the few free-lance, independent producers, by far the most successful was Joe Meek, who was strongly influenced by the enterprising studio devices and business acumen of the American producer, Lee Hazelwood. (Based in Phoenix, Arizona, Hazelwood pioneered use of tape delay and echo chambers on a long series of hits by guitarist Duane Eddy.)

Working from studios he designed and built himself, Joe Meek issued his first productions on his own Triumph label which was absorbed by EMI after one Top 10 Hit in 1960. For the next five years Meek produced hits for various companies including Decca, EMI, and Pye, all of them making adventurous use of echo (notably John Leyton's "Johnny Remember Me" and the international hit "Telstar" by the Tornadoes).

But more representative of the period were Cliff Richard and the Shadows. Most of Cliff Richard's hits werre custom-written for him, some by members of his backing group, the Shadows, and others by established writers of the time. The Shadows also had a parallel career as an instrumental group, recording a succession of hits with a disarmingly simple formula

Table 2 **Ratio of British Ten Top Hits Between Two and Four Firms**

	Two Firms Hits		Four Firms Hits		
Year	No.	%	No.	%	Total No.
1955	62	77.5	78	97.5	80
1956	60	79.0	76	100.0	76
1957	52	73.2	69	97.2	71
1958	64	87.7	72	98.6	73
1959	55	74.3	71	96.0	74
1960	64	75.3	79	92.9	85
1961	61	71.8	85	94.4	90
1962	64	76.2	84	98.8	85
1963	74	79.6	93	100.0	93
1964	79	76.0	102	98.1	104
1965	72	65.5	99	90.0	110
1966	61	57.6	92	86.8	106

Companies in Order (number of hits)							
1		*2*		*3*		*4*	
Decca	(37)	EMI	(25)	Philips	(5)	Pye	(1)
Decca	(33)	EMI	(27)	Philips	(9)	Pye	(7)
Decca	(37)	EMI	(27)	Philips	(4)	Pye	(4)
Decca	(37)	EMI	(27)	Philips	(4)	Pye	(4)
Decca	(31)	EMI	(24)	Philips	(10)	Pye	(6)
EMI	(34)	Decca	(30)	Pye	(10)	Philips	(5)
Decca	(31)	EMI	(30)	Pye	(17)	Philips	(7)
EMI	(34)	Decca	(30)	Pye	(14)	Philips	(6)
EMI	(37)	Decca	(37)	Philips	(11)	Pye	(8)
EMI	(46)	Decca	(33)	Pye	(13)	Philips	(10)
EMI	(41)	Decca	(31)	Pye	(16)	Philips	(11)
EMI	(41)	Decca	(20)	Pye	(16)	Philips	(15)

of medium-paced rhythm under a guitar melody, often enhanced with a few note-bending tricks on a tremelo device. Professional-sounding but unadventurous, the reliably *neat* Shadows replaced the Lonnie Donegan skiffle group as the models which aspiring musicians imitated. A lot of groups during the early 1960s never sang a word.

Similar in style and appeal to American TV star Ricky Nelson, Cliff and the Shadows had good clean-cut, boy-next-door images, and there was a homey character to most of the British-made pop music of the time, which the radio favored over the more raucous contemporary American hits. So Britain missed many records which have stood the test of time much better, including several produced in New Orleans by Allen Toussaint ("Ooh Poo Pah Doo," "Mother-in-Law," "I Like It Like That"), early American hits from the new Detroit-based Motown company ("Shop Around," "Please Mr. Postman," "Heatwave") and almost all the hits by gospel-style singers such as Bobby Bland, Jerry Butler, Clyde McPhatter, and Solomon Burke.

Recognizing the energy and emotion of these American hits compared to the music available on the radio, adventurous collectors and musicians began hunting down obscure rhythm-and-blues records from the previous ten years, and in London and on Merseyside two parallel music movements emerged. In London, the emphasis was on blues: intense singing, wailing harmonica, amplified guitar, a heavy beat. On Merseyside, they favored the rhythm: frantic drummers racing the bass player to the end of the number with everybody in the group singing the words.

MERSEY BEAT

At first the Mersey groups played for tolerant relatives and friends, but gradually basements, youth clubs, and church halls found that audiences would pay money to see these wild four-piece bands and by the end of 1962 there was a flourishing music paper in Liverpool, *Mersey Beat*, whose editor counted 350 different groups in existence at the time.

On the comparatively vast continent of the United States locally distinct musical cultures have been taken for granted, but there was no precedent in the recent history of the British music business for the Liverpool phenomenon, whose activities were confined exclusively to London. By tradition, any ambitious artist had to move to London to attract the attention of an agent, a manager, a publisher, or a record company. Larry Parnes, manager of Marty Wilde, Billy Fury, and several other established artists, recently ruefully recalled that in 1961 Billy Furty reported astonishing audience reaction to a four-piece back-up band he had hired in Liverpool to support him on a date in Glasgow. Parnes ignored the report but recognized the oddly spelled name of the group when he saw it in the Top 20 a year later: the Beatles, "Love Me Do" (Parlophone).

No overnight success story, the early years of the Beatles were distinguished mainly by persistence, their own and their manager's. Brian Epstein was working at the record counter of his father's department store in Liverpool when he first heard of the Beatles. Young kids kept coming in to ask for their records, but they hadn't made any. Epstein investigated and discovered a seething network of basements and town halls, presenting live groups seven nights a week and lunchtimes too. After going to hear most of the reputed groups, Epstein settled for the one he had heard of first, mainly for their own songs.

The Beatles were unusual in having the confidence to write some of their own material. The typical attitude of the time was nicely caught in the movie *That'll Be the Day*, where a British musician offering songs to a group is derided as being impertinent—only the Americans know how to write good songs. Several British compositions of the time proved otherwise, notably Ian Samwell's "Move It" for Cliff Richard, and Johnny Kidd's "Shakin' All Over," but the myth remained, there was something more authentic about American songs.

The Beatles played American songs as all the other groups did, but it was their own material which fired Brian Epstein's confidence, and enabled him to keep trying after audition tapes were turned down. Ironically, George Martin, who took on responsibility for producing the new group, was at first skeptical of their songwriting ability, but yielded when "Love Me Do," their self-composed first record, made the Top 20.

Although their first record was a relatively modest hit, it brought enough exposure to the Beatles to reveal the potential of a *singing* group, in contrast to the standard Shadow-type instrumentalists. For the first time, record companies sent staff men out on scouting trips, to check out the "Mersey Beat." Tony Hatch, a young producer with Pye Records, signed several groups including the Searchers, and kept bumping into A and R men from Decca, Philips, and EMI. But EMI got the best haul, largely through their relationship with Epstein, who brought them Gerry and the Pacemakers, Billy J. Kramer and the Dakotas, and Cilla Black from his own "stable." From nearby Manchester, EMI signed Freddie and the Dreamers, the Hollies, and Herman's Hermits.

Although groups in name, most of these acts were focused on the lead singer and actually were not much different from the already established hit-makers of the time. The Searchers and the Hollies were genuine harmony groups with a distinct, enduring sound, but records by the others showed few changes, in style or material, from those by Helen Shapiro or Frank Ifield, solo artists who were swallowed by the group era.

The publicity surrounding the Mersey groups suggested that most of them were self-contained units who wrote, arranged, and played their own songs. Actually, most of them were still carrying on the tradition of covering recent American records, not always hits, more often B-sides or R and B obscurities. The biggest Searchers' hits included two songs first recorded by Jackie DeShannon, one by the Drifters, and an Orlons B-side; the Hollies' first three British hits revamped records by the Coasters, Maurice Williams, and Doris Tory. The groups which didn't find such material were usually supplied with songs written by established professional songwriters, produced and arranged by the record company A and R staff. Of all the Mersey groups recording in the years 1962 to 1966, only the Beatles really did almost everything themselves, writing not only all their own hits but several others for Billy J. Kramer, Cilla Black, the Fourmost, and even for the London-based Peter and Gordon and the R and B group, the Rolling Stones.

LONDON R AND B

The R and B movement in London was only coincidentally parallel to the Mersey Beat. As live music, it also was played mainly in basements and clubs which were the stronghold of the jazz groups. However, the R and B groups and their audiences much more consciously rejected "pop music" and "rock 'n' roll" with their associations of an exploitive commerical record business, banal disc jockeys, and gullible pop fans. R and B represented authenticity, much as skiffle had a few years earlier, and it shared a similar American base.

The material of the R and B groups was unearthed from records which had sold well in some black American ghettoes during the 1950s, mixed with more contemporary gospel-style hits from the current R and B charts in the States. Where skiffle had drawn primarily from acoustic folk-oriented material (mostly pre-1950), R and B now focused on the amplified, urban derivatives of the country blues. Chicago was the main center for combos featuring electric guitar, harmonica, drums and bass, played mostly by migrants from the Mississippi Delta, notably Muddy Waters, Little Walter, Howlin Wolf, John Lee Hooker, and Jimmy Reed. The music was loud and crude, 12-bar blues and boogie shuffles, exciting and emotional. American pop radio almost totally ignored it, although Chuck Berry and Bo Diddley successfully exploited the potential danceability of the rhythm by putting more open-ended, teen-oriented lyrics over it. In Britain, even the keen collectors, used to looking far beyond the music supplied on the radio, allowed their prejudices to prejudge R and B, which was too heavily rhythmic for the jazz fans and too heavily amplified for the folk tunes.

Chris Barber, whose band had spawned skiffle leader Lonnie Donegan, also supported R and B as best he could, bringing Muddy Waters on a European tour in 1958. Audiences were skeptical, but Barber encouraged blues enthusiast Alexis Korner to open up his gigs with sets of blues songs, accompanied at first by acoustic instruments but eventually introducing electrically amplified guitar. By 1961 clubs began to book Korner as an act on his own, whose gigs were "jams" where other musicians could join in on stage to sing, play harmonica, guitar, or whatever would fit. Through these jams various musicians discovered others with similar interests and eventually formed their own units. In 1962 Decca recorded Alexis Korner's Blues Incorporated, a similar ensemble called John Mayall's Bluesbreakers, and the first of these groups to make the pop charts, the Rolling Stones.

More open-minded and eclectic in their choice of material than the purists Korner and Mayall, the Rolling Stones also stressed the entertainment aspect of live gigs more, with lead singer Mick Jagger parodying the extravagant stage actions of black American singers. Word-of-mouth recommendation carried the Rolling Stones from the suburbs to the center of London where the Marquee Club changed its musical policy from jazz to R and B and drew bigger audiences than before.

Other groups emerged in the wake of the Stones, each taking a distinct direction. Despite Decca's headstart, EMI signed the best of the rest. Georgie Fame and the Blue Flames played at the Flamingo Club, a favorite haunt for West Indians and American GIs stationed near London, who favored a lighter, jazzier musical menu played by a line-up featuring keyboards and saxes. Jazz-trained pianist Manfred Mann mixed Cannonball Adderly tunes into his group's basic R and B repertoire, and the Yardbirds featured a succession of virtuoso blues-inspired guitarists, Eric Clapton, Jimmy Page, and Jeff Beck. From Newcastle in the northeast of England, the Animals brought a similar repertoire, arranged by Alan Price and sung with surly confidence by Eric Burdon.

Compared to most of the Mersey groups, these R and B groups had a stronger musical identity; but most of them still first made the pop charts with covers of American songs. Manfred Mann's group wrote their first two hits before embarking on a successful series of covers, but the others followed the familiar formula, boosted by two new media outlets, ITV's *Ready Steady Go* and "pirate" radio.

Ready Steady Go was the first TV music show which attempted to represent an existing live music scene, in contrast to Jack Good's various showcases of his own theatrical concept of musical excitement. Coinciding with a visually distinct youth life-style ("mod"), *Ready Steady Go* reinforced and extended it, introducing the homebound audience to American soul records and Jamaican ska music, which the radio had ignored, as well as launching the new groups.

Meanwhile, radio itself changed, with the founding in 1964 of the first offshore radio station. Anchoring outside the three-mile limit of "British" sea territory, Radio Caroline introduced twenty-four-hour, all-record radio to Britain for the first time, sponsored by advertisers. There were soon enough pirate radio ships dotted round the island to provide most of the nation with an alternative to the BBC's mean treatment of pop music on the Light Programme and to Radio Luxembourg's rigid, promotional, even shows. By the end of 1964 a new era of pop music did seem to have arrived in Britain. But more astonishing than that, it had hit America too.

TRANSATLANTIC REBOUND

Right up to the end of 1963 Americans were still oblivious to the bizarre British interest which kept alive songs and singers most Americans had forgotten about or had never heard of in the first place. In 1963 Chuck Berry, out of favor for some years in America, made the Top 10 in Britain with a reissued 45, "Let It Rock"/"Memphis Tennessee," while a demo of one of his songs, "Brown-Eyed Handsome Man," recorded at home in 1956 by Buddy Holly, made the Top 3 the same year. Singles by John Lee Hooker and Howlin Wolf appeared in the Top 30, and these artists were booked for club tours, playing to audiences who had been introduced to their songs by the British groups who made a point of crediting the originators.

The American record business was skeptical of British artists, regardless of their international success. Cliff Richard and the Shadows between them had more than thirty hits around the world, yet only three Cliff Richard 45s received any significant radio play in the States and not one record by the Shadows made Billboard's *Hot 100*. A few one-offs made it, so rare as to be flukes: "Telstar" by the Tornados, "I Remember You" by Frank Ifield.

Capitol Records, owned by EMI of Britain, had first option to release EMI records, but turned down the Beatles. Vee Jay, a Chicago-based label which specialized in R and B records, took up the option on the first two Beatles' singles, but passed on the third, which the Philadelphia label, Swan, took up with no better luck. Once more, the astute and persistent Brian Epstein stepped in, insisting that EMI force Capitol to take the group seriously in America, not only to release the fourth single but invest in its promotion. "I Wanna Hold Your Hand" was duly released, and, boosted by the group's personal appearances on radio and TV across the country, raced to the top of the charts, followed by the belatedly acceptable releases on Vee Jay and Swan.

Suddenly, British artists were hot property in the States, although Capitol, with access to the huge EMI roster, was slow to follow its own lead. All the other American companies grabbed what they could, and for a while it seemed that anything by a British group would be an American hit, even the cover versions of previous American hits. And then it didn't have to be a group, just British, so Pet Clark, Dusty Springfield and Tom Jones made it.

From having no faith in British records, the American business swung around within six months to having no faith in its own. Or rather, no faith in its own *pop* records. R and B companies pressed on regardless, redefining their music as "soul." The Motown organization in Detroit survived particularly well, launching several acts in the teeth of the British gale—the Supremes, Temptations, Four Tops—while reinforcing the earlier advances made by the Miracles, Marvin Gaye, and Martha and the Vandellas, whose records had been admired, imitated, and publicly praised by the Beatles, Rolling Stones, and other British groups.

Musically and technically, the Motown records were a major inspiration for the Beatles. Gospel music was the basis of the chords, harmonies, and infectious energy of the "Detroit Sound," and influenced most of the early Beatles hits. Having achieved a good performance in the recording studio, Motown followed through by mastering their records with a lot of volume, especially in the treble register. In London, the Beatles listened in awe and made their engineers listen too, arguing that if Motown could overload the recording levels and get away with the resulting distortion, why couldn't the Beatles? On the radio, the result was a sound that jumped through the speaker, in sharp contrast to the conservatively recorded British productions.

The Beatles were more than slightly baffled by the American reaction to their records, which were universally greeted as something new. All too aware of their own sources, the Beatles fended off the praise with unsolicited testimonials to the artists who had inspired them, in particular Buddy Holly and the Crickets (a self-contained unit of musicians who supplied most of their own material, inspired equally by R and B and country music), the Everly Brothers, Little Richard, and the current R and B style of gospel-based call-and-response harmony groups.

America already had two comparable groups established in the charts, the Beach Boys and the Four Seasons. If the Beatles had not done the Radio/TV promotional tour, America might never have acknowledged them. The difference was that the Beach Boys and the Four Seasons fit established marketing conceptions, West Coast sand-and-surf playboys and East Coast Italians making their break off the streets.

The Beatles confounded the American stereotype of the pop-music performer. Articulate, witty, unpredictably impolite, they not only awoke long-dormant interest within the music business and its existing audience, but attracted the attention of people who had consigned pop music to the lowest level on the scale of social prestige in the popular arts, somewhere below comic strips and TV soap operas.

The visit of the Beatles to America, the next year which brought several more hits, and two movies (*A Hard Day's Night* and *Help*), set off a chain reaction whose effects have not yet worn off or even slowed down, on both sides of the Atlantic. In America the immediate reactions were to swamp the radio with British records and to slip in a few homemade copies of the "group sound," under deceptive names like the Knickerbockers, the McCoys, the Beau Brummels, and the Sir Douglas Quintet. The long-term effect was that many musicians for the first time considered recording for the world of commercial formulas, teen idols, and subteen record buyers; and record companies became interested in musicians and songwriters who would previously have been turned down as being too clever or complicated. The folk movement in particular took a sideways jump into the pop mainstream, launching Bob Dylan, the Byrds, Simon and Garfunkel, the Lovin' Spoonful, the Buffalo Springfield, and from 1967, the San Francisco scene, all of them directly inspired by the British reinterpretation of American pop music.

A third effect of British success in America was a marked increase in American participation in the British music industry, by individuals and by companies.

THE INVISIBLE AMERICAN INVASION

Occasional Americans had participated in British music even before 1964, particularly in the folk scene. Parallel with the traditional jazz movement, folk clubs around the country featured troubadors who kept alive the narrative ballad tradition which had "died" as popular music by the end of the nineteenth century. The radical American folk-singer Pete Seeger was a regular visitor (his sister Peggy became a British resident) and among other Americans Ramblin' Jack Elliott, a former associate of Woody Guthrie, was particularly popular. On Eliott's advice, Guthrie-disciple Bob Dylan made the trip from Greenwich Village to London, and another New York folksinger, Paul Simon, recorded his first album in London in 1964.

More immediate contributions to British pop music were made by a couple of American independent producers, Bert Berns and Shel Talmy. Bert was a songwriter who had learned production at Atlantic Records in New York before launching his own Bang and Shout labels, which he licensed to Decca's London label in Britain. Recognizing the new circumstances of competing in the American market, Decca commissioned Berns to produce a couple of their British artists in London, resulting in hits for Lulu and Them, whose lead singer Van Morrison later left Britain to record for Berns's own label in New York.

Shel Talmy had, according to his own recent admission, little experience in producing when he persuaded Decca to assign him to a project midway through 1963. His success with the Bachelors (an Irish cabaret act who even managed a couple of American hits) launched Talmy as a creditable independent producer, whose work with the Kinks and the Who launched a new direction for British music.

The solid, pounding rhythm of the Kinks' "You Really Got Me" made a virtue out of a common weakness in British musicians, their inability to play strong dance rhythms with a lilt. A drummer from New Orleans such as Earl Palmer or Charlie Williams would intuitively play a fraction after the beat in a 2/4 or 4/4 rhythm, creating a relaxed feeling in a dancer even at a fast tempo. A British drummer would tend to play *on* the beat, causing tension in the listener. Many American drummers could only play on the beat too, but were rarely encouraged to record—until the Kinks made the stilted style acceptable. Actually, there had been an earlier "freak" American hit with a similar feel (or lack of feel), "Louie Louie" by the Kingsmen, a Seattle group whose record took over a year to hit the chart in late 1963, and may have given Talmy the idea of stressing a primeval rhythm by having drums, guitar, and bass all play the same beat. Having launched the Kinks, Talmy used a similar approach on the early Who records, marshalling the wayward rhythms of the group's drummer and guitarist to a "heavy strict tempo." So Heavy Rock was born, witnessed by Talmy's engineer Glyn Johns, who went on to become a notable producer in his own right, with the Rolling Stones among others.

The Rolling Stones also played with a more rigid rhythm than Americans were accustomed to, and soon after their first American hit they abandoned British studios in favor of American studios. They returned to British studios in 1967, by which time British engineers had absorbed the American recording techniques (but the Stones still favored Glyn Johns or an American, Jimmy Miller, as producers).

The few folksingers and producers and a handful of American artists who saw an opportunity to launch their careers in Britain (.J. Roby, the Walker Brothers, Jimi Hendrix) were easily absorbed into the existing British record business. A more fundamental change was less obvious: American record companies began setting up United Kingdom operations.

When Britain was just a market for records, the American companies had been content to license their releases to British companies. When it became clear during the late 1950s that the British companies were tending to favor their homegrown productions over the material licensed from America, American companies began insisting on their own label identities. Capitol, MGM, and Mercury were among the first American companies to have their records issued under their own logos (trademark and label design), followed by RCA in 1958, Warner Brothers in 1960, Liberty and CBS in 1962, and United Artists in 1963. But they were all still licensed to the four major British companies (EMI, Decca, Philips and Pye), until the group invasion of America in 1964 redefined Britain as not simply a minor market for record sales but a major source of talent. Having been forced to pay high advances and royalties to sign up British acts, most of the major American companies decided to set up British-based subsidiaries with their own A and R, promotion, distribution, marketing, and sales forces.

For a few years the American companies were much more successful in Britain with records produced in America than with local material (see Table 3), but gradually the proportion of British productions increased, overtaking the number of Top 10 hits produced by the major British companies in 1972. Since 1969 at least half of Britain's hits have emanated from American companies, either released through their own subsidiaries or licensed through British outlets.

PROGRESSIVE INTEGRATION

Every company with a "major act" in Britain or America now launches a full-scale campaign to launch the act in the other market. Invariably these campaigns are based on tours of the territory, making the name known through billboard posters, ads and interviews in the press and on the radio, and word-of-mouth recommendations from the audiences.

The prototype act launched by tours was Cream, formed in 1966 by three breakaway musicians from London R and B, Eric Clapton, Jack Bruce, and Ginger Baker, who were frustrated by the limited structure and rhythms of three-minute R and B songs. Playing a few college gigs, a jazz festival, and at the Marquee in London, Cream discovered an unexpectedly large audience with similar feelings and surprised the record business by making the singles and albums charts with their first records, made for the independent Reaction label (distributed by Polydor).

America in 1967 was at the height of the Flower-Power movement, which had been launched in San Francisco by previously unknown groups playing long solos and by FM radio stations which favored album tracks and fostered the identity of a new freethinking, drug-taking youth culture with its own ways of reaching decisions. Cream was imported into this scene by its American record outlet, Atlantic, and took it by storm, topping the album charts with its third album in 1968, in the wake of national tours which drew unprecedented audiences. Guitarist Eric Clapton openly acknowledged his debt to records made in the 1950s and early 1960s by black American blues guitarists B. B. King, Otis Rush, Albert King, Freddy King, Buddy Guy and others, whose careers all benefited from the new attention of Clapton's audience, without ever matching the drawing power of Cream.

FM radio spread across the States, British and American bands found audiences wherever they played, and *Rolling Stone* magazine confirmed and consolidated the market for the new "progressive music" (previously "underground," but now definitely on the surface). Several music festivals, notably at Monterey, California, in 1967 and Woodstock, New York, in 1969, presented many of the leading live groups of the time, lacking the Beatles, the Rolling Stones, Bob Dylan and Simon and Garfunkel, but offering the best of the rest—many of whom were British.

Despite their adroitly established British outposts, the American companies missed signing most of the enduring British live acts, and so did the British majors. Independent British producers signed up the majority of them, forming their own labels in Britain and licensing their records to majors in America, where they consistently outsold most of the homegrown alternatives and imitators.

Although they wrote most of their own material, Cream and the other leading British bands of the late 1960s mostly stayed close to the formulas of postwar amplified guitar blues—heavy rhythmic chords, with space for virtuoso guitar solos. The Jeff Beck Group, Led Zeppelin, Status Quo, Free, Ten Years After, Fleetwood Mac, Deep Purple, and Black Sabbath all worked the same field, making their records with British and American audiences in mind, often spending a larger part of each year working in the States than in Britain. Surprisingly few American groups sprang up in retaliation, although the heavily promoted Grand Funk Railroad proved that the American audience could be persuaded to accept a local substitute for the British bands. Steppenwolf, Guess Who (from Canada), and the southern bands like the Allman Brothers, Lynyrd Skynyrd and Z. Z. Top have also proved the enduring effectiveness of the boogie-and-blues formula, in live performance and on record. It would take a connoisseur of the style to distinguish British from American records, and the difference would be academic—aiming to perform the same function, assaulting their audience with huge PA systems and mind-numbing solos, the bands have no motive to stress their individuality, a difficult task which is left to enterprising PR offices.

While those heavy riff bands subdue their audiences with grotesquely exaggerated blues, a more genuinely "European" contribution to music has been made by bands playing Concept Rock, introduced into homes across the world during the summer of 1967 via the Beatles' album *Sergeant Pepper's Lonely Hearts Club Band*. Although the thematic relationship of the songs on the album was tenuous, they shared an atmosphere of hidden meanings and exciting implications, a suite of intricately arranged ballads and celebrations.

Table 3   U.S. and U.K. Share of British Top Ten Hits Market, 1965-1975

| Year | Total Hits | Records Produced in U.K. | | | Total |
| | | Major U.K. Co. | Independent U.K.Co. | Subsidiary of U.S. Co. | |
	(1)	(2)	(3)	(4)	(5)
1965	110	77	—	1	78
1966	106	65	4	1	70
1967	104	60	13	5	78
1968	97	43	11	12	66
1969	100	31	19	8	58
1970	111	24	23	11	58
1971	105	21	28	15	64
1972	109	16	31	17	64
1973	120	27	32	24	83
1974	127	18	38	34	90
1975	137	18	41	34	93

| U.K. Label | Records Produced in U.S. (licensed to own logo) | | Total | Total Subsid. of U.S. Co. (4 + 8) | Total All U.S. Companies (4 + 9) |
| | With U.K. Co. | Subsidiary of U.S. Co. | | | |
(6)	(7)	(8)	(9)	(10)	(11)
12	10	10	32	11	33
13	17	6	36	7	37
5	11	10	26	15	33
6	11	14	31	26	33
6	18	16	42	24	50
5	27	21	53	32	67
6	17	23	41	38	54
6	18	21	45	38	62
1	15	21	37	45	61
6	21	10	37	44	71
3	25	16	44	50	78

Sergeant Pepper was particularly welcomed by the middle-class audience who had shunned popular music before the Beatles and who had found their earlier records intellectually inadequate, too closely tied to pop music's traditional functions as dance music and emotional soundtrack. Looking for a record to listen to on sophisticated stereo equipment at home (maybe a little high on drugs), they got what they wanted with *Sergeant Pepper*. The record was partly a triumph for George Martin, producer and musical arranger for the Beatles, but after following through with the similar *Magical Mystery Tour* soundtrack, the Beatles themselves returned to musical styles closer to the traditional pop mainstream, leaving other musicians to explore the territory discovered in *Sergeant Pepper*.

For the first time, Americans had accepted a distinctive British musical style which was not a direct derivative of one of their own, and their interest created a market which other British musicians began to supply, not only with concept albums, but with theatrically conceived stage shows as well. Pink Floyd, Jethro Tull, Nice, Yes, Emerson Lake and Palmer, Genesis, and the Moody Blues evolved various styles, often borrowing harmonic ideas from classical composers and tending to lose the emphasis on rhythm which previously characterized contemporary pop music. The Who still stressed rhythm, but harnessed it to a double-album epic called *Tommy* and belatedly achieved a prestige which "mere" hit singles had failed to give the group. More recently, David Bowie, Roxy Music, and Queen have further exploited the theatrical and visual aspects of live performance and press coverage, effectively promoting hit singles and albums. Americans have so far accepted most of this music as consumers, without coming up with any satisfactory alternative of their own.

Despite the acute awareness from musicians on each side of the Atlantic towards the other, most records are still distinctively American in style. A few are distinctively British. Fewer still are a genuine mixture of the two cultures. This resilience of established forms partly reflects the market divisions of American radio into "black," "country," "easy listening," "FM progressive," and "AM pop." Each of those markets has its formula expectations, and records are obliged to meet them. The Average White Band (from Scotland) gets play on black stations by sounding exactly like a black American band; Olivia Newton-John, an Australian who records in London, gets play on country stations because her records sound as if they were made in Nashville.

In Britain, radio playlists are more eclectic, reaching for all the family and aiming at a younger audience than American radio caters to. Black American styles are accepted much more quickly than they were ten years ago, but funk was delayed by an anachronistic alternative British dance music based on rock 'n' roll. T. Rex, Slade, Gary Glitter, Mud, and several other groups had a succession of hits using crashing drum rhythms in 4/4 time and old-fashioned boogie bass lines. No amount of promotional tours could persuade Americans that this music had more than a short-lived novelty appeal, and most of the bands have made drastic stylistic changes in order to meet the more sophisticated musical standards of the American market, sacrificing their British popularity in the process.

The artist who comes closest to bridging the gaps in style and taste between the British and American markets is Elton John. Singing in a strangely rootless style, Elton John sounds neither British nor American, neither urban nor rural, neither happy nor sad; suspended in unreality, his well-recorded, technically competent, emotionally unspecific records are played more widely on American radio than those of any artist since the Beatles.

Elton John and his lyricist, Bernie Taupin, typify and embody the influence and effect of America (in general and its music in particular) on Britain. Virtually surrendering their own identity, they have assumed the character of a person who grew up simultaneously in a small southern town, a northern ghetto, and a London suburb, absorbing gospel and country roots into the youthful energy of R and B and the mature melancholy of pastoral rock. The album titles are properly symbolic: *Madman Across the Water*; *Captain Fantastic and the Dirt Brown Cowboy*. Provided the listener is not concerned with pinning down a more precise identity behind the evasive, shifting persona, the records represent the most complete synthesis of twentieth-century British and American music.

If the listener prefers a more personal vision, then Van Morrison may be more satisfying. Similarly influenced by all aspects of American music, Van Morrison has a stronger personal musical base (in Irish folk music) and a more self-obsessed, experience-based attitude to his songs. In contrast to the meticulous perfection of Elton John's records, Van Morrison's are more loosely arranged and improvised, making brilliant use of the intuitive rhythmic sense of American musicians to capture the instinctive insights of a singer first inspired by America from far away. Recording in New York and California since 1968, Van Morrison has sold fewer records than Elton John because he has refused to promote each release with a series of concerts, as the system currently requires. But his records suggest a more optimistic future for the collusion between American and British musical cultures than the coldly impersonal million-sellers of Elton John.

PLATE 1. A Panel of Speakers at a 1976 Conference Session. *Left to right*; Sulak Sivaraksa from Thailand, Göran Hermerén from Sweden, Mbulamwanza Mudimbe-Boyi from Zaïre, and Marcus Cunliffe from Great Britain. (*Photograph courtesy of the Smithsonian Institution, Washington, D.C.*)

PLATE 2. An A & W Root Beer Stand in Kobe, Japan. Notice that "Root Beer" is translated, but the brand name remains in English. The American soft drink—Coca Cola, 7-UP, Pepsi Cola—is another aspect of American life style exported around the world. (*Photo courtesy of A & W International, Inc., Santa Monica, California*).

Avis springt ein, wenn Ihr Wagen ausfällt.

Weil er zum Beispiel in die Werkstatt zur Wartung muß.

Weil er vorübergehend seinen Geist aufgegeben hat.

Weil zur Zeit ein anderer damit unterwegs ist.

Oder weil es zum Beispiel einen Betriebsunfall gegeben hat.

AVIS

Avis Autovermietung GmbH
Eschersheimer Landstraße 55 · 6000 Frankfurt am Main · Tel.: 0611/55 05 61

Wir vermieten PKWs und LKWs.

PLATE 3. Avis Advertisement in Germany: "Avis will come to the rescue when your car quits; when it is laid up in the garage; when it repeatedly gives up the ghost; when someone else takes it on the road; when an accident has taken place." Avis, American Express, Hilton, and other American companies are as familiar in Germany as Volkswagen is in the United States. (*Photo courtesy of Avis Rent A Car System, Inc., Garden City, New York*).

Plate 4. Heinz Ketchup made in the Netherlands, Heinz, like many American companies, has established factories abroad and develops special advertisements for its foreign clientele. This advertisement for Ketchup made in Holland is in German, but the brand and the product are unmistakedly American. (*Photo courtesy of H. J. Heinz Company, Pittsburgh, Pennsylvania*).

PLATE 5. Heinz Soup Billboard in Tokyo: "Heinz soup is full of youthful vitality." While American products and American advertisements are familiar sights in Japan, Japanese Toyotas, Sonys and Minoltas capture a portion of the American market. (*Photo courtesy of H. J. Heinz Company, Pittsburgh, Pennsylvania*).

PLATE 6. Levi's Advertisement in Spanish. American jeans like American music, American movies, and other aspects of American youth culture have penetrated every corner of the world. This advertisement for Levi's in Spanish says simply: "The brand that created the jean." (*Photo courtesy of Levi Strauss & Co., San Francisco, California*).

PLATE 7. McDonald's Advertisement in Sweden promoting the traditional American meal of hamburgers and french fries. McDonald's Golden Arches are a common sight in many parts of the world. (*Photo courtesy of McDonalds Corporation, Oak Brook, Illinois*).

Plate 8. Purina Advertisement on a Truck in Mexico: "Feed your animals with Purina and make more money" is the message. (*Photo courtesy of Ralston Purina International, St. Louis, Missouri*).

PART 2

Technology, Business, and Foreign Policy

INTRODUCTION

"From the Model T to the multinational corporation, America's inventive genius and corporate know-how have reshaped societies and the lives of men and women everywhere."[1] In an even more sweeping generalization, Zbigniew Brzezinski, national security adviser to President Carter, wrote: "Rome exported law; England parliamentary party democracy; France culture and republican nationalism; the contemporary United States, technological-scientific innovation and mass culture derived from high consumption."[2] We live in a "technetronic era," Brzezinski argues, a postindustrial society shaped by technology and electronics. American technology, American business, and American foreign policy are closely related. American-based corporations build factories in France, Brazil, and Taiwan; American research laboratories and computer companies influence decisions around the world. American investment and trade help dictate policy toward Chile, Iran, South Africa and Saudi Arabia. "The global corporation is transforming the world political economy through its increasing controls over three fundamental resources of economic life; the technology of production, finance, capital and marketing," a recent study concludes.[3]

The following essays describe various aspects of the American technological and business influence on other parts of the world and spell out some of the implications for the future. The first essay by Isaias Flit-Stern, scientist, professor and general director of the Institute for Industrial Research and Technical Standards in Lima, Peru, explores the impact of

American technology on Peru. "Whether one concludes that the influence of American technology has been beneficial to Peru," he writes, "depends on one's perception of possible alternatives for developments and how much one likes the society and culture that American technology has helped to shape. . . . If the United States really wants to help the technological development of its neighbors, first it has to try to understand the complexities of the problem and to learn how to compromise."

The next essay by Pehr Gyllenhammar, lawyer, businessman and president of Volvo, describes the influence of American industrial and business methods on the Swedish auto industry. He credits the United States with many inventions and innovations, the assembly line, efficiency studies, and management techniques which have helped to produce modern industrial systems in many parts of the world, but he also suggests that Swedish management practices have gone beyond the American model. "There seems to be a new defensiveness on the part of Americans," he writes, "and a reluctance to have their own technologies blended in the European mix, and shipped back to the United States."

The next essay by Marina Menshikova, formerly a professor of economics at the University of Moscow and later a consultant to the United Nations, is a Marxist analysis of American agriculture and its international impact. She concludes that although American agriculture and agricultural techniques have had a large impact on the world's economy, the American experience is not exportable especially to the developing countries of the world. "The experience of American agriculture was in many ways unique, and determined by the particular combination of vast, easily exploitable virgin lands with scarce, but highly productive labor resources," she writes. "This particular combination has rarely been repeated elsewhere in the past, and it is not likely to be repeated in the future."

The last essay by Eqbal Ahmad of Pakistan who is currently a fellow of the Institute for Policy Studies in Washington, is an angry indictment of American foreign policy and the influence of American business and the multinational corporation on the Third World. It is with some irony that he uses the work of a number of American historians and political analysts to document his attack on American foreign policy.

One does not have to agree with all of the points in these essays to understand that the United States is entering a period of crisis in its relationship to the rest of the world.

NOTES

1. Robert Gilpin, "Exploring the Technological Revolution," *Saturday Review* (13 December 1975): 31.

2. Zbigniew Brzezinski, *Between Two Ages: America's Role in the Technetronic Era* (New York: Viking Press, 1970), p. 25.

3. Richard Barnet and Ronald Müller, *Global Reach: The Power of the Multinational Corporations* (New York: Simon and Schuster, 1974), p. 26.

AMERICAN TECHNOLOGY AND PERUVIAN DEVELOPMENT: HOPES AND FRUSTRATIONS _____

Isaias Flit Stern

> Meddling with a nation's technology is indeed meddling with a nation's future form and character.
>
> Eugene B. Skolnikoff
> *Science, Technology and American Foreign Policy*

INTRODUCTION

We live now in a technological era. Technical knowledge permeates the whole tissue of our present civilization, and the United States plays *the* leading role in the shaping of this technological civilization. From nuclear power plants to digital wristwatches and managerial techniques, we find an American birthmark on almost every technical development in current use.

American technology influences almost every human activity despite the fact that the United States world leadership in technological matters is relatively recent; it only encompasses a little more than one quarter of its two hundred years as an independent nation. Since technology affects the ways in which we communicate, produce, manage, govern, use our leisure time, and solve our problems, it becomes clear that to have influence on the technological development of a country is to be able to affect its economic, social, and cultural development.

The technological influence of the United States is strongest in developing countries like Peru, which are in the political and economic sphere of the United States and have only a limited capability to create and handle their own technology. By demonstrations, lectures, international meetings, foreign aid, and advice, Peru has been gradually convinced of the need to acquire technical knowledge as a means of becoming a modern industrial nation. Here the word *acquire* is used in its broadest sense, which means buying, leasing, borrowing, adapting, copying, creating, or developing technical knowledge.

The following discussion is based on my direct experience in technological problems in Peru and on my involvement of almost fifteen years in the design of technological policies and technologically-oriented organizations and instruments for development in Peru.

TECHNICAL ASSISTANCE

There are three main ways by which technical knowledge from the United States reaches Peru: (1) through the operation of the subsidiary of an American enterprise; (2) through license agreements between Peruvian and American enterprises; and (3) through United States technical aid to Peru.

The American influence started when American companies began to exploit Peruvian natural resources (oil, mining) and to organize public services (such as telecommunications) through subsidiaries of American firms. Later, when Peru adopted a "substitution of exports" industrial-development policy, many American enterprises set up subsidiaries to produce what they had been exporting to Peru. Through this involvement of American enterprises in the Peruvian economy, Peruvian nationals, mainly in the lower and middle technical and managerial echelons, gained some technical knowledge. On the other hand, access by Peruvian nationals to the high decision-making levels and to the most sophisticated techniques was restricted, and the most important decisions were made at the United States headquarters.

As a result, not only was it difficult for Peru to develop a national capability for handling the more important means of production and public services, but this practice also linked the development of the country not to Peru's own needs but to the needs, plans, and policies of foreign enterprises. Many times this policy has been reinforced by United States government interference.

The question is whether there could have been any other alternative open to Peru for utilizing its natural resources or organizing its telecommunications network. These undertakings would have required large amounts of capital, technical knowledge not available at the time in the country, and marketing and managerial skills beyond Peruvian capabilities. Some will argue that the activities of American subsidiaries created jobs and income as well as providing a means to learn the technical capacity to handle these matters. The fact that after the Peruvian government nationalized American-owned oil companies, mining businesses, and the telephone company (a subsidiary of ITT), there were nationals able to operate them supports this argument.

On the other hand, there is little doubt as to who got the lion's share in those operations. Furthermore, the question is: was the learning process due to a conscious policy of the multinational enterprise, or was it rather hampered by a careful withholding of relevant information?

In any case, capital and technology were used by American-based multinational corporations as trumps to gain or retain privileges or to increase profits. It also has to be mentioned that the United States State

Department applied additional, and sometimes unbearable, pressure in favor of those corporations' interests. In the 1960s, for example, the United States Embassy in Lima used great pressure to help a foreign company retain control of the Peruvian telecomunications system.

The second method of American influence, license agreements, is becoming increasingly important as Peru struggles for industrial development. Most economists agree that improvements in technology are at least as important as increases in capital and labor for the economic growth of a country. Coupled with the growing recognition, at the state level, of the importance of technology in development is the need, at the company level, of the knowledge to start production, to keep it going, and to take advantage of the current developments in other countries.

As the process of "transfer of technology" is studied in more detail, especially by the developing countries, it becomes obvious that there are many drawbacks in type, quality, conditions, and costs. In 1974, following a proposal made by Henry Kissinger, a group of government experts was created "to study the possibility to create an Inter-American Commission for Science and Transfer of Technology." The group had several meetings. In the first meeting, held at Brasilia in July 1974, the official record of the proceedings mentioned "abuses in the transfer of technology" from the United States to Latin America. These minutes were approved by the American delegation without reservation, but the abuses were not corrected.

A recent study made in Peru shows that from a sample of 404 technological-transferral contracts 181 (that is, 44.8 percent) were with enterprises based in the United States. The sample was taken from the manufacturing sector. Furthermore, during 1972 and 1973, the gross royalties paid for those 404 contracts was 12.4 and 11.4 million dollars, respectively, of which the United States contracts amounted to 44 percent and 38 percent.

Most of those contracts had clauses that condition the transfer in such a way as to make the words *lease* or *hire* more appropriate than *transfer*. These restrictive clauses deal mainly with:

a) The interference of licensor in licensee's managerial decisions such as price-fixing, hiring of personnel at top managerial or technical levels, marketing, ownership of shares, volume and structure of products, etc.

b) Obligation of the licensee to buy from or through the licensor equipment, raw materials, or any type of goods or services necessary for production.

c) Restriction on the countries to which the licensee could export what is produced with the technology or under the trademark licensed.

In the above-mentioned 404 contracts 1,677 restrictive clauses were found, of which 875 (52.2 percent) were with American licensors.

The profit-motivated firms of the Untited States "transfer" the technology they have available without taking into account the real needs of their clients and the peculiar social, economic, and physical environment of Peru. In addition, they usually overcharge for a commodity that, in the words of J. J. Clark, "is the only instrument of production that is not subject to diminishing returns."

The third method of American influence—technical aid through official agencies—has been concentrated mainly in rural development, agriculture, light industry, public health, and military assistance.

It is difficult to assess the effectiveness of United States technical-aid efforts in Peru. Sometimes they have helped to solve a problem, but many times they have been part of a general program developed in Washington and exported to many other countries on a "take it or leave it" basis. This type of program leads to an assistance that is seldom geared to the specific characteristics of the political, cultural, and social environment of Peru. As a result, very little concern has been given to the need to adapt technology to the local environment or to take into account the effects of technological innovation on a particular society.

Many times the United States technical aid to Peru has come with the same restrictions and ties that have made economic aid a way to enhance the business that United States corporations do with Peruvian agencies. From war surplus to textile equipment, many things have been sold to Peru as a result of technical-aid programs that have not really been needed in Peru.

TRADE

The equipment and products that a country buys have an effect on many other things. For example, the equipment chosen affects the mix of production factors required in industry, determines the type of raw materials or intermediate goods to be used, and creates the need for certain skills and resources for maintenance, adaptation, and repair.

The imported products create new problems for the economy and the society of the country. These products may require new marketing techniques, may create a demand for local production, and may force a change of habits or social behavior. These imported items may even displace local products which have long been in use. Thus, the United States government's technical aid helps to increase the amount of equipment, goods, and services that Peru buys from the United States. At the same time, the flow of those productions to Peru increases Peru's demand for technical assistance. This whole process is reinforced by the "demonstration effect" created through magazines, films, cultural events, educational exchange, and other means of selling "life styles" that crate cultural, social, and economic needs. There seems to be no way out of the circular trap.

In the case of Peru, much of the equipment and new products has come from the United States, with an obvious influence on patterns of production and demand, cultural and industrial development, and the society's internal development. For example, in 1973, Peru imported consumer goods worth about 3.4 million United States dollars, of which about 13.5 percent came from the United States; 9.5 million United States dollars worth of raw materials and intermediate goods, of which about 32 percent came from the United States; and about 9.1 million United States dollars worth of capital goods, with about 37.5 percent from the United States.

EDUCATION

Technical knowledge is processed information, and this process takes place mainly through the educational system. Hence, the use, transmission, growth, and diffusion of technical knowledge in Peru has been influenced by scholarships, training in the United States, student-exchange programs, visiting professors, assistance to Peruvian technical universities, and other similar activities of the United States AID program for education.

In many cases, all of these activities have been useful to Peru, but they have also had definite drawbacks. A particular technology shapes the society that uses it, and this is specially true when it comes to managerial techniques. Many of the best-trained technicians from Peru have been trained in United States universities or companies. Many of them now live in the United States or work for American enterprises.

The point is that Peru's technocratic elite has been strongly influenced by American aid and technical education. This has been highly beneficial for the technological development of the country; at the same time, it has reinforced the cultural, economic, and technological dependence of Peru on the United States. Whenever Peruvians trained in the United States return to their own country, they bring not only technical knowledge with them, but also American cultural values, a preference for American equipment and know-how, and attitudes about the way men and things should be managed. How good or bad this is, is an open question. The point is that a technologically sophisticated and powerful country exerts a great influence over a weaker and less-developed country, and that influence is structured through education.

ADVICE ON TECHNOLOGICAL POLICY-MAKING

The United States has been, in the past fifty years, a showcase for the idea that a nation's growth and security depend on research and development.

American technicians, scientists, and government officials have been outspoken supporters of the theory that developing countries need to spend money on science and technology if they want economic growth.

In Peru, as in other countries, the United States involvement goes further than the mere promotion of the benefits of science and technology. United States agencies have given special support or advice to their Peruvian counterparts on matters related to scientific and technological policy-making.

Among the most important actions has been the assistance in creating research and development capabilities in the armed forces, particularly in the navy. Also with American support, The National Academy of Sciences has sponsored Peru-United States workshops on science and technology in economic development. These workshops, supported by AID, were held in 1966 and 1967, and they brought together "scientists and government representatives of the United States and Peru to discuss informally the development of an organizational structure and policy necessary to accelerate scientific and technological progress essential for Peruvian development." As a result of the workshops, many Peruvian scientists, technicians, and government officials interested in the development of a scientific and technological structure met for the first time. Many useful relationships between them were started, and scientists and technicians realized the benefits of creating a "pressure group" to call the governments' attention to technological matters. A National Research Council and a Peruvian Association for the Advancement of Science were created as a result of these meetings.

On the other hand, the Peruvian group, when trying to duplicate United States organizations without fully understanding them and their real purpose, endangered the development of a technological policy more compatible with the Peruvian reality and the essential problems of Peruvian technological development. It took some time for Peruvians to realize that policy-making and institutional arrangements cannot be transplanted, and that the American advice should be taken with careful consideration of the special characteristics of the environment in which it has to be put to work.

INSTITUTIONS

American involvement in the development of a scientific and technological structure in Peru has not been limited to the universities or to the policy-making efforts. In some cases, it has supported and even helped to create research institutions.

The most interesting example is the Institute Geofisico del Peru, which was founded in 1919 by the Carnegie Institution under the name Huancayo Magnetic Observatory. During the International Geophysical Year

(1957-1958) its work was increased considerably, and numerous additional observatories and observing posts were established elsewhere in Peru. Later, under a cooperative agreement with NASA, the satellite tracking station of Ancon was built and, under an agreement with the NBS, the radar observatory of Jicamarca was created.

Although all those efforts were directed mainly to the collection of data that were of interest to the American institutions involved, the activities of the Instituto Geofisico made it possible to develop scientific activities of direct interest to Peru, such as seismology, and to train a highly qualified group of Peruvian engineers and scientists in fields related to electronics, communciations, earth sciences, and physics. In this case, the decisive role was played not by the Americans, but by their Peruvian counterparts who realized that the interests of American scientists in the special geophysical conditions of Peru could be used to further the development of some technical activities necessary to their country.

Not all United States technical and financial aid for research institutions has had similar benefits. There are institutions in Peru and the rest of Latin America that stand as sad examples of what happens when a technical organization is created because of an external impulse, depends too heavily on foreign resources, and is unable to find a legitimate place in the technical structure of the country before the foreign resources stop coming.

CONCLUSION

It is clear that the United States has had a strong influence on the development of technology in Peru. This influence is the result of the economic, cultural, and political power of the United States, not only over Peru, but over much of the world.

As technology becomes an increasingly predominant factor in American society, the effects of American technology on countries like Peru become overwhelming. Whether one concludes that the influence of American technology has been beneficial to Peru, depends on one's perception of possible alternatives for development, and on how much one likes the society and culture that American technology has helped to shape. Even setting aside value judgments, it is obvious that much more could have been achieved by Peru if the United States government and the American corporations had paid closer attention to Peru's needs and hopes.

If the United States really wants to help the technological development of its neighbors, first it has to try to understand the complexities of the problem and to learn how to compromise.

THE IMPACT OF AMERICAN CULTURE ON MANAGEMENT ORGANIZATION AND THE TRANSPORTATION INDUSTRY _____

Pehr G. Gyllenhammar

Present-day American culture and life-style have had a larger impact on European development than many Europeans want to believe. The American way has been reluctantly, and sometimes unconsciously, accepted in eating habits, fashion, social life, and leisure activities. In fact, a growing criticism of the United States has gone hand in hand with the ever-increasing acceptance of American life-styles. The basic acceptance of American values in a variety of fields has made Europeans sensitive and defensive. The same defensiveness has not been apparent in the fields of American dominance. American management science, organization development and industrial technologies have in many ways not replaced the European way but rather have filled a vacuum. American leadership has in many new fields been unchallenged and the benefits to the recipients clearly seen. This is not the case where strong European cultures based on long histories and traditions have given in to American influence.

The United States has given enormous and frequent stimuli to innovative technology, to a rapidly increasing material wealth, and to increasing international trade. The early take-off of the United States as a wealthy nation impressed a slow-moving and poverty-stricken Europe. Most Europeans also had close relatives or friends who had emigrated to the United States, thereby creating interest in and motivation for maintaining a close relationship in the exchange of information between the old country and the new country.

Europeans took a personal interest in what was happening on the other side of the Atlantic ocean. Sweden, for example, saw almost one-third of its population move to the United States during the middle and latter part of the nineteenth century. This means that almost every individual in Sweden today has relatives in the United States.

The United States' impact on the transfer of technology, the transfer of capital, the monetary systems, and the accounting practices of various activities in other societies has had an enormous impact. The monetary system, designed at the 1943 Bretton-Woods Conference was, in essence, an American system, arising from the fact that the United States controlled a major share of the world economy. It was maintained by the policing of the United States. The collapse of the monetary system in 1971 was a logical consequence of the relatively diminishing power that the United States could exercise in the late 1960s and early 1970s. Strong American supervision faltered and the monetary system was destroyed. The United States is now emerging from its external and internal political problems and is seeing a recovery of her economy. This will no doubt again give more stability to the monetary system in the world.

The United States was the first country where the science of management was taught in college. Since the 1950s other countries have followed this practice and have built their curricula on the American system.

In product development and production technologies, the United States has made innovations of historical importance. One such innovation was the assembly line concept, so successfully introduced as to make possible mass production of complex products and the availability of such products to almost every individual. However, the assembly line technology became so successful that few efforts have been made in the United States to introduce new production techniques to succeed it.

In the area of management techniques, it was the United States that gave birth to "Taylorism" and "scientific management." It was in the United States that the "human relations theory" was created and developed. It was in the United States that the expressions "Economic Man," "Social Man," and "Complex Man" were coined. It was in the United States that Douglas McGregor developed his theory "x and y."

In the study of behavioral sciences and the social structure of the organization Abraham Maslow launched his theories on basic needs and self-fulfillment, whereas Frederick Herzberg separated motivators from hygiene factors. In organizational development the United States has introduced group dynamics, T-groups, and modern psychoanalysis.

What has then happened to American breakthroughs in production technologies, to United States theories on management and organizational development? They have been transferred to Europe.

Let us first look at the production technology and, specifically, the assembly line concept. The culture of the United States is very achievement-oriented. This is a natural consequence of the motivation behind the European emigration to the United States. The people who left were mainly dissatisfied with the political, economic, or religious situations in their home countries. They left to become independent and to create that independence partly through accumulating wealth. The European establishment, on the other hand, was left with a combination of ancient traditions, repressive values, and old wealth. Europe, particularly in the industrial areas, was less innovative and certainly much less achievement-oriented. When democratic ideas penetrated to Western Europe the push for equality started. A way was sought to make distribution of wealth and income fairer by adopting more achievement-oriented management and production methods. This laid the foundation for the transfer of United States technology to Europe.

The simplest and most obvious transfer of technology was in the production area which, however, had little influence on cultural values that affect infrastructure and education. The science of management had long to wait before it was applied in European countries. The assembly line technology was, at first, uncritically accepted. In the 1950s when capital and technology were transferred from the United States to Europe, American consultants were everywhere in European industry. They were experts on material handling, tool making, and in production organization. When the European automobile industry finally took off after World War II it was based on doing what the Americans had been doing but on a smaller scale, both in product design and in the number of cars produced. Sweden generated enough money from its abundance of raw materials and through its expertise in processing them to be able to apply American technological systems in new areas of business. The manufacture and assembly of mechanical products increased in the 1950s and the 1960s. In the late 1960s, however, a fairly significant movement started against the uncritical acceptance of the imported production technology.

The northern European workers, specifically people in Germany and Sweden, had reached a level of income and education which led them to question focusing on achievement only in economic terms. The average period of education for a young Swede had gone from seven years to an average of ten to twelve years in less than two decades. This education did not primarily provide new skills and new know-how, but it had the effect of changing values fairly rapidly. Life-styles became important, as did the structure and components of jobs. Attention was focused on the monotony and boredom of modern industrial works symbolized by the assembly line technology. Strong union organizations put pressure on management to change work patterns and modify the technologies used. More significantly, both union leaders and management were surprised by the phenomenon of workers leaving industrial jobs to seek other employment opportunities. Affluence and economic growth made it possible for them to spend a very short time on each job. In a way, this turnover of workers could be seen as a new escapism, where one would not give up one's standard of living, but could escape from being bound for a lifetime to a job that never changed and seemed meaningless. The growing size of labor organizations contributed to widening the communication gap between management and workers and thus caused alienation and frustration.

These are the reasons why, in Sweden, management has focused on retaining workers by improving their jobs. Efforts have been made to attempt to change the jobs themselves. Traditional technology has been challenged on the assumption that a new technology will provide flexibility for organizational development. Thus, within Volvo, we have designed new production patterns, new work organizations, and new material-handling systems—all directed at giving management and employees an entirely new flexibility when organizing resources. The assembly line has been broken up. First of all, it has been recognized that it is fairly humiliating and not very efficient to have people running after a product that moves constantly and continuously on a conveyor belt. Secondly, it has been recognized that a conveyor belt, or the assembly line principle, is based on the assumptions that work should be fragmented and that each operator would be used to the maximum if he specialized on a specific operation—not to say a specific movement. We have had the paradoxical development of man being better-and-better educated and less-and-less able to utilize his talents in his work situation.

Within Volvo we have designed plants where people work on stationary products, where they perform many different functions, and where they are encouraged to extend their responsibilities and capabilities. They are asked to work in groups, instead of as isolated individuals on a production line. With increased skills and competence come a higher involvement and more aggressiveness of the individual, which can be used in his own work. The role of factory and plant management has thereby changed to focus more on the management of people than on the management and flow of material.

In this transition of production-technology and management it is not primarily European or Swedish management and organization theories that have been used. It is, to an amazing degree, American research that has been applied to change American-based technologies and organizational structures. One could say that the cultural base of Europe, and particularly Sweden, has been the driving force behind applying American science and developing, in a European way, the imported American technology. We have gone through the phases of Taylorism, the human relations schools, and modern theories by McGregor, Herzberg, and Argyris to come to grips with the growing danger of a high rate of turnover of people. Motivation of workers has been one of the key preoccupations, as well as the design of new jobs and job opportunities.

American studies of the structure of organizations have been applied, not so much to maximize profits in the short term through greater productivity but to decentralize and thus encourage individuals to take larger responsibilities. American organizational structures have been adapted to include such features as the Swedish Work Council design and the integration of employees in decision making. Structures have been changed to promote a new flow of information from management to employees, and vice versa. A decision-making process has been created to use the employees either on a consultative basis or with veto-making power in company developments that may be contrary to their interests.

American educational systems and methods have been applied in training employees for their new roles. Employee representatives are encouraged to use the new and extensive education provided them and to acquire a broader understanding of the role and the functioning of their organization. The role of management has changed in Sweden, where previously a traditional conflict of interest existed between employee and employer and between shareholder and worker. Common interests have been stressed as the key principle in managing a successful corporation. The profit motive is still heavily stressed and has, if anything, become more important in these recent years of recession and financial problems for many corporations However, one of the important ways to maintain high productivity and exceptional quality is through involving and motivating the whole work force. They should participate in, criticize, and stimulate the corporate development in the common interest.

This new element of Swedish and European management development has gone beyond American practice. The American attitude towards the Volvo development has been either coldly observing or somewhat critical. A Ford Foundation study was made of American workers in a Swedish plant. The study's objective and methodology seemed less aimed at impartial findings, than at supporting the prejudice that new developments in production technology were unsuccessful and unproductive. There seems to be a new defensiveness on the part of Americans and a reluctance to have their own technologies blended in the European mix and shipped back to the United States.

Why should the United States accept a diffusion of Swedish or European ideas into its systems? Certainly one should have reservations about serious cultural differences. Certainly one should have an open mind to the variations in local conditions and life-styles. But one should not assume that an American worker has entirely different basic needs from a Swedish worker. That is going too far. My previous argument was that United States values and technologies were almost uncritically accepted in Europe. This means also that Europe had few difficulties in going through the dramatic change from being tied to their traditional power-structure to accepting an entirely achievement-oriented system. The acceptance of American researchers' ideas of human development in Europe should encounter no serious cultural barriers in the United States except as these obstacles are of a psychological nature.

We may thus be contemplating a transition in American corporate organization, where Europe, as was the case two hundred years ago, can make important contributions to American development.

THE AMERICAN WAY IN AGRICULTURE AND ITS INTERNATIONAL SIGNIFICANCE

Marina Menshikova

It is not generally realized that the analysis of American agriculture plays an important role in the general Marxist interpretation of the evolution of capitalism. In his *Das Kapital*, Karl Marx explains how laws of capitalist accumulation lead to the creation of anticapitalist trends and forces within the system and eventually to the "expropriation of expropirators." This, indeed, posits a "double ending." Marx then discusses the theory of colonization.

Colonization is looked upon by Marx as an inevitable outcome of the same laws of accumulation which govern the evolution of capitalism in general. The concentration of large masses of capital at one extreme and of unemployment and misery at the other led to exports of both capital and labor from the western European cradle of capitalism. Colonization served as a means of partially resolving economic and social conflicts in some countries, while reproducing them elsewhere on a larger, worldwide scale.

Relevant to a study of American agricultural ways and their international significance is the mass emigration of skilled labor from western Europe to America and to other "white colonies." For a long time the settlement of European capital and labor on the vast, unexploited, and relatively free and rich virgin lands of the New World remained one of the principal forms of colonization. Because of this international process the peculiar nature of American agriculture was created.

From its very beginnings American agricultural use, quite unlike that in the Old World, was based on a practically unlimited supply of land. The land was available to the settler and its was virtually free. For decades giving away land to anyone who wanted it, for only a nominal amount of money, was the undisputed American public policy. As a rule the free land was not gobbled up by large owners who would then use it as their means of making small unpropertied farmers work for them, but was available to independent farmers who tilled their own land. Some attributes of private property, such as the high price of land and land rents, were something that did not yet exist.

This unique combination of circumstances, according to Marx, tended to create the relatively uninhibited free movement of labor between industry and agriculture. Whereas in the Old World labor was being forced off the land and drawn into the grinding wheels of urban civilization, in the New World at least for many decades there existed a possibility of the opposite free movement from the proletarian industrial position to one of a relatively well-to-do farmer-owner.

This possibility helped to create a relatively high level of wages in industry which, even by the middle of the nineteenth century, were about twice as large in real income terms as in the leading western European countries. The effect was important, multifaceted, and long-lasting. Higher industrial wages contributed to the continuous supply of highly qualified immigrant labor in America, thus providing one of the most significant inputs to its fast economic growth. Relatively expensive labor also had the effect of stimulating technical progress by inducing industrialists to introduce labor-saving capital equipment, contributing to the fast growth productivity. On the demand side, wages helped create greater consumer demand, creating yet another growth factor.

The very simple fact of the availability of cheap and abundant land in America had effects reaching far beyond the borders of the United States. While the family farm became the mainstay of agriculture in the West and Far West, the large cotton plantation with its vast dependence on cheap labor was the bulwark of agriculture in the South. For the plantation class, slavery became a basic means of capital accumulation. But capitalism and slavery were having their honeymoon in a much wider sense. The Industrial Revolution had started in the textile industry, and its fast growth was impossible without cotton. Thus the American cotton plantation became a necessary component of world capitalist development throughout a major part of the nineteenth century.

This dual nature of American agriculture encompassing both the plantation and the family farm was doomed, however, even during its most flourishing period. As the plantation expanded westward, it became a direct competitor of the family farm in the quest for free land. The two types clashed in a deadly battle, and the plantation had to recede to a secondary role. Slavery was abolished, but the cheap labor of yesterday's slaves remained the plantation's financial basis for many decades. When the use of machinery finally managed to infiltrate the plantation it started the great exodus of black labor to the North, which set the stage for a new act in the history of capitalist urban civilization.

In the second half of the nineteenth century, American cotton and wheat became important factors in the development of world agriculture. Cotton from the United States was in sharp competition with cotton grown in the African colonies of the European countries, while American wheat became a new threat to grain production in western Europe itself.

In the 1880s and 1890s American production helped to create what is known in Marxist economic history as the first crisis of overproduction in capitalist agriculture. The crisis struck western European grain production, which became noncompetitive relative to the cheap grain coming from the virgin prairies of the New World.

The relative cheapness of American grain compared to European grain was not due exclusively to natural conditions. The prairie soils were rich, but crop yields there, on the average, were not higher than in Europe. The main difference stemmed from economic and social conditions. Land rent was absent from the production costs of the wheat from the prairies, while in western Europe wheat costs were burdened by high land rents due to the specific conditions prevailing in the area. Grain exports from Russia were also highly competitive with western European grain, but the reason for their lower price was different—it stemmed from the cheap labor of the Russian peasant who had recently emerged from serfdom.

The influence of cheap imports caused drastic restructuring of western European agriculture by the end of the nineteenth century. There were three principal changes. Many countries became highly specialized agriculture producers and net exporters of livestock products. Their crops were reoriented toward growing feed grains with an emphasis on intensive investment in land productivity. In a relatively short time, crop yields were exceeding the yields in the American prairies by a factor of two or three. At the same time, these countries remained net importers of overseas wheat for uses other than as feed grain.

With this restructuring accomplished, the agriculture of western Europe was competitive once again even with higher land rents. Western European countries were able to retain their basic social structure, which was still very different from the American type.

By this time, Vladimir Ilyich Lenin appeared as a leading Marxist writer. A substantial part of his economic books and articles was devoted to agriculture and its role in the economic development of capitalism. This was no coincidence, since Russia was a predominantly agricultural country. Russian agricultural statistics, organized by the *zemstvos* (local associations of large landowners), were well developed and lent themselves to detailed and scholarly analysis of socioeconomic conditions in agriculture. For a similar reason, another country attracted Lenin's interest: the United States. In *New Data on the Evolution of Capitalism in Agriculture* Lenin pursued two lines of analysis: types and paths of agricultural development; trends in the evolution of the family farm.

A serious problem, which Russia was then facing, was the choice of direction for developing its agriculture. The abolition of serfdom opened possibilities of various types of capitalist evolution. Another widely shared view was that because of the traditional communal organization of Russian peasantry known as *obschina* the country was not ready for capitalism and should instead pursue a different, noncapitalistic path.

Lenin showed that there could not be two different socioeconomic structures at the same time—one being capitalist in the cities and industrial centers and another being noncapitalist in agricultural areas. Given the predominance of capitalism in industry, the communal organization in agriculture would be rapidly transformed into one of two distinct types of capitalist organization. Accordingly, he spoke of two possible paths of capitalist evolution in agriculture.

One path, which he called Prussian, was to transform the big landownerships which were previously also serf-ownerships, into large-scale estates of a capitalist type. In this case, the peasantry would gradually be eliminated or proletarized. Another path, which he called American, was to eliminate the big semifeudal estates through land reform, and transform the peasant households into family farms.

Lenin did not imply that there were no other capitalist ways of organizing agriculture. In fact, the classical way as described in detail in Marx's *Kapital* was the English type with its predominantly capitalist labor-hiring farm using rented land. What Lenin meant was that in Russia the realistic alternatives were different.

Lenin's choice was the American way. He felt that the Prussian path would be long, unfair, and painful for the millions of landless peasants. It would also tend to strengthen the economic base of the most conservative class in Russian society which was totally opposed to any radical reforms. He felt that the American way, which for Russia meant land reform, would be much more efficient economically in bringing about a rapid increase in agricultural production.

Actually, the policy pursued in Russia, up to 1917, was a combination of the predominantly Prussian type with a half-hearted attempt to create a dual structure of large estates and strong capitalist farmers.[1] The outcome was total support given by the peasantry to the ideas of socialization and nationalization of land in the October Revolution of 1917.

By choosing the American way, Lenin was not saying that the family farm was a stable type of agricultural organization. He pursued this subject in a number of his works, including *New Data on American Agriculture*. Here he showed that the traditional mainstay of American agriculture, namely the family farm with its accent on family labor and farmer-ownership of the land, was being rapidly washed out by market forces, giving way to large capitalist farms based on hired labor (or a combination of family and hired labor) and generating the mass exodus of the less-fortunate farmers to the ranks of industrial labor. This analysis was borne out in the next decades.

The total number of farms in the United States rose rapidly in the second half of the nineteenth century: 1.4 million in 1840 to 5.7 million in 1900. There was still some growth in these numbers in the beginning of the twentieth century but practically no change occurred between 1910 (6.4 million) and 1930 (6.5 million).

The problems of the family farm were exacerbated by the prolonged period of agricultural overproduction, which started in the early 1920s and continued until the mid-1940s. The exodus from the farm was next to impossible during the Great Depression of the 1930s, but resumed in even greater numbers after it was over. From an overall peak of 6.8 million farms in 1935 their number declined rapidly to 4.7 million in 1955 and 2.8 million in 1975. Average land per United States farm practically remained constant between 1880 and 1910 (at 135 acres), but increased thereafter—to 155 acres in 1935, 258 in 1955, and 385 in 1975. In 1910 only 19 percent of total agricultural land was in large farms of a thousand acres or more but the proportion reached 29 percent by 1935, 46 percent by 1955, and 54 percent by 1969. There are only 150 thousand of such farms in the country—a tiny percent of the total number.

Writing in 1915, Lenin remarked that American agriculture was yet in its premachine stage. Since then, particularly after the mid-1940s, that industrialization of the farm has proceded rapidly. Grain production, animal products, and finally, cotton were mechanized to the extent that complete machine systems are being used. This was particularly fostered by rural electrification. The use of chemical fertilizers and pesticides increased enormously. Irrigation became widespread.

As a result of this technological revolution the American farm became highly capital-intensive: labor productivity increased by seven times from 1929 to the early 1970s, land productivity (measured by total agricultural output per cultivated acre) increased twofold.

In the course of this revolution, the socioeconomic type of American agriculture also changed rapidly. The farms were being integrated into a system of industrial, agricultural, commercial, transportation, and financial enterprises called "agribusiness." The dominant and leading role in this integration was assumed by the industrial and trade corporation and the bank, rather than the farm. In the case of contract farming, the vertically integrated farmer found himself left as only a hollow shell of an independent proprietor. Agriculture became closely interwoven with the overall economic system of financial and industrial monopoly capitalism. Thus, the old agricultural system, based predominantly on the independent family farm, virtually ceased to exist.

The American way of agricultural development was not followed in most other countries of the world. In developed capitalist regions such as western Europe the American way could not be followed because of the complex mix of large-scale landownership and old-styled peasantry into which the more modern capitalistic farm had to merge and adjust, but over which it had not the power to dominate. With the advent of the age of agribusiness this socioeconomic structure became even more complex and substantially different from the type of agribusiness prevailing in the United States. Land reform came to western Europe rather late and in many countries was not successful. But even where it was, the underlying relationship between farm labor, farm land, and farm capital was very different from the conditions in American agriculture.

In Japan the land reform, which was one outcome of World War II, destroyed much of the feudal system in agriculture. However, because of the specific relationship between abundant farm labor and scarce farm land, the predominant socioeconomic type is a very small farm using intensive irrigation and labor with little machinery.

A large part of eastern Europe and the Soviet Union chose yet another path, which is even further from the American way than in the cases of western Europe and Japan. The present socioeconomic structure of the agriculture of these centrally planned countries is based on state farms and production cooperatives (collective farms). This was a logical development from their previous structures. The land reforms in these countries were radical and sweeping. They eliminated the large landed estates and passed a substantial part of the land on to the peasants. In some of these countries land was nationalized; in others, private ownership of land was drastically limited. In spite of the vast redistribution of land, most of the individual farms remained very small, their productivity level very low. This became a major barrier to policies of rapid industrialization. The predominance of small private ownership in agriculture was seen to be in deep conflict with large-scale state-owned industry. This dual system was considered incompatible with fast economic growth and, in fact, with maintaining economic and political independence. The outcome of this conflict was collectivization, or the merging of small individual peasant farms into production cooperatives, and the creation of state farms wherever the cooperative form was inapplicable (that is, on some former large estates, in the virgin lands, and so on).

Thus, the choice in these countries was no more between the American and the Prussian types, but between the slow capitalist evolution of small landowners on the one hand, and a socialist type of agricultural organization on the other hand. The choice was made in favor of socialism.

Where does the evolution of agriculture in the developing countries stand? Which path are they expected to choose?

The basic problem of agriculture in the developing countries is to provide conditions for a rapid increase in output so as to satisfy the food demand of the growing population. In order even to maintain the current extremely low levels of food consumption, it is necessary in the developing regions, as a whole, at least to double agricultural output by the end of this century. This implies an annual compound growth rate of 2.5 percent (equal to the United Nations "medium" projected rate of population growth). If a significant improvement in nutrition standards were envisaged, a fourfold increase in output would be necessary.

According to a recent United Nations study this is a technologically feasible target, provided that some 550 million acres of arable land are brought into cultivation, and that adequate additional investment is made in land improvement, irrigation, fertilizer production and distribution, research and development, and maintenance of the natural environment. Land productivity could at least be doubled or even trebled.

The United Nations study indicates that success in this endeavor is contingent on adequate institutional arrangements:

The success of the new technological revolution in the agriculture of the developing regions depends to a large extent on land reform and other social and institutional changes, which are necessary to overcome nontechnological barriers to increased land use and productivity. It also depends on creating, by special measures of agricultural policy, a favourable economic environment for agricultural development, including incentives aimed at eliminating inefficiencies in the use of land, labor, and technology.[2]

It is worthwhile meditating about which course will be pursued in the agriculture of the developing countries. Will it be the American way as described above, or the Prussian way, or the Socialist way, or a combination of these, or other possibilities?

One thing is obvious; each developing country will hopefully make its own choice, which will be based on the specific conditions and cultural values of that country.

It is not possible simply to transplant development models from one continent or country to another. Even transferring technology is not that easy. For example, to increase drastically wheat yields in Mexico, India, and Pakistan Norman Borlaug, the American father of the "Green Revolution," had to spend years developing the kinds of plants that would yield the best results in the peculiar natural environment of those countries. There are vast areas such as paddy production where American agricultural technology is simply not applicable. If a technology is to be imported, it has to be Japanese or some other workable method, and in all cases the imported technology has to be adjusted to the specific conditions of the region.

In the more difficult area of socioeconomic organization, a few points clearly show the inadequacy of the American way for the developing world.

First, there is a large excess labor potential in these regions, indicating that agricultural development should be based on labor-intensive, rather than labor-saving technologies. As historic experience indicates, labor-intensive technologies are consistent with small-scale peasant farms, production cooperatives, or large-scale plantation-type enterprises. It is hard to envisage the capital-intensive family-size capitalistic family farm as a prevailing type in these circumstances.

Second, in most developing areas technological progress in agriculture is impossible without widespread irrigation. It is inconceivable, given the prevalence of small-scale peasant farming at the outset, that irrigation could be organized otherwise than centrally (that is, in some form of state or collective enterprise).

Third, the formidable task of bringing under cultivation vast new lands that are not easily and immediately exploitable, and that need intensive preparation, irrigation, resettlement of labor, and road-building among other things, is not going to be accomplished unless special programs are adopted involving large public investment, and possibly the creation of publicly owned farms.

Thus, the path of agricultural evolution in the developing countries will probably be predominantly non-American and noncapitalistic.

It was not our intention to diminish or underestimate the international role of American agriculture. Quite clearly, it has deeply affected the evolution of the world economy and world agriculture. However, the experience of American agriculture was in many ways unique, and determined by the particular combination of vast, easily exploitable virgin lands with scarce, but highly productive labor resources. This particular combination has rarely occurred elsewhere in the past and it is not likely to be repeated in the future.

NOTES

1. This was the so-called "Stolypin" reform.
2. These and other figures relating to growth projections are derived from Wassily Leontief, et al., *The Future of the World Economy: A United Nations Study* (New York: Oxford University Press, 1977), p. 5.

POLITICAL CULTURE AND FOREIGN POLICY: NOTES ON AMERICAN INTERVENTIONS IN THE THIRD WORLD

Eqbal Ahmad

At the close of World War II, the United States enjoyed, in the words of Wendell Willkie, an "inexhaustible reservoir of goodwill" particularly in Asia and Africa. For the colonized peoples of the world America symbolized the possibility and the promises of liberation. Americans had waged the first successful struggle against colonialism, had declared their unequivocal commitment to the right of self-determination, had asserted as inalienable the people's right to revolution and charged them with the duty to exercise that right, had founded a prosperous republic dedicated to the exciting proposition that all men are created equal, and had even engaged in a bloody civil war to uphold that principle.

Subsequent developments tended to confirm in these distant lands the image of America as a unique Western nation dedicated to the universal application of democratic and republican ideals. Anti-imperialist idealism continued to characterize the popular culture and political rhetoric of the United States, reflecting the origins of the nation as well as the clash of interest between it and the old colonial powers. American rivalry with the British, French, and Spanish colonialism in the Far East and Latin America was often construed in the non-Western world as an expression of anti-imperialism. The Open Door policy, for example, was hailed by most Asian nationalists as a triumph of anti-imperialism. Hardly anyone noted Woodrow Wilson's candid admission that America's concern was "not the Open Door to the rights of China, but the Open Door to the goods of America."[1] Similarly Woodrow Wilson's Fourteen Points, with its ringing support for self-determination, had an enormous impact in Asia and Africa. American entry in the war against German fascism and Japanese militarism further confirmed our *préjudgement favorable* for the United States. The only exceptions to the Third World's Americophilia were some Latin Americans made wiser by experience.

Historically, in the development of Asian and African national movements and during the crucial years of our struggle for independence America served as an inspiration and an example. Faith in its friendship and support was part of our rising expectations. As a schoolboy in British India, my first act of rebellion had been to substitute the phrase "American Rebellion" for the "American War of Independence" in a history reading-class. George Washington was a popular hero among us. Words from the Declaration of Independence adorned the constitutions of several new republics in the Third World including the Democratic Republic of Vietnam. Belief in an anti-imperialist America was part of our nationalist mythology. The persistence of this belief through more than a century of counterrevolutionary American interventions in the Third World is a poignant witness to the universal appeal of the principles upon which this republic had been founded.

THE END OF AN ILLUSION

The realities of American foreign policy stood in sharp contrast to the myths we had nourished. For over a century successive American governments and major American corporations abroad have flagrantly betrayed the principles embodied in the Declaration of Independence, in the Bill of Rights, and in George Washington's First Inaugural Address. Their policies have been consistently antinationalist, opposed to revolutions, supportive of dictatorship and fascist states, and violently interventionist in the American sphere of influence (which, until World War II, was limited to Latin America and parts of the Pacific). Between 1900 and 1917, for example, the United States intervened militarily on more than twenty occasions from Columbia to China in an attempt—so Woodrow Wilson would have the world believe—"to make the world safe for democracy."

After World War II, when the United States emerged as the paramount world power, there occurred a Latin Americanization of the Third World. The rhetoric of American policy makers has been dominated by images of bipolarity. The public is told that the policy is concerned with national security, as it is directed at rival powers such as the USSR. However, the reality is different. Since 1945 United States forces have engaged more frequently, lost more lives, inflicted more sufferings, and expended greater amounts of arms and money in suppressing social revolutions in poor countries than they have in defending America's security from enemies or rivals. Between 1947 and 1970, as America stood "watch," in the ringing phrase of John F. Kennedy, "over the walls of world freedom," Washington intervened against local revolutions and nationalist regimes on an average of once every sixteen months. During this period the United States spent more than fifty times more money on its military operations in under-developed countries than on its so-called economic aid to them. At the same time, its investments abroad grew from 7.2 billion dollars in 1947 to more than 60 billion in 1970; the Pentagon and the armaments industry collaborated to make the United States the biggest merchant of death in the Third World (11 billion dollars in United States arms sales to the Third World in 1975); the United States, representing less than one-fourteenth of the world's population, consumed an estimated 40 percent of the world's resources; and each successive year its war budget increased until, in 1976, it surpassed every defense budget in American history. Yet, except for a handful of pacifists and Marxists who suffered severe reprisals for exercising their right to dissent, few Americans protested and fewer challenged the assumptions and objectives of this policy. Total consensus on matters of policy may be an anomaly in a liberal democracy; yet it lasted until the relentless escalation of an undeclared aggression, and the Indo-Chinese peoples' heroic resistance to it, put intolerable strains on the country as a whole, and particularly upon the young. To us, in the Third World, America began to appear as a status-quo-seeking, interventionist monolith whose allies were the Saudis and the Shah, the Samozas and the Trujillos, and the Phnom Penh, Vietnam, and Saigon generals who had once collaborated with colonial France and then sanctioned the systematic destruction of peoples and countries they pretended to represent. The "war" in Vietnam laid to rest the Third World's myths and illusions about the United States.

A PROFILE OF INTERVENTIONS

Americans interventions in the Third World have been noteworthy for the following characteristics:

First, there has been a tendency to escalate the violence out of proportion to the natives' resistance. Two examples should do. The American colonization of the Philippines was the bloodiest in colonial history, followed closely by the French colonization of Algeria, involving the massacre of an estimated two-thirds of the native population. In Indochina, United States intervention entailed widespread crimes against humanity that were surpassed in our times only by the Nazis.

Second, these interventions have been carried out in support of unrepresentative, dictatorial regimes, against revolutionary and popular movements, and often against constitutional regimes such as those of Mossadeq in Iran and Allende in Chile. This is understandable because right-wing dictatorships tend to be especially attractive to foreign capital. The denial of distributive justice under such regimes assures a high rate of return on investments; their repressiveness secures a quiescent labor force; their ruling class, being antagonistic to and fearful of the masses, covets external support, and thus they become dependable allies.

Third, the United States, the protestations of its leaders and academic functionaries notwithstanding, has been opposed to Third World nationalism, historically in South America and in recent years throughout the world. However, this opposition has been clearly expressed not in the initial stage of a country's demand for formal independence from Spanish, French, or British colonialism, but in the stage when a particular nationalism begins to acquire economic and social content. For good reason: radical nationalism (that is, one not contained by the mere transfer of formal power from the metropolitan to the indigenous bourgeoisie) threatens the interests of those who shape United States foreign policy. For example, nationalization of natural resources is the primary economic expression of nationalism. It appears to threaten American corporations, which exercise a near monopoly of influence over United States foreign policy and which continue to have a stake in a policy characterized by militarization at home and interventions on behalf of right-wing oligarchies abroad. Similarly, an independent foreign policy and rejection of foreign military ties are expected of radical-nationalist governments; this displeases the American national-security establishment whose growing power is based on the accumulation and expansion of military power and political leverage over other nations.

Fourth, Washington's tolerance for Third World governments which seek to exercise their full sovereignty appears to be inversely proportional to its business investments in a country. In client states like Guatemala, Iran, the Dominican Republic, Brazil, and Chile the United States has preferred exploitative elites and dictatorial governments. American-sponsored coups d'etat or sharp, swift armed interventions have suppressed radical expression of nationalism or any efforts to overthrow an oppressive regime. In nonclient states a radical expression of nationalism is tolerated if it occurs unexpectedly or if change occurs gradually under a popular leader. Egypt under Gamal Abdel Nasser was an example of the first type; Tanzania of the second. But relations with such regimes remain reserved, often strained. When conditions permit, subversion is encouraged as it admittedly was in Indonesia (1957-1958) and British Guiana (1962-1963). In the decade of 1965 to 1975 there was an inclination to tolerate radical governments in zones of French influence, in response to De Gaulle's national ambition to free France from American tutelage. But only in eastern Europe has America consistently welcomed and encouraged assertive nationalism.

ROOTS OF AMERICAN FOREIGN POLICY

In locating the sources of American foreign policy, I should first acknowledge the argument of those American historians and economists (William A. Williams, Paul Baran, Harry Magdoff, Gabriel Kolko, and others) who situate the roots of American foreign policy in monopoly capitalism, and identify it as a policy in the service of corporations rather than of the public-at-large. Their argument on the historical relationship between the corporation and the state in America is by no means dated. To the contrary, the multinationals' need for imperial states may be greater now than in the past, for their investments abroad are increasing rapidly; and today they have no better candidate for policing the globe than the United States.

Foreign investments of the international corporations, a majority of which are United States-based, are increasing rapidly. The more famous of the giants—IBM, Uniroyal, Squibb, Coca-Cola, Mobil, Gillette, Reynolds, Pfizer, and others—draw over 50 percent of their profits from outside the United States. And, as a study of the Business International Corporation shows, profits abroad are increasing at a much faster rate than at home. American corporations have also been shifting their assets abroad. According to Barnet and Müller about one-third of the total assets of the chemical industry, two-fifths of the consumer industry, and three-fourths of the electrical industry have moved out of the United States.[2] More, in every sector, are on the way. As labor costs have risen in the United States and western Europe, the Third World countries from which the metropolitan corporations have historically extracted a bulk of their raw materials are now becoming a source of cheap labor also. The richer among them are the targets of corporate concentration as "export-platform countries."

It is understandable that partisans of big business should herald the dawn of a new era of corporate globalism. The chiefs of the capitalist giants are being portrayed, and portray themselves, as transformers of the world—the new internationalists. They pronounce the nation-state an anachronism. A 1967 research report of Business International Corporation warns that ". . . the nation-state is becoming obsolete; tomorrow it will in any meaningful sense be dead—and so will the corporation that remains essentially national." Jacques Maisonrouge, the articulate president of IBM World Trading Corporation, relishes pointing out that "Down with Borders," a slogan in the Paris uprising of 1968, is also a company slogan of IBM. He views the world as an "extension of a single market" and contemplates the making of "one world" under the aegis of international business. Aurelio Peccei announces the corporation to be the "most powerful agent for the internationalization of human society." Courtney Brown, Dean of Columbia University Business School, rhapsodizes them as "the prologue to a new world symphony." And Roy Ash, Nixon's budget director, affirms that the multinationals represent "transcendental unity."[3]

Yet, like Henry Kissinger's, Gerald Ford's, or Jimmy Carter's professions of peace, the internationalist cant of business magnates is no Orwellian hoax. Their claims to internationalism and transcendence are belied by a mundane reality; big businesses have much to protect in the world especially from the forces of national liberation, but few means of doing so except to employ the coercive capabilities of certain states. No corporation owns an army, air force, or navy. Yet, one knows from three centuries of experience that these military forces are ultimately necessary to protect corporate investments and perpetuate the exploitation of peoples and their resources. Nothing has changed this fundamental reality which, since the advent of modern imperialism, has defined the symbiosis between monopoly capitalism and imperial states.

It is not surprising, therefore, that such seemingly diverse entities as ITT, the State Department, CIA, Naval Intelligence, and the World Bank collaborated to destroy Allende's government, or that David Rockefeller's way to Egypt was paved by his brother's protégé, Henry Kissinger. Or that a majority of the countries chosen to be regional marshals under the Nixon doctrine (for example, Iran, Indonesia, Brazil, South Africa) are precisely the ones in which the international corporations are investing massively and which are targeted to be the "export-platforms" of the Third World.

CULTURE AND DIPLOMACY: THE MAKING OF CONSENSUS
AND THE LOGIC OF INTERVENTION

Although its motives have been imperialist, United States foreign policy has generally enjoyed popular support because its ideology and practice have been in harmony with some dominant features of American political culture. The language of realpolitik offers a poor basis for constructing a popular consensus behind a corporate ideology. Hence, modern imperialism has needed myths to legitimize itself. A policy which responds to the interests of the few but needs the support of the many must necessarily invoke a peoples' sense of mission and fear. The British carried the white man's burden; the French had their *mission civilizatrice*; and America stood watch over the world's freedom. Each, in its mission, was threatened by the forces of evil—the yellow, the black, and the red perils. Take the myth away, and domestic support for imperialism will begin to disintegrate— unless a new, equally effective set of myths replaces the old. This is what Kissinger meant when he complained that every former colonial power of Europe, except fascist Portugal, had lost its imperial avocation not so much because it lacked power but because it had lost "a certain view of its own destiny" and with it the will to play a "global role."[4]

AN "EXTRAORDINARY" CONCEPTION OF MISSION

A sense of power is congenial to any people. Its exercise becomes morally acceptable when it is believed to be employed in behalf of a noble cause and against a mortal enemy. In the United States after World War II, the doctrines of necessity and moral responsibility combined to produce a compelling ideology whose most important single component was the invocation of the threat of conspiratorial communism. From Truman and Acheson to Nixon and Kissinger, officials have contended that the United States was reluctant to assume the stewardship of the world; but the nation, come of age, could not shirk its historical responsibility of defending itself against communism. History and metaphysics had crowned America to become the world's watchman. "We did not choose," explained President Johnson helplessly, "to be the guardians at the gate." Yet the stake in the struggle, as President Kennedy put it, was nothing less than "sway over the destiny of man." The principal battleground is said to have shifted in the late 1940s to the underdeveloped countries. Hence, every local area acquired a global significance; countries became dominoes.

The globalist, destiny-ridden outlook feeds on what Edward McNall Burns has described as America's "extraordinary" conception of mission. It is a product, at least in part, of a deeply and popularly held belief in the uniqueness of America and its perfection as a political model. The American Revolution gave the world, Abraham Lincoln contended in 1842, the final "solution" to the political problems; hence it must "grow and expand into the universal liberty of mankind." His contemporary, William Seward, contended that if America were weakened mankind's hopes would be "disappointed," and all progress would be "indefinitely postponed," for it was the "ark of safety in which are deposited the hopes of the world," and the "key to progress of freedom and civilization." Since 1945, no president, secretary of state, or secretary of defense in the United States has failed to repeat and exploit this theme.[5]

AMERICA'S SELF-IMAGE AS AN "ISLAND POWER"

William Appleman Williams attributes the Americans' "intense consciousness of uniqueness" to the "colonial achievement of founding and consolidating a society on the edge of a vast wilderness; the deep religious convictions and intensity of the early settlers; the secular pride in having purified the tradition of the 'Rights of Free Englishmen'; the country's rapid economic growth; and the Founding Fathers' awareness that by establishing a Republic in such a large state, they had carried out a theoretical breakthrough."[6] A more important, if less obvious, reason for the American sense of uniqueness, but also of isolation and insecurity, may be that despite their large population, vast territory, and historic position as a hemispheric power, Americans view themselves as an island nation. It is a major source of the American's deepseated and recurring, if ever suppressed, isolationism; aggressive globalism draws on it as well.

For two centuries—from George Washington's First Inaugural Address through the Monroe Doctrine to the Nixon Doctrine—the self-image of island America has conditioned Washington's diplomatic and military policies. For example, among the few basic and commonly held concepts to which Henry Kissinger adhered for two decades is the distinction between "island power" and "continental power." For this reason, he, like other American policy makers since 1917, was obsessed with the challenge of the Soviet Union. The USSR, being the largest, richest, and politically the most integrated land mass in "Eurasia," was viewed as the leading "continental power." As such, it was the natural enemy and permanent threat to the United States, which Kissinger described as the foremost "island power" (that is, one in need of access to the resources of Europe, Asia, and Africa). Hence, he argued that in relation to the USSR the United States was confronted by the traditional problem of an island power—"of Carthage with respect to Italy, of Britain with respect to the continent."[7]

This perception produces a compelling domino theory and an unavoidable role for America as the guardian at the gates. "If Eurasia were to fall under the control of a single power or *group of powers* and if this hostile power were given sufficient time to exploit its resources, we should confront an overpowering threat.[8] This view of America's geopolitical predicament also defines the American concern with preventing the emergence of western Europe as an independent and cohesive center of power. Similarly, for nearly two decades, the policy of halting the imagined rise of China as the Pacific power conditioned American policy in Indochina. At the popular level it reinforced the sense of national anxiety and insecurity which the salesmen of militarism and intervention were adept at exploiting. "Everything that happens in the world affects us," said Lyndon Johnson in a typical justification of the intervention in Vietnam, "because pretty soon it gets on our doorsteps."

A CONSPIRATORIAL VIEW OF HISTORY

What Richard Hofstadter has described as the paranoid strain in American politics is undoubtedly related to the feelings of uniqueness and insularity. It constitutes the most important component of a conspiratorial view of history, a Manichaean outlook which panics over imagined subversions by the forces of evil of the forces of good. Hofstadter states: "The distinguishing thing about the paranoid style is not that its exponents see conspiracies or plots here and there in history, but that they regard a 'vast' or 'gigantic' conspiracy a *motive force* in historical events. History *is* a conspiracy, set in motion by demonic forces of almost transcendant power, and what is felt to be needed to defeat it is not the usual methods of political give-and-take, but an all-out crusade."[9] This phenomenon contributes to the crusading zeal which realists like Morgenthau, Kennan, and Fulbright have bewailed. It may also account for the tendency to escalate violence beyond rational limits. The deep hold among the people of an almost theological anticommunism becomes more understandable when viewed in this light; so does the easy acceptance of the official ideology of foreign policy.

The habit of viewing historical events in ad hoc, technical terms also derives in part from the conspiratorial view of history. The bulk of recent American writings on revolution is a case in point. Revolutionary warfare is viewed as a technical problem—of plotting and subversion on the one hand and of intelligence and suppression on the other hand. As the chief conspiratorial group, the communists are believed to be the most likely initiators and beneficiaries of revolution. This belief produces a pessimistic posture toward a transforming world and underlies America's obsessive commitment to maintaining the status quo in the countries under its influence.

A logical extension of this attitude is the puppeteer view of the world. In complete disregard of the forces of nationalism as well as revolution, it assumes that any revolution and every radical movement is inspired, directed, and controlled from abroad. Dean Rusk's colorful description of the People's Republic of China as a "Slavic Manchuko on a large scale" expressed a view commonly held in the 1950s. Similar to it were the claims made by senior officials in three successive American administrations that the northern Democratic Republic of Vietnam was a puppet of Russia (or China, in some versions), the NLF was a puppet of DRV, and the Cambodian and Laotian national fronts were the puppets of the Vietnamese. Such assertions often fly in the face of facts and eventually prove wrong; but the attitude which produces them persists tenaciously and, when they are made, the allegations are popularly accepted.

The combination of globalism and paranoia yields a rhetoric so senseless and a vision so apocalyptic that were it not coming from serious and successful politicians one would tend it dismiss it as insane. Thus, at the beginning of his remarkable second campaign to win the presidency, Richard Nixon warned in a letter to the *New York Times* that "the victory for Vietcong . . . would mean ultimately the destruction of freedom of speech for all men for all time not only in Asia but in the United States as well. . . . We must never forget that if the war in Vietnam is lost . . . the right of free speech will be extinguished forever."[10] Three years later, while the war still raged, he was elected president after announcing only—and rather conspiratorially—that he had a "secret" plan for peace. Whatever opinion one may hold of the role of the military-industrial complex or of corporate influence on American foreign policy, it would be difficult to deny that such a statement by a serious aspirant to the presidency, and the Republican party's and public response to it, reveals more about the political pathology of America than it reveals about the economic interests of America's ruling class.

A TRADITION OF BARGAINING AND COOPTATION

Owing, perhaps, to its immigrant character which required the successful integration of diverse groups, the American political culture is management oriented. Historically, group demands have been met through the process of political bargaining and selective rewards. Ideological and political dissent has been managed by the cooptation both of individuals and ideas. The politics of management within a pluralistic framework was made possible by expanding resources (largely through territorial aggrandizement and colonial exploitation) and an extremely mobile social structure. It was further facilitated by the existence of a national consensus to which all aspiring groups tended to subscribe.

Yet the same forces which produced a flexible tradition of bargaining and cooptation also encouraged an emphasis on consensus so strong that the system would admit differences but not an agreement on how society was to be organized. Unmanageable dissent has, therefore, encountered swift and ruthless repression in America. The case of the Industrial Workers of the World immediately comes to mind. Furthermore, those groups which were defined as being outside of the political boundary either faced extermination, as did the American Indians, or were forcibly kept on the outer limits, as were the blacks. The result is an authoritarian superstructure, allowing for a well-defined but extremely permissive infrastructure. This characteristic has important ramifications for American response to the stresses of social change in the Third World countries.

First, there is the expectation that the African, Asian, and Latin versions of robber barons and political bosses will, out of self-interest, get around to introducing reforms and achieve an orderly resolution of conflicts arising from the pressures for political participation and income distribution. Hence, the tendency to cling obstinately to the hope that political institutions shall be promoted and social progress shall be achieved under a Shah, a Wiem, the Thai generals, or Philippine politicians. This view misconstrues the value systems and class characteristics of what the social scientists fondly call "elites" in the traditional feudal societies. It is one reason for America's alliance with reactionary, status-quo-oriented regimes whose legitimacy erodes as social pressures mount and foreign involvements increase.

Second, since bargains and rewards are essential aspects of this tradition, the United States increases its economic and military commitment to client states in the hope of using these as leverages to press for political and economic reforms. Yet students of American foreign aid have noted that in most countries American pressures for reforms backed by United States economic and military aid inducements fail to produce the desired reforms, often promote the expansion of the American presence, and sometimes culminate in United States military intervention on behalf of the defaulting client. This phenomenon, called "incrementalism" in academic parlance, obviously results from transposing American style and expectations of behavior to relationships with feudal elites and comparable bourgeoisie, whose interests, motivations, and techniques of insuring political and economic survival are quite different from those of the mercantilist and capitalist Americans.

Third, the consensus upon which the American system of bargaining and boundary management is predicated does not exist in underdeveloped countries. It is particularly likely to be lacking in the client states; foreign alignments tend to exacerbate internal divisions. There is a growing trend in our part of the world toward the radicalization of conflict. The superimposition and infiltration of modern technology and values are drastically altering the social and economic configurations which had, in the traditional societies, circumscribed discontent within the boundaries of religiosity and rebellions. Third World countries are witnessing a fundamental shift in the equation of the human condition, and this change marks their transition from rebellion to revolution. The basic drive becomes not merely the fulfillment of limited goals such as raising the per capita income and the level of food consumption but the transformation of all relationships—political, economic, and social—between groups and individuals. As new groups of people, previously outside the political realm, force their way into politics the common man becomes politically relevant. For many newcomers in politics this mass constitutes their only capital. Politics, thus, ceases to be a mere struggle within a privileged minority for spoils of power. Politics becomes, progressively, a contest between the contenders from different social systems and political ideals. The opposition in such societies is frequently unmanageable because it does not share the values of an often ill-defined and sometimes illegitimate authority.

When faced with unmanageable dissent in countries within its paramount influence, the United States tends to intervene, responding in a traditional American style. The opposition is defined as being outside the legitimate political boundary (it often does not matter if legitimacy as well as a defined boundary are absent). Paranoia seeks plausible enemies: radical nationalists, socialists, all become communists; repression against "outside agitators" is carried out. If the clients are unable to defeat the opposition with American aid and advice, then direct intervention appears to be a necessity. After listening to a State Department official's defense of Vietnam at Tougaloo College, Mississippi, a black woman remarked that he spoke exactly like the white leaders in the South: there was the assertion that people in the south were generally satisfied; trouble began only when agitators from the North infiltrated; there was communist subversion. For the same reason, Ambassador Nolting in Saigon came to "remind" the *New York Times*'s correspondent, David Halberstam, "of some white community leaders in Mississippi and Tennessee."

THE LEGACY OF LATIN AMERICA

Before becoming a superpower, the United States had exercised power outside of its own boundaries mainly in the Latin-Aemrican countries; and this seems to have shaped its attitudes and methods of dealing with weaker nations. "What the C.I.A. has done in Indo-China, Iran, and Chile is no different in kind from the way marines turned patriots into bandits and puppets into presidents in Central America and the Carribean."[11] There, radical nationalism had been the greatest threat to vested American interest; there, the pattern of alliance with right-wing oligarchies was established and paid economic and political dividends. Even the practice of labelling radical nationalists as "communists" developed in Latin America long before the cold war had begun. For example, in 1933 the American ambassador in Cuba found the ill-fated Grau San Martin government "communistic"; in 1937 Cordell Hull condemned the Mexican government intent on nationalizing oil intrests as "those communists down there." The dialectic of American intervention developed in that hemisphere. There, too, was confirmed the belief in the efficacy of violence as an instrument of foreign policy.

BELIEF IN THE EFFICACY OF VIOLENCE

There has been some discussion in recent years of the role of violence in American culture. However, I have not seen a sufficient analysis of the extent to which a belief in the efficacy of violence appears to be an important aspect of the historical outlook and socialization in the United States. As a newcomer I was struck by the thematic consistency of films on American colonization and the audiences' reaction to them. The whites are depicted with human emotion and failings. Tension builds up around the pioneer group united by a common enterprise, threatened by an invisible, elemental enemy. The Indian is an outsider and dehumanized. One does not learn of his family life, hopes, fears, and grievances. Indians come in hordes. They are screaming primitives. Wipe them out. They fall in stylized movements which bring smiles or laughter to the audience. Efficiency and superior technology in the service of a mission overcomes the Indian; violence is seen as an instrument of national purpose, with culturally and racially alien groups perceived as being inferior and expendable. One is reminded of Mark Twain, when Huckleberry Finn was asked if anyone was hurt in the steamboat accident. "No'm," he replied, "a couple of niggers was killed though." An Asian people were the victims of American atomic bombs. And it was in Southeast Asia that crimes against humanity were committed (in the opinion, among others, of the chief American prosecutor at Nuremberg)—while the men responsible for these crimes are being honored at and preside over the Bicentennial celebrations. When reinforced by racism, the belief in the efficacy of violence augments interventionist tendencies and brutalizes the resulting conflict beyond legal and human limits. It also produces a tendency to miscalculate the will and tenacity of the presumably inferior people. It is not surprising that the United States has experienced a significant stalemate (Korea) and its first defeat (Indochina) in Asia.

NOTES

1. John Gittings, "The Origins of China's Foreign Policy," in David Horowitz, ed., *Containment and Revolution* (Boston: Beacon Press, 1967), p. 186.

2. Richard J. Barnet and Ronald E. Müller, *Global Reach: The Power of the Multinational Corporations* (New York: Simon and Schuster, 1975), pp. 16-17.

3. Ibid., pp. 13, 20.

4. Henry Kissinger, *United States Foreign Policy: Three Essays* (New York: W. W. Norton Company, 1969), pp. 41-72. "Today the poorest Western country—Portugal—has the widest commitment outside Europe because its historic image of itself has become bound up with its overseas possessions. This condition is unlikely to be met by another European country—with the possible exception of Great Britain—no matter what its increase in power."

5. Edward McNall Burns, *The American Idea of Mission* (New Brunswick: Rutgers University Press, 1957), p. 90.

6. I owe the quotations and the argument in this paragraph to William Appelman Williams, *America Confronts a Revolutionary World: 1776-1976* (New York: William Morrow, 1976).

7. Henry Kissinger, "Defense of the 'Grey Areas,'" *Foreign Affairs* 33 (April 1955): 416-28.

8. Kissinger, "Grey Areas," p. 423.

9. Richard Hofstadter, *The Paranoid Style in American Politics* (New York: Alfred A. Knopf, 1965), p. 29.

10. *New York Times*, 29 October 1965.

11. I. F. Stone, "The Threat to the Republic," *New York Review of Books* (27 May 1976): 3.

PART 3
Missionaries, Educators, and Writers

Many nineteenth-century Americans believed they had a special mission to help the unfortunate and less-civilized people of the world. None were more committed than the thousands of missionaries who went out to civilize and Christianize the people of Africa and Asia. They did not win a great many converts, but as Daniel Boorstin has pointed out, "Religious conversion pure and simple was no adequate measure of the meaning of American missionary effort abroad. Missions became a way of hallowing American democracy and the American Standard of Living." Just as important, American missionaries carried the "gospel of education to the farthest corners of the world." They founded schools and colleges. They taught the English language, and they introduced American books, magazines, and newspapers, as well as the American way of life to the people they educated.[1]

American books were not universally admired in the nineteenth century. In fact American literature was usually considered a minor branch of English literature. Despite an isolated few who read Cooper, Melville, or Hawthorne, it was not until after World War I that American writers were recognized in most parts of the world as masters of prose and poetry. Sinclair Lewis won the Nobel Prize in 1930, T. S. Eliot, Ezra Pound, and Robert Frost were recognized for their poetry in many parts of the world. Faulkner and Hemingway had their admirers, as did the writers of the Harlem Renaissance, but Jack London and Upton Sinclair were probably more popular.

The missionaries may not have had much to do with publicizing American fiction but they did teach many students English, and English was the only path to the appreciation of American

literature before World War II. Since that time American
literature, like all products of the United States, has intrigued
and often dominated the world's consciousness. This happened
not only because of American power and wealth, although they
were obviously important, but, as Marcus Cunliffe has pointed
out, "ultimately, the conquest of the world by this literature has
come about because in both the world's imagination and that of
America, the United States seems to sum up the miseries,
ironies and aspirations of modern man."[2]

Some of these ironies and aspirations are described in the
following sections. In the first essay, Sahair El Calamawy, a professor of literature of Cairo University, emphasizes the positive
aspects of American foreign aid to Egypt. She stresses the nineteenth and early twentieth century contributions of American
missionary educators. The American schools, she argues, were
not only more flexible and effective than were the French and
English schools, but they also helped to encourage the education of women and the use of Arabic as well. She decides that
Egypt could not have done without American help.

In the next essay Anthony Ngubo, a black South African
scholar at the University of California in San Diego, traces the
influence of the American Methodist Episcopal Church on the
blacks in South Africa. It is a fascinating and little-known story
of black Americans helping black Africans—an ironic counter to
the massive aid to white South Africans from the American
business and financial communities. "The contributions of the
A.M.E. Church to African social and political development in
South Africa cannot be measured in figures," he concludes. "Its
leadership role in the field of higher education produced the first
group of articulate national figures, Through their link with
American and European intellectual leaders they helped bring
the African community out of centuries of parochialism and
isolation. With the help of the church, the African was brought
into the world of community."

In the next essay, Mudimbe-Boyi Mbulamwanza, a professor
of languages and literature at the National University of Zaire,
traces the influence of a group of black American writers on the
literature and on the movements for black consciousness in
France, Africa, and in other parts of the world. It is a complicated and little-known story of cultural links and influence
across many miles.

The last essay by Sulak Sivaraksa, author, professor, and
editor from Bangkok, Thailand, traces the important contribu-

tions of American missionaries and intellectuals on Siam over nearly two centuries. But he concludes that the overall impact of the United States on his country since World War II has been negative: "By making us their junior ally for three decades the American Government has made us lose confidence. We have become materialistic, superficial, and lacking in self-respect. With such characteristics, we cannot even produce any first-rate literature—not to mention other political, social, cultural, and spiritual implications. If the U.S.A. would only leave us alone or allow us to be ourselves once more, we should be able to develop our own thinking, writing, and publishing for our own benefit and perhaps for the benefit of the outside world."

Sivaraksa's plea to "leave us alone" raises an important question for American policy makers and for the American sense of mission as the nation begins its third century.

NOTES

1. Daniel Boorstin, *The Americans: The Democratic Experience* (New York: Random House, 1973), p. 562.
2. Marcus Cunliffe, "America's Impact on the Arts: Literature," *Saturday Review* (13 December 1975): 86.

THE AMERICAN INFLUENCE ON EDUCATION IN EGYPT _____

Sahair El Calamawy

When the United States sponsored the European Recovery Program (Marshall Plan) after World War II, it was not aware of the great need for educational aid in many countries. Forty-five percent of the funds of this plan went to military aid; 3.5 percent went for long-term loans; and only 1.5 percent went for education, health, and social welfare. After thirty years it is now an accepted fact that American foreign aid, especially technical aid, to any country should be mainly educational. Any long-range resolution of international problems must have economic, political, cultural, and educational development as its paramount elements. As long as we are convinced that the lack of development of any country is in itself a threat to world peace, all effort and aid helping this country to bridge the gap to prosperity should be basically educational.

Half of all the nations in our world today are less than twenty years old. They all have rising educational expectations and aspirations. The United States, a nation that has emerged from isolation to world leadership, is fully aware of what this leadership has imposed upon her shoulders. It realizes and sympathizes with other nations' aspirations for economic development, self-education, and a modern style of life. The change from an agrarian (the nature of almost all of these countries) to an industrialized society, from traditional to modern, is basically an educational process. The development of manpower is a basis for economic development and these nations, so young in independence, can no longer blame colonialism as the single cause for all their misfortunes. They have to depend upon themselves, to use their own natural resources, which are often rich and abundant. To realize their dreams of freedom from foreign exploitation, with all that this freedom implies, they badly need to be industrialized. They need technical and development aids which must come through education. The developing countries do not need the importation of fixed programs or traditional European systems. They need their own methods and technologies, carefully planted and nurtured on their own soil.

The United States began a new approach to foreign aid in the early 1960s. It sponsored many educational programs for newly independent nations. The Agency for International Development, the Teachers of East Africa, the Peace Corps, and other agencies all work in cooperation and coordination to extend the educational service programs, as an integral part of American foreign aid. These services and programs are not entirely new in the history of America; and if the United States government is taking new steps, American citizens have long extended educational services as individuals or members of religious or social groups. In the Middle East, these contributions in education are more than 130 years old. The steadfast efforts in the field of education during this long period are worthy of the greatest consideration and appreciation. The new agencies and councils in foreign education have a tradition to look to and be proud of.

Education in the Islamic world had deteriorated badly by the nineteenth century. Negligence, poverty, and unrest had disastrous effects upon the traditional religious system of education. The kuttabs (primitive village schools), formerly run by devoted Muslims who held teaching as a form of worship, were not able to continue and they finally disappeared. The generous donations by the pious rich for teaching the Koran were transferred to the national budget to be spent on the armies. The crumbling kuttab with its miserable teacher became a poor place, where children recited the holy script mechanically. Not only did the boys know nothing of its meaning, but the teacher himself was almost as ignorant. Cases where the teacher was illiterate were not uncommon.

The big mosques were considerably better than the kuttabs and above all there was the oldest university, the famous Al Azhar. Yet even Al Azhar had become so stereotyped in its methods and materials of education that the enormous reforms carried out by Mohammed Abdou at the end of the nineteenth century were to no avail.

The doors of Egypt were wide open for foreigners to come and settle by the middle of the nineteenth century. The area was suitable for economic enterprise which increased after the opening of the Suez Canal and the British occupation. These foreigners soon formed large communities. In addition others took refuge in Egypt from Ottoman persecution. They all wanted to educate their children in their own way. They were not only allowed to do so, but they were generously encouraged. Italians, Greeks, Armenians, besides the French and the English, had their own schools which taught their languages and followed the school curriculum of their homelands and preserved their national traditions.

When the American missionaries arrived, their help with education was badly needed. Copts and Muslims alike were suffering from deterioration in the national school system. Upper and middle-class parents were in search of any new schooling, and in their desperation they had to turn toward the foreign schools. There were only two foreign systems available. The foreign-run community schools were quite alien and never met the educational needs of the natives, except for a very few schools like the Italian polytechnical college for boys (still functioning today).

The French and English schools were attended by many, despite all their drawbacks. They prepared their graduates to fill some coveted jobs in the administration or in the native and foreign agencies. These French and English schools, however, had many deficiencies. The English, snobbish and selective, tended to reserve their schools for members of their own community, permitting only 20 percent non-British enrollment and asking for very high tuition fees. The examinations came from and were corrected in England. The conviction that Egypt needed only a very few educated natives to run, or rather to help run the administration was a persistent colonial belief which by the end of the century had completely corrupted the national educational system. The English stood steadfastly against all endeavors to establish a native secular university. The French as colonizers did not permit any other foreign or national culture to exist. In Egypt the French were not political but cultural colonizers. Their examinations came from France and when they opened a college for law (the only foreign university college aside from the American University), it was part of the School of Law in Paris. These two systems, sponsored by their respective influential governments, cared very little or not at all for the national Egyptians. And worst of all, they did not care for the Arabic language.

In the American missionary schools things were quite different. The American consulate was opened in 1848. There was an occasional American trader and a few American mercenaries in the Egyptian army. Yet as late as the beginning of the twentieth century the United States had no political or economic relations with Egypt. With the British infiltration and then occupation of Egypt, the English language became more and more the language of trade, administration, and politics. The elite could still remain French-orientated, but the young seeking a job or a career needed the English language. The British schools did not welcome local students, so American schools came to fulfill the ever-growing need for instruction in English. While the British fought hard to suppress the call for a native secular university, the Americans were planning the opening of an American university in Cairo (for Egyptians and other nationalities) similar to the American University in Beirut, the first higher education institute in

the whole area, founded in 1866. The American University in Cairo, founded
in 1922, was the first secular university in Egypt.

Both English and French schools had the goal of training students to pass
an external general examination in order to obtain preferred jobs (a deadly
defect we still suffer as a relic from British colonialism). American schools,
however, had independent local systems. Responsible to no government,
they were flexible and changeable, designed to supply the native Egyptian
needs. When the Egyptian government adopted the general public-
examination certificate and opened its doors to students from foreign
schools in 1943 it was the American schools that responded. Sixteen
American schools sent 1,110 of their students to sit for these examinations.
The high percentage of success of these students demonstrated how well the
American schools prepared their students.

Most important, American schools were not obliged to echo any political
or cultural propaganda for their country. They did not feel superior or in-
vincible. Even their Christian evangelistic goals took second place to their
educational pursuits. America's tradition valued human dignity and the
right to be a free citizen in one's country and in the world. Moreover, the
Protestant missionaries had much in common with the devoted Muslims.
They both believed in the need to purify actual religious practices and to
eliminate all aspects of idolatry. Moreover, they both believed in the absolute will of God and in predestination, and they disliked the presence of
statues and pictures in the house of God (church or mosque). On some occasions when friction between the Coptic church and the missionaries led to
trouble and force was used, the Muslims joined the missionaries in destroy-
ing the idols and tearing down the pictures. In the "Faris Hekim" affair,
which led to a correspondence between Said Pasha and President Lincoln,
the Muslims supported the missionaries and even rejoiced with them when
they were released after the intervention by the American government.

Most educational institutions in Egypt were concentrated in the urban
areas. The Americans, however, devoted most of their educational efforts
in the rural areas. Their schools were scattered in many villages along the
banks of the Nile, especially in the south which was neglected by nationals
and foreigners alike. For example, they concentrated their efforts in Assiut,
historically known as a stronghold of the Coptic community. As early as
1865 they opened a men's college and the famous Pressly Memorial girls' institution in that city.

The need of the whole area for a proper high school was met by opening
boarding hostels in these two American schools. More than 160 small
villages sent their young men and women to these institutions. This boarding facility not only opened an educational door otherwise closed for
women but it also saved them from breaching tradition and all that would
have been involved if they had crossed the streets, even when they were veiled.

Later this encouraged students from other Arab and African countries to enroll in the American colleges and at the American University in Cairo. In the girls' college, twelve nationalities and at the university, thirty-five nationalities are now represented.

By the end of the nineteenth century, the Americans had established 186 schools—thirty-three of which were for women. The American missionaries not only established schools and colleges, but they also introduced new fields of study. The first school of commerce in Egypt was opened in Alexandria in 1910. The Department of Journalism at the American University in Cairo prepared a large number of journalists for the leading journals and newspapers all over the Arab world. The Division of Extension, with classes to teach foreigners Arabic began at the American University and has been copied by Egyptian universities. In 1976 this division had an enrollment of 6,405 students who attended 264 classes.

The free and flexible American methods which were adopted by the Egyptian system of education have left a marked impact upon education and all that education leads to in changing the life of the community. Two major endeavors in particular have left a marked influence.

The first is the teaching of the Arabic language from the earliest grades in all American schools, in contrast to what other foreign schools did. When Ottoman rule began openly to disregard its Arab subjects Turkish was imposed as the official language and by the end of the nineteenth century the British occupiers tried to do the same. Arabic is not only the native tongue but it holds a certain sacred status because it is the language of the Koran. For sixteen centuries it remained alive, holding the people of the whole area together, despite differences in religion or race. The people "from the Gulf to the Ocean" had nothing to bind them together except the Arabic language. Any attempt to suppress its learning would call for a vehement protest or revolution. In Syria, it was American missionaries who introduced the first Arabic press. They began printing books and issuing a whole series of translations, the Holy Bible being first on the list and appearing in Arabic for the first time. These early missionaries who introduced the printing of Arabic books, at the time when Egypt's rulers were despising Arabs and their language, certainly contributed to the rise of Arab nationalism. George Antonius concludes that: "The educational activities of the American missionaries in the early period had among many virtues, one outstanding merit. They gave the pride of place to Arabic, and, once they committed themselves to teaching it, put their shoulders with vigour to the task of providing an adequate literature. In that, they were pioneers, and because of that, the intellectual effervescence which marked the first stirrings of the Arab revival owes most to their labours."[1] Munir Bashshur supports this opinion.

True to its Protestant-American tradition of freedom of thought and propagation of individual and social welfare, A.U.B. became a fertile ground for radical ideas, for Arab nationalism and anti-imperialism, which were not welcomed by the Turks nor by the French after them. In contrast, the USJ [St. Joseph University] had a different development. In political attitudes it remained largely subservient to French interests, the same interests which gave it protection. Instead of producing radicals and nationalists, its graduates turned out to be (at least until World War II) outstanding theologians, Orientalists, and professionals.[2]

J. B. Glubb has written: "It was through these [educational] institutions that Western ways of thought penetrated Syria. The most potent of these new ideas were nationalism and democracy."[3]

But not every scholar agrees. Joseph S. Szyliowicz, after an elaborate presentation of his own ideas, quotes A. L. Tibawi as a scholar who places the profound impact of missionary activities in a more appropriate context:

Unfortunately both the character and the forces that contributed to the rise of the [great educational and literary] movement have long been obscured by partisan or uncritical presentation. By some writers the rise and development of the movement is ascribed exclusively to Protestant or more particularly American missionary effort; by others to Catholic missions; by most to Christians to the exclusion of Moslems; but by none to a combination of native development and foreign efforts. . . . The claim . . . that the missionaries were instrumental in the rediscovery of the Arabic literary heritage, is untenable.[4]

Tibawi is correct in stating that the Arabic educational and literary movement should be ascribed to a combination of factors. No popular movement can be attributed to only one factor, however great. But it should be remembered that the Muslims of the area were at first very reluctant to join with their fellow Arab Christians against a Muslim Caliph, no matter how corrupt his reign was. This fact, coupled with other factors, kept Egypt for a long time from joining the Arab nationalist movement. In addition, fanatic zeal for Turkish nationalism was not clearly or officially expressed except in the early twentieth century, which also delayed Muslim Arabs of the area from joining the nationalist movement. This factor is neglected by all. The pioneers of the movement were almost exclusively Christian. Bustani, one of the two pillars on whom the activity of the Arabic-American press depended, was the father of Ibrahim whose nationalistic poem served as the secret appeal, to be orally extended, calling for a rise against the Turks and the establishment of an independent Arab state. The five who founded the "Scientific Learning Society" (the official name which hid the real aims of the group) were all graduates of the American University in Beirut.

One general summary of the effect of missionary schools concludes:

It is not necessary to exaggerate their contribution to recognize the important role they have played in the region. Missionary schools did serve as important models for local governments to emulate; they did represent benchmarks of educational quality; they did introduce many important subjects including medicine, dentistry and engineering; they did pioneer in the field of women's education; and over the years they trained many persons who came to occupy important administrative, political and cultural posts.[5]

The second major change made in the Egyptian system of education through American influence was in the field of women's education.

When Mohammed Ali opened a maternity school for women in 1836 he could not enroll one Egyptian woman. Ten Abyssinian slaves were recruited and housed to pursue their studies and justify the existence of the school Even the suggestion of a school for women was considered a heresy. The pioneer reformer, "Al Tahtawi," in his book about his mission to Paris, called for the education of women to prepare them for jobs when widowed. His book, published in 1826, was the cause of his exile in Sudan as soon as his patron, Mohammed Ali, died. American missionaries, as early as 1830, opened a school for girls in Syria (the first girl's school in the whole area) and their missionary schools were a major factor in the emancipation of women. In Egypt, beginning in 1856, missionaries opened one school after another until by the end of the nineteenth century there were over thirty-three schools for women. These schools were mainly in the crowded poor areas of cities and in villages or faraway towns. In 1856 a school in Alexandria opened in a back street; in 1860 another opened in Cairo, also in a crowded street. These were followed by the opening of a large college in Assiut and schools in Mansura, Tanta, Fayyoum, and so on. The Muslim women, as well as the Copts, enlisted in these schools and colleges. The first school in Cairo in Haret al Sakkayin had 349 women students, 195 of whom were Muslims. Some of these schools are now renowned colleges having not only Egyptian Muslim students (in 1957, for example, Ramses College had 807 Muslims out of a total of 1,203 girls), but also Arab and African women. (The number of non-Egyptian women in Ramses College is greater than those enrolled in all other government schools put together.)

American officials seemed to be more interested in schools for women than for men. The former president Theodore Roosevelt, returning from his African hunting tour in 1909, passed through Egypt. The only two educational institutions he visited were women's colleges. At Luxor he addressed the women during his dedication of the new college building:

I think that, more and more, everywhere, it is growing to be realized that you cannot raise part of humanity while neglecting the other part, and that above all, it is idle to try to raise the man unless the woman is raised at the same time. . . . There has been too much belief that education was purely a matter of books, of learning to read, write and cipher, and then go into the higher branches. The woman, which your girls here are to become, must have a brain which shall not be a torpid brain, which shall make her the intellectual equal of husband and brother. . . .[6]

In Cairo in March 1910 he attended the dedication of the new college which started with twenty-nine students, seventeen of whom were Muslims. The celebration was in a very large tent attended by over 1,400 persons, and the women appeared on the platform unveiled for the first time in their lives.

The education of women is only one example of the way American missionaries and educators influenced Egyptian life. If on the occasion of the Bicentennial of the independence of America, the question was asked, What difference did it make? we answer by asking another question, How could we have done without it?

NOTES

1. George Antonius, *The Arab Awakening: The Story of the Arab National Movement* (New York: G. P. Putnam's Sons, 1946), p. 43.

2. Munir A. Bashshur, "The Role of Two Western Universities in the National Life of Lebanon and the Middle East" (unpublished Ph.d. thesis, University of Chicago, 1964), p. 59.

3. J. B. Glubb, *Syria, Lebanon, Jordan* (New York: Walker, 1967), p. 117.

4. Elie Kedourie, "The American University of Beirut," *Middle Eastern Studies* 3 (1966), 87; J. S. Szyliowicz, *Education and Modernization in the Middle East* (Ithaca: Cornell University Press, 1973), pp. 121-22; A. L. Tibawi, *Modern History of Syria* (New York: Macmillan, 1969).

5. Szyliowicz, *Education*, pp. 121-22.

6. Earl Edgar Elder, *Vindicating a Vision: The Story of The American Mission in Egypt, 1854-1954* (Philadelphia: Board of Foreign Missions of The United Presbyterian Church of North America, 1958), p. 133.

CONTRIBUTIONS OF THE BLACK AMERICAN CHURCH TO THE DEVELOPMENT OF AFRICAN INDEPENDENCE MOVEMENTS IN SOUTH AFRICA _____

Anthony Ngubo

The history of the African church independence movement has been covered extensively by Allen Lea and B. G. M. Sundkler.[1] It is therefore not necessary to give a blow-by-blow account of its evolution and development. It is sufficient to mention but a few salient events so as to place the movement in a proper perspective, and to provide a framework within which to evaluate America influence on and contributions to South African society.

The religious schism that erupted during the last decade of the nineteenth century was not born out of doctrinal controversy but out of a combination of sociopolitical and economic forces that had become increasingly acute after the discovery of sizeable deposits of diamonds at Kimberley and gold at the Witwatersrand.

The beginning of large-scale mining operations attracted both Europeans and Africans to the mining and industrial centers where the two groups began to compete on the job market. White workers began to demand some form of protection from African workers in the form of job discrimination. At the same time the white community began to retreat from a commitment to political multiracial democracy that had been instituted in the Cape when the colony was granted responsible government in 1853.

It is important to note that religious independence movements arose among those Africans who had actually achieved high positions within white-controlled multiracial mission churches. This seemingly paradoxical development calls for comment in order to reveal some of the forces that contributed to the social ferment.

The first point to be noted is that while white missionaries worked among Africans, they did not abandon their racial status within the larger South African society. Theoretically, they were equal partners with the African clergy in the service of the church but in reality they were Europeans who enjoyed all the exclusive privileges that attached to their racial group. Church teachings of Christian brotherhood were contradicted by racial segregation within the church. The African minister, his elevation within the church notwithstanding, was not free from racial humiliation.[2]

African ministers were subject to discrimination at the hands of white secular authorities and of their religious superiors. Racism within the church was in violent conflict with the values and ideals that white missionaries taught in the schools, religious classes, and clerical seminaries. The discrepancy between teaching and practice was too flagrant not to engender African rebellion against and rejection of white leadership even in the church. The religious revolt can be viewed as a manifestation of the pervasiveness of discontent not just against church authorities but also against white South Africa in general. What led to the identification of religious discrimination with that in the secular society was that religious subordination paralleled political subordination. It was within the context of increasing racial discrimination in the society as a whole that the religious schism occurred.

It was in the year 1892 that the Ethiopian Church broke upon the scene with a dramatic suddenness that startled white missionary bodies throughout the South African mission fields. That year the Methodist Church of South Africa held its conference in Pretoria to which black and white ministers were invited. When the conference opened, the board of directors of the conference "resolved that the representatives of the two races should meet separately," and that black deliberations would be open to whites. Black ministers were not granted a reciprocal privilege to attend white meetings.[3] African reaction was swift and decisive. They left the conference, retired to a nearby vacant lot, and proclaimed their ecclesiastical independence. For the new body they chose the name "Ethiopian Church."

The young church was immediately beset by a number of problems. It had neither churches, schools, nor central administrative organs; it was no more than a collection of disenchanted former Methodist ministers and their followers. The church was not recognized by government authorities in the area. When the movement seemed on the verge of extinction, a series of coincidences that were to have lasting effects on South Africa unfolded in the United States.

During the 1893 Chicago's World Fair, a group of African singers was brought to America to sing at the fair. After the engagement at the fair they had a brief tour of a few American cities; but the venture failed. Within a few weeks they were stranded in Cleveland, Ohio, where they were rescued by the Reverend R. C. Ransom of the African Methodist Episcopal Church. He advised them to go to Wilberforce University and, with the help of Bishop B. W. Arnett and Dr. S. E. Mitchell, was able to gain them admission to that university in the fall of 1894. This was the first group of African students in an American university.[4]

The second significant event was a letter written by one of the students to her sister in South Africa. By coincidence it was written on the official church letterhead. The young girl in South Africa showed the letter to her uncle who was a leading figure in the Ethiopian Church. He immediately wrote to Bishop Turner asking for informaiton about the African Methodist Episcopal church. It was this incident that brought the attention of the members of the Ethiopian Church to the existence of a black American independent church. After some correspondence between Bishop Turner and the Reverend Mangena Mokone, the South African church decided to seek affiliation with the American church. In 1897 a South African delegation was sent to the United States to present a formal application for acceptance into the A.M.E. church. The application was accepted and Bishop Turner was dispatched to South Africa the following year for purposes of solidifying the two bodies.

The union of the two churches gave the young South African body access to American administrative talent and guidance as well as to financial support. Had the American church not come to the rescue of the Ethiopian Church, it seems certain that it would not have survived because its leaders lacked administrative experience and organizational skills. This point can be illustrated by the 1899 defection of the Reverend James Dwayne, one of the leading ministers of the Ethiopian Church after the American parent body had appointed him general superintendent for South Africa.

After a tour of the United States at the invitation of the A.M.E. church, Dwane returned to South Africa and, within a few months, called a meeting of the church at which he urged the members to disaffiliate with the American church. There are conflicting explanations of Dwane's actions. One is that when he left the United States he understood that he would be sent a sum of ten thousand dollars for the establishment of a South African college. When the money was not immediately forthcoming, he concluded that the Americans had gone back on their word.

The second explanation offered by Dwane himself is that, after reviewing the history of the A.M.E. church while he was in America, he found irregularities in its priesthood which made him doubt its validity. He also said he found that fair-skinned blacks "would not have a very dark man as their minister."[5]

On receiving the news of trouble in South Africa, the A.M.E. church dispatched the Reverend I. N. Fitzpatrick to investigate the cause of dissension, hold the church together if possible, and give direction to those who did not defect with Dwane. Having accomplished his mission, he returned to the United States accompanied by a contingent of African delegates to the General Conference of the church in Columbus, Ohio. It was at this conference that Levi J. Coppin was elected as the first bishop for the South African district.[6]

The arrival of Bishop Coppin resulted in the conclusion of negotiations for the recognition of the church by the Cape authorities. After recognition was granted and the schism arrested, Bishop Coppin proceeded to buy a

piece of property for the church in Cape Town. This property became
Bethel Institute with a church and a school offering academic and industrial
training to African and colored children. The founding of the Bethel Institute marked the beginning of the church's illustrious history of educational endeavors on behalf of the African people in South Africa.

African ministers received their training in American theological schools
that demanded as a prerequisite a higher level of precollege preparation
than was available in South Africa at that time. The success of the A.M.E.
church in that regard generated an increasing demand for better and higher
education among Africans. That is not to say that other missionary bodies
did not provide educational facilities for their African converts. On the contrary, it was the white missionary societies that pioneered in African education, providing both academic and industrial training for their pupils. What
was not available were avenues to higher education. The A.M.E. church
provided leadership by sending Africans to its colleges in the United States
at a time when no such facilities for them existed in South Africa.

The transatlantic movement of African students strained the resources of
the church and taxed the generosity of its American congregations. But
rather than retreat from the challenge, the church embarked upon a program of providing both academic and industrial training for African and
colored students. This combination was by no means unique; other missionary schools offered similar facilities. What was unique was that Bethel
was independent and black. It was the first independent black school of its
kind in South Africa. For the first time in the history of racially mixed
South Africa, the black community had a modern institution whose founding, maintenance, and survival depended on its own initiative and support.
It is true that most of the money came from black Americans; nevertheless,
the school was black-financed, black-controlled, and black-staffed.

In later years the church established other schools among which the most
successful was the Wilberforce Institute at Evaton in the Transvaal. Its
educational offerings were more varied than those of the Bethel Institute. In
addition to the elementary and industrial schools, it had a teacher-training
and a high school department. All operating expenses and teachers' salaries
were borne by the church. For a long time the school operated without a
government subsidy—its survival resting squarely on the shoulders of
Africans and their American brethren. The existence of Wilberforce as an
independent black school had important psychological and social consequences for the African community.

While the A.M.E. church labored to provide elementary and secondary
education, it did not lose sight of the need for higher education. When it
became clear that there was a great need for college-educated Africans, the
church did all it could to send as many young Africans to the United States
as was possible. The costs of transporting and maintaining these students in
America were prohibitive. The church then decided to build the South

African College in the Cape Colony. The idea was that if the college was located in South Africa, more Africans could be trained than was possible at American universities.

It is important to note that the idea of a college in South Africa was born before the turn of the century. It would be a facility that would offer training in a variety of fields and disciplines including agriculture, medicine, and engineering.[7] The site was a twelve-acre piece of land that Bishop Turner had purchased during his visit to South Africa in 1898. The college was to be an African institution with an African faculty whose nucleus was already in training in the United States. The rest of the faculty was to be trained at the South African College. It was a good idea, but the college was never built because the church could not raise enough money for the project.

The initiative taken by the A.M.E. church in the field of higher education, especially in encouraging the stream of African students to the United States, was not lost on local governments and missionary societies. After the South African War of 1899-1902, the four British colonies of the Cape, Natal, the Orange Free State, and the Transvaal and representatives of missionary bodies convened an intercolonial conference at which the idea of a college for Africans was discussed. The discussion led eventually to the establishment of the South African Native College (Fort Hare University) in 1916 near Alice in the Cape. Although its own college did not materialize, the church did not cease to train Africans in higher education.

The greatest impact of the A.M.E. church on South African society was in the field of education. The church responded immediately and practically to the educational needs of the African community. The aim of the church was twofold: to spread the Gospel and to improve the quality of African life in South Africa. It needs to be emphasized that at that time there were no facilities in South Africa for African higher education and no organization, public or private, that believed that Africans were ready for college education.

In a broader context, the impact of the A.M.E. church on South African society can be discerned in two areas whose significance has had wider implications in the development of African self-expression. These are education and emancipation from psychological dependency on the white community. Although the two are interdependent and mutually reinforcing, they are nonetheless analytically distinct.

The infusion of college-educated Africans into the African community opened new vistas which, up to that time, had not been thought possible. College education was now seen as not only attainable, but also desirable. Other missionary bodies began to send promising young Africans to overseas universities and colleges. The American Board of Missions, for example, sent gifted young Africans to the United States for college training and two of the American-trained Africans, P. Seme and John L. Dube, were later to play leading roles in the formation of the African National Congress in 1912.

The impact of the A.M.E. church on South African Society went beyond the field of education. It was felt in the political field as well. The foundation laid by the church by drawing its support and membership from all African ethnic and linguistic groups can be viewed as a forerunner of African political unification. At the time the Ethiopian Church was founded in 1892 and affiliated with the American church in 1897, existing African organizations tended to be localized within each of the British colonies and the Boer republics. The church extended its influence across territorial boundaries and gave Africans the first organizational structure that embraced all groups.

Before the return of Africans from overseas universities, there were in South Africa a number of independent and regional political sssociations but no common body that articulated broader African interests. The experience gained abroad gave such figures as Pixley Seme and John Dube, for example, a new perspective that enabled them to see a need for an African national organization. It is no accident that these two men played an important role in the formaton of the African National Congress in 1912. The Congress was to be an instrument for the unification of all Africans in the fight against the racial discrimination that had been written into the South African constitution of 1910.

There was a feeling among educated Africans that regional differences had to be dissolved in a new spirit of nationalism. The driving force behind this thrust was P. Seme, a young attorney who had recently returned from universities in the United States and England.[8] The organization he proposed was to embrace all Africans without regard to province, language, religion, and education. His objective was to bring together all Africans into a united political force and at the same time forge a trans-ethnic consciousness.

The influences of the American church on South African politics must not be seen as operating in a vacuum. The leaders of the new movement had had contact with black secular organizations and intellectuals during their sojourn in the United States. There were also other forces in the country that contributed to the rise of African race consciousness and nationalism. The path to African personal and social development was hampered by racial discrimination whose institutionalized rigidity set severe limitations on opportunities for personal advancement and fulfillment.[9] Widespread social and psychological discontent provided the setting within which the church functioned as a social catalyst.

At the time that Africans were redefining themselves as members of the South African political community, the United States was experiencing similar black reactions to racial discrimination. Responding to an increasing volume of discriminatory laws, especially in the South, black Americans were regrouping under new and radical organizations such as the Niagra

Movement that was led by a group of young intellectuals like W. E. B. Du Bois and W. M. Trotter. The founding of the Niagra Movement took place when some of the future leaders of the South African congress movement were attending American universities. It is not unreasonable, therefore, to assume that radical movements in America had some influence on African political leaders.

The connection between attendance at American universities and the radicalization of African political thinking led some white South Africans to fear that the transatlantic movement of African students was introducing dangerous ideas that would change race relations in South Africa.[10] That blacks in the United States were sympathetic toward Africans was a sign of their recognition of the similarities in the subjugation of the black man in the two countries.

The movement of ideas across the Atlantic tended to generate a new consciousness of a common Africanness among some segments of the two societies. It was this common self-image that led to the rise of the Pan-African movement that claimed to speak for black people all over the world. Despite this interaction between America and Africa, the initial link between blacks on two continents was forged by the A.M.E. church by exposing young Africans to black intellectuals in American colleges.

The new political consciousness and the claims of the African National Congress to speak for all Africans were in a way echoes of black leaders in the United States. Once a new local political leadership emerged, the role of the church as a political catalyst receded. Political articles in the *Voice of Missions*, the official journal of the A.M.E. church, on race relations in South Africa prompted a white missionary to chastise the church for suggesting that Africans would one day drive the French and the British out of the continent.[11] The church was forced by missionary and government suspicions of its "subversive" influences to retreat from a direct comment on the South African political situation. Its work could easily be threatened by the denial of permission to American officials to enter the country.

Government suspicions against the church were evidenced by the questioning of the Reverend Allen H. Attaway about the aims of the church in its South African missions. His responses emphasized evangelization and the training of Africans, especially for manual labor in the country.[12] While the church disclaimed any political intentions or involvement, its influence cannot be denied. On the other hand, caution must be taken against crediting any or all political unrest to it. Nevertheless, its successful application of the principles of self-help and independence could not but have an effect on African political perceptions and reactions to their condition of social and political subordination.

We must now return to a discussion of the significance of Wilberforce Institute at Evaton, Transvaal. The impact of Wilberforce Institute was not so much in its outstanding record as an educational institution as it was in its psychologically emancipating effect on the African people. A political subordinate group often develops a psychological dependency on the dominant group for its well-being. This dependency relationship tends to stifle initiative and to engender a sense of social impotence and helplessness which, in turn, reinforces dependence. To break out of the vicious cycle, the subordinate group needs to experience a crisis from which it eventually extricates itself without the assistance of the dominant group. The events surrounding Wilberforce Institute illustrate the rejuvenating effects of a challenge successfully met by the subordinate group through its own efforts and sacrifices.

Between the departure of Bishop D. H. Sims from South Africa and the arrival of Bishop R. R. Wright in November 1936 the Transvaal Department of Education ordered the Wilberforce Institute's teacher-training and high schools closed because the buildings in which they were housed had deteriorated to a dangerous state of disrepair. The Department of Education would not permit the institute to reopen the two departments until the buildings had been brought up to government standards. Up to that time, Africans had always looked to the white community or to the American church to provide the necessary support for their schools and other modern institutions. In this case there were no funds either from America or from local whites. This was a crisis and a challenge for both the newly arrived bishop and the African community.

Bishop Wright immediately began to negotiate with the Transvaal authorities for the reopening of the school. He was informed that such permission could not be granted until the buildings in question had been upgraded to government specifications. Instead of appealing to the parent church, Bishop Wright turned to the African community. This time the challenge had to be met from local resources. Africans were asked to save the school from extinction through their efforts and sacrifices. The response was enthusiastic and generous. Building materials that could be made by the institute's technical school were fashioned from local sources. Bricks were molded and baked on the institute's premises and, instead of retaining a white building contractor, the church called upon one of its members to draw up the plans and execute all the work in accordance with the specifications of the Department of Education. The whole project cost about ten thousand dollars, of which three thousand dollars came from the United States, and the balance from Africans themselves.[13] Through the self-help project under the direction of the church, Africans saved the school and assured its independence.

The saving of the Wilberforce Institute was a practical and visible demonstration of African community power that lay dormant, unrecognized, and untapped by local leaders. The success of the campaign aroused a sense of self-confidence in a community that had grown accustomed to looking to others to provide for its needs. The realization that something as big and important as building a school could be accomplished without the ever-present European hand and supervision had a psychologically emancipating effect on the community. Under the leadership of the A.M.E. church, the community broke out of the cycle of dependence that had for a long time characterized its relationship with white missionaries and the government.

The saving of the Wilberforce Institute started a rash of community self-help programs that resulted in the construction of several buildings on the institute's premises. One of these was to house a clinic which was a donation from black Americans to the community. Although the money for the project came from the United States, the local people donated their labor. The clinic brought medical health services to a community that had had to travel miles to the nearest town. Although the idea of a clinic was initiated by the church, it generated interest among some doctors, three of whom offered to man the facility during their free time. One of them was an African whose medical training in the United States had been made possible by the A.M.E. church.

The self-confidence evoked by involvement in self-help programs was to manifest itself in other spheres of African life. The buying of land by the church was followed by other African independent religious bodies. They began to venture into land-buying activities wherever that was possible. While it is true that Africans owned land in certain areas before these developments, it was the A.M.E. church that pioneered in the use of collective resources through the instrumentality of the church organization.

Once the pattern was set, religious and secular "land-buying syndicates" adopted the practice.[14] In the South African context land has been one of the main points of conflict between races since the extension of white dominion over the whole country during the second half of the nineteenth century. Since that time there have been four types of land on which Africans could live. They could attach themselves to a white farmer and live on his land in exchange for labor; they could live in mission reserves provided they became members of the particular religious denomination; or, if they were urban workers, they could live in compounds or locations (townships) provided by local authorities. In all of these cases they could be evicted for a variety of infractions of prevailing regulations. Lastly, they could live on reservations specifically set aside for them. In none of these areas, except in some mission reserves and peri-urban areas, did they have a right to own real estate.

Land ownership complemented psychological emancipation by strengthening the community's sense of independence and social efficacy. Dependency on the white farmer or city government for a place to live was a constant reminder and reinforcement of African dependency and impotence. Reliance on others for a place to live tended to act as a restraint on personal aspirations and ambitions. The ever-present threat of eviction kept the level of aspiration in check because of the knowledge that the pursuit of personal goals must not bring conflict with the landlord.

The few who could get land through the church or some other syndicate were free from the dilemma of having to measure their personal ambitions against those of the landlord, except that in the context of the larger society they were still a defenseless subordinate group. The hopes of liberation through land acquisition were crushed in 1913 when the Union Government enacted the first of a series of land laws that culminated in the restriction of Africans to approximately 13 percent of the country.

The contrbution of the A.M.E. church in this regard must be viewed as part of a process of psychological emancipation. What had seemed impossible became an attainable goal under the leadership of the church. The confidence gained in this area reverberated in other spheres of South African society and brought about a realization that collective power could be used effectively toward the amelioration of some of the social conditions.

Although the African had experienced a steady decline in his social and political position over the years, the self-confidence gained as a result of involvement in the activities of the church helped him initiate and sustain a drive for equal rights in society. The rise of an African national consciousness has already been noted. The new nationalistic spirit also led to the formation of a labor organization, the Industrial and Commercial Union (ICU) in 1919.[15] The ICU began among dock workers in Cape Town and spread to other industrial centers. Its aim was to seek ways to improve working conditions and wages for all African laborers. Although the ICU was a direct response to industrial conditions it was, like the Congress, a nationwide union that claimed to speak for all Africans.

It is our contention that, although the A.M.E. church was not the only force in South Africa, it was the first black organization to bring different African groups into a common association, pursuing common objectives. Its work and influence transcended linguistic and territorial boundaries and initiated an organizational pattern that united Zulu, Xhosa, and Sotho groups in a common cause.

The church gave a divided and bewildered people access to organizational expertise, financial support, and an external reference group with which it could readily identify. Black Americans offered Africans an example that supported and gave legitimacy to their claims. African political isolation was thus broken and the race conflict internationalized by the Pan-African movement. From then on, the South African problem could no longer escape scrutiny by the world community.

Before the arrival of American blacks, African groups were divided by language and colonial boundaries with the result that each colony dealt with its subjects with little regard for developments in the other territories. The American church presented itself to various colonial governments as a single body with a membership in all areas. Its officials travelled from colony to colony with no regard for African ethnic divisions. The experience gained by Africans in the multiethnic church helped facilitate later political unification. While white mission churches drew their members from all African groups, they were non-African bodies representing, in the main, white ecclesiastical authority. Membership in a white-controlled mission church did not carry with it social, and more importantly, racial identification.

The white church could not offer a sense of social belonging because of prevailing white attitudes. Social differentiation in the white church could not give Africans equal status with white members for fear that such equality would carry with it full and equal membership in congregations that were otherwise exclusively white.[16] For this and other reasons an African could only gain limited organizational and administrative experience. All important policy and other decisions were made in his absence.

The A.M.E. church offered Africans full participation in decision-making and administration. Through such participation, they not only gained practical experience but also confidence in their ability to manage their affairs. The experience gained in church administration helped in the organization and management of political associations without the assistance of American blacks. It is interesting to note that some of the leaders of new African political organizations were ministers.

Prior to the union of the Ethiopian and the A.M.E. churches, the only "advanced" group that could be used to make legitimate African claims was British society, which served the same purpose for the colonists. Since British interests tended to coincide with those of the colonists, the imperial government often supported local contentions that Africans were not ready to assume responsible roles in a modern state. By and large, there was an agreement between the imperial government and the colonists that the only safe and practical policy for South Africa was to maintain white supremacy and keep the African in his proper place.[17]

The contributions of the A.M.E. church to African social and political development in South Africa cannot be measured in figures. Its leadership role in the field of higher education produced the first group of articulate national figures. Through their link with American and European intellectual leaders they helped bring the African community out of centuries of parochialism and isolation. With the help of the church, the African was brought into the world community.

It was also the American church that helped break the chains of linguistic and ethnic parochialism that separated Zulu from Xhosa and from other groups. Through participation in the church, the African came to a realization that he was a member of a larger community whose well-being depended

156   MISSIONARIES, EDUCATORS, AND WRITERS

as much on individual effort as on collective action. It was the church that
gave him organizational and administrative experience which was to stand
him in good stead in his political efforts. Involvement in self-help projects rekindled in him a sense of peoplehood and confidence in his ability to
define objectives and to seek fulfillment through his own efforts and
initiative.

NOTES

1. Allen Lea, *The Native Separatist Church Movement in South Africa* (Cape
Town: Juta, 1928); B. G. M. Sundkler, *Bantu Prophets in South Africa*, 2d ed.
(London: Oxford University Press, 1964).
2. V. Lanternari, *The Religion of the Oppressed* (New York: Mentor Books,
1963), p. 20.
3. F. B. Bridgman, "The Ethiopian Movement and Other Independent Factions
Characterized by a National Spirit," *Christian Express* 33, pt. 1 (1 October 1903):
151.
4. Richard R. Wright, *87 Years Behind the Black Curtain: An Autobiography*
(Philadelphia: Book Concern, 1965), pp. 226-27; Charles S. Smith, *A History of the
African Methodist Episcopal Church* (Philadelphia: Book Concern, 1965), p. 182.
5. *South African Native Affairs Commission* 2 (1904): 709.
6. Richard R. Wright, *Centennial Encyclopedia of the African Methodist
Episcopal Church* (Philadelphia: Book Concern, 1916), p. 286.
7. *Voice of Missions*, July 1899.
8. Peter Walshe, *The Rise of African Nationalism in South Africa* (Berkeley:
University of California Press, 1971), p. 8.
9. G. R. Norton, "The Emergence of New Religious Organizations in South
Africa: A Discussion of Courses," *Journal of the Royal African Society* 40 (1941): 49.
10. L. Elwin Heane, "Ethiopianism: The Danger of a Black Church," *Empire
Review* 10 (1905-1906): 264.
11. Bridgeman, "The Ethiopian Movement," p. 152.
12. *South African Native Affairs Commission* 2 (1904): 252-56.
13. Wright, *87 Years*, pp. 238-40.
14. Sundkler, *Bantu Prophets*, p. 33.
15. Edward Roux, *Time Longer Than Rope* (Madison: University of Wisconsin
Press, 1964), p. 153.
16. T. Karris and G. Carter, eds., *From Protest to Challenge: A Documentary
History of African Politics in South Africa, 1882-1964* (Stanford: Hoover Institution
Press, 1973), vol. 1, pp. 18-29.
17. Arthur P. Newton, *Select Documents Relating to the Unification of South
Africa* (Frank Cass & Co., 1968), p. 206.

AFRICAN AND BLACK AMERICAN LITERATURE: THE "NEGRO RENAISSANCE" AND THE GENESIS OF AFRICAN LITERATURE IN FRENCH _____

Mbulamwanza Mudimbe-Boyi

Translated by J. Coates

THE AMERICAN CONTEXT

One of the most important moments of self-assertion and emergence for the black personality in the world was the Negro Renaissance or, as it is also called, the Harlem Renaissance. It was the reflection and the remarkable expression not only of a peculiar culture but also the living proof of a particular cultural longing. This literary movement demonstrates the integration of black American culture with American society and, to a very great degree, with the black world as a whole.

It was Margaret Butcher who noted with some force that:

By setting up an inveterate tradition of racial differences in the absence of any fixed or basic differences of culture and tradition on the Negro's part, American slavery introduced into the very heart of American society a crucial dilemma whose resultant problems, with their progressive resolution, account for many fateful events in American history and for some of the most characteristic qualities of American culture. On all levels, political, social, and cultural, this dilemma has become the focal point, disruptive as well as constructive, of major issues in American history. In the pre-Civil War period, the issue was slavery versus anti-slavery; in the Reconstruction era it was discrimination and bi-racialism versus equalitarian nationalism. In the contemporary era, it is segregation and cultural separatism versus integration and cultural democracy.[1]

Summed up in this passage we find the most important points of contradiction in American society, which essentially boil down to certain basic modes of life and dynamics in the American context.

My thanks to Dr. V. Y. Mudimbe and Dr. Ngandu for the help they have given me towards the completion of this work. My thanks also to the translator of this paper.

Yet what was the point of making appeals if one was black and living in the America of Lothrop Stoddard and Madison Grant, who were adopting and revising the racial theories of Gobineau, Schultz, Wagner, and Chamberlain? And what was the point of making demands if, just at the very moment when the purity and power and beauty of New Orleans music was bursting upon the world, the ideas and the violence of a regenerated Ku Klux Klan were being paraded and spread about? For during the 1920s, as during the final quarter of the last century, black musicians and black writers, like all black people who "were trying to make their voices heard, carried a heavy burden marked with all the signs of inferiority which every single black bore, no matter which tradition had lent its character to his plays or poetry or novels."[2]

It was in this climate of derision toward anything black that the Negro Renaissance in America emerged to give some direction and significance to the black personality both in literature and in the culture as a whole.

THE HARLEM RENAISSANCE AND THE BLACK PERSONALITY

The Harlem Renaissance movement which Arna Bontemps brought to life in 1921 is, in fact, the philosophical, spiritual, and artistic result of a number of movements and actions beginning at the turn of the century.[3] Among them we should note: W. E. B. Du Bois's organization of the National Association for the Advancement of Colored People (NAACP), his editing of the *Crisis*, and his organization of several Pan-African congresses; Marcus Garvey's creation of the Black Star Steamship Line and the founding of the review the *Negro World*; and Carter G. Woodson's founding of the Association for the Study of Negro Life and History. All these projects and creations, with their fair share of generosity and radicalism (and sometimes, of utopia), directly helped the rehabilitation of black Americans.

The "Black Renaissance" was thus brought about by blacks for blacks. It was himself that the American black put forward as a subject for his own literary creations, and he went to great lengths to express for himself his own particular problems and his own aspirations and rights in a form which seemed to correspond best with his own fate.

Jean Wagner has summed up this new perspective: "The Black Renaissance rises as a whole from a new vision of the past which the whole race shares together."[4]

The movement was composed of many themes: there was revolt against the injustices suffered by blacks; the demand for a new personality and for a cultural identity; and finally there was nostalgia and fascination for the far-off land of Africa. The movement expressed the feelings and thoughts of blacks. And thus where literature is concerned one may speak of a realistic, engaged literature, yet it was also romantic. The nostalgia for Africa appears in fact as a wish to return to roots, coupled with a great love for the history and life of the African people. Africa also appears as a mythical continent, a lost paradise; but at the same time it is also a representation of a black past before all the denials and distortions of slavery. So by turning back and resurrecting Africa there was a possibility for self-assertion: the extent to which black Americans could feel certain about their past governed the extent to which they could place their hope in the future.

This movement for self-assertion, racial rehabilitation, and recognition of the links of solidarity with Africa was centered in Harlem and crystallized around three writers—Claude MacKay, Countee Cullen, and Langston Hughes—to which one should add the voices of Jean Toomer, James W. Johnson, Sterling Brown, Jessie Fausset, Nella Larsen, and others.

These writers produced an eminently American, but also an explicitly black, literature. The writing reflects the material conditions of existence of black writers, as well as the ideological and spiritual expression of a special group in American society. There are two principal themes: first, the rehabilitation of black history and of blacks in contact with "white" and "Anglo-Saxon" culture; and second, the reappraisal of the black race and its art in a world of cultural interaction.

This unique revolution was to be achieved through the efforts and work of the *exiles*. Although effectively exiled from their fatherlands like other blacks, the blacks in America who were to rise up were also exiles within their own culture. Many of them came from places other than Harlem: Claude MacKay was Jamaican; E. Wabrond was Guyanese; Langston Hughes came from Missouri; and Arna Bontemps was from California. And several of these poets were not from the black middle class. They were academics who, through learning, had moved away from their origins: Claude MacKay came from the State University of Kansas; Jean Toomer from Wisconsin and City College; Jesse Fausset from Cornell; Langston Hughes from Lincoln University; Rudolph Fisher was a professor from Howard University.[5] So they were a minority within a minority; first, because on the level of social relations, they were black in a white-dominated country; and second, because they were the privileged among the blacks. What they began to shout out was: "I am different because I'm Black" and "I, too, am America." These shouts were to launch an important literary movement which was to have considerable influence in the United States and in other parts of the world.

THE NEGRO RENAISSANCE AND NEGRITUDE

During the 1920s there appeared in Paris a series of publications on Africa: in 1920 there was *L'Anthologie Nègre* ("The Negro Anthology") by Blaise Cendrars, a collection of stories, legends, fables, poems, and songs from black Africa; in 1921 there was *Batouala, Véritable Roman Nègre* ("Batouala, A True Negro Novel") by Réne Maran; and finally in 1927 there was *Le Voyage au Congo* ("Journey to the Congo") by André Gide, followed by *Retour du Tchad* ("Return from Chad") in 1928.[6] In these last two books, as Jean Wagner notes, "Black America thought it had found confirmation of its idea that France was turning back toward genuine life forces. Postwar American writers, rebels against both the system and the Victorian prudery that dominated small-town life, thought they had found in the black man a kind of noble savage whose primitive spontaneity had somehow been left untouched by the horrors of the civilization which they were surveying."[7]

It was a period in which among the intellectuals and liberals in Europe there was a distinct interest developing in Africa and African people. The black man, in his innocence and splendor, became a kind of curiosity. This approach pervaded both the colonial administration and applied anthropology. There was a search, on the one hand, for the most efficient means of colonizing Africa and, on the other hand, to fill in the gaps in the ancient history of European man which meant describing "African savages" in terms based upon models taken from Western prehistorical accounts.[8] Yet at the same time, the West was discovering that it was no longer the norm in history and thought, that it was not the prime incarnation of either civilization or culture, and that rational thought as an absolute value and major reference was nothing but a myth. The subjective philosophies set off by German romanticism in the eighteenth and nineteenth centuries were beginning to spread, while the notion of relativity on which specialists in the exact and natural sciences were working began to invade the social sciences and the humanities. The human and spiritual misery at the end of the 1914 to 1918 war also led to a serious questioning of the values of that Western culture which in practice could so effectively set the instruments of death in motion.

It was at this moment that white Europe discovered the American black, jazz, African art and, above all, masks. Certain ethnologists (Frobenius, Delafosse, Monod and so on) kept a wary distance from the ideology of applied anthropology and described a sympathetic, dynamic, and original African culture quite different from the mistaken images put out by colonial propaganda. At the same time there also started to be some deep questioning in the works of African scholars who had felt only satisfaction and pride up to then: what actually was African culture?

Leopold Senghor, in an excellent little book entitled *Pierre Teilhard de Chardin et la Politique Africaine* ("Pierre Teilhard de Chardin and African Politics") has described the astonishment of young black students in Paris and elsewhere in Europe who suddenly discovered good reasons for feeling pride in being Africans.[9] And Lilyan Kesteloot has shown in her book that one of the main causes of this confidence was being in touch with black American writers.[10]

Whenever they speak about the beginnings of their literary movement, the poets of Negritude (or, more precisely, the three apostles Césaire, Senghor, and Damas) give recognition to the leading role that the black American writers played in arousing their general sense of awareness and the sense of racial awareness that was worked out in the Negro Renaissance. Therefore it was with good reason that Senghor, in his paper to the Colloquium on Negritude held in Dakar in 1971, rightly called them the "fathers of Negritude."

To understand the influence of the black American writers on France, it should be remembered that they brought their rebellion to Paris. There, like other writers such as Ernest Hemingway and Gertrude Stein in this period, they had fled from the dehumanizing system of racial segregation and the dryness and conformity of American culture during the 1920s. There were three focal points to their demands—rebellion, violence (both literary and political), and racial awareness.

First, they rebelled against the structure of American society (see, for instance, *Banjo* by Claude MacKay), a society into which they had been thrust but yet one which disowned them ("I, too, am America," exclaimed Langston Hughes). They made claims for their rights; for the rights of American citizens; for their human dignity (as in "If we must die," for example, a poem by Claude MacKay); for the right to live; and for the recognition of Africa (as in Countee Cullen's poem "Heritage"). And they denounced racial hatred by both blacks and whites.

Second, one can understand why their tentative gropings would often be toward a sort of religious mystique in which evil (sin, the devil, hell) would be symbolized by the fall of man (especially in the work of Countee Cullen, but also in that of Claude MacKay). They were tempted by communism as a social system, as an ideology, and as an epistemology, insofar as communism claimed to resolve all contradictions, to end man's alienation, and to give freedom not just to the proletariat but to blacks—crushed through exploitation, destroyed through racial discrimination, and denied through poverty.

Third, there was the inner assertion of the exile, which is to say the intense existential anxiety that without doubt sprang from the rejection suffered by the black in American society, but which was equally caused by the very fact of Americanism. This can be seen in the rebellion and misery and bitterness which had been sung about ever since the first Negro spirituals, such as "Nobody Knows the Trouble I've Seen." This torn black conscience ("the shock of Americanism on the Negro conscience," in Chester Himes's words) would only find itself properly by going over all the psychological conflicts, frustrations, and traumas that had been endured by blacks since slavery.

The poets of the Negro Renaissance were the first to show signs of a wish to discover and develop their own culture: American jazz erupted in Europe and brought with it a new violence in art and, more particularly, in music. The phenomenon of Josephine Baker made a deep impression on the French ballet in 1925 with the dazzling spectacles that she made, for example, at the Folies Bergères. This had prompted the majority of observers to think that the black African poets involved in the Negritude movement had only taken up the Negro Renaissance rebellion in order to assert the "African Presence."

First of all, there was *La Revue du Monde Noir* ("The Black World Review") published in Paris (1931-1932) which established a point of focus for all the blacks in the French capital. Previous meetings had been organized where most black writers had worked toward one goal: the reappraisal of black culture.

What we want to do is offer to the intellectual elite of the Black race and to the friends of the Blacks an organ in which they may publish works of art, literature and science; to study and make known through newspapers, books, conferences or classes, everything that concerns *Negro civilization* and the natural riches of Africa—the fatherland that is three times sacred to the Black Race; to forge amongst Blacks throughout the world, drawing no distinctions between nationalities, an intellectual and moral link that will help them to know themselves better, to love each other as brothers, to defend their collective interests more effectively and to lend honour to their Race.

This statement was directly inspired by the manifesto of the Negro Renaissance. The contribution made by poets such as Claude MacKay and Langston Hughes is by no means negligible.

Thus *La Revue*, in wishing to identify Negro values and reappraise black culture with an eye on historical truth, brought about a kind of cultural awakening through justifying its own myths. It talked about the "cultural unity of the black world" which was a unity presented as a belief in oneself and as a force acting in the face of the colonial powers. It should, however, be noted that in *La Revue*, in contrast to the Negro Renaissance, there was to be neither aggressiveness nor polemics, but rather the demand for a return to oneself—a demand made with greater serenity through writing that was sometimes not so much racist as rather conciliatory. There remained nevertheless something of the atmosphere of Alain Locke's "New Negro Movement" in the attitude of understanding and sympathy and responsibility in respect to blacks.

In 1932, when *La Revue du Monde Noir* ceased to appear, the young people from the Antilles who were studying at the universities of Paris declared themselves "suffocated" by the system of exploitation and denial which was making the black man "less than his master's object." They founded the review *Légitime Défense* ("Self Defense") which in one single issue effectively inaugurated the "New Negro" movement. Against the great alienation that the black writer experienced (because of his "borrowed personality"), protesting over the muddled poet (for whom "being a good copy of light-skinned man is meant to stand for social as well as poetic reason"), the authors of *Légitime Défense* in their own way took up the aims of the Negro Renaissance. Speaking about the militant function of the literature that they were trying to start up, E. Lero stated: "The wind that is rising from Black America will, we hope, swiftly sweep our Antilles clean of the fruits fallen from a decayed culture. Langston Hughes and Claude MacKay, the two black revolutionary poets, have brought to us, steeped in red alcohol, the African love of life, the African joy in love and the African dream of death. And already the young poets from Haiti are beginning to bring us verses inspired with the dynamics of the future."

The development of the black rebellion can be traced from Negro Renaissance to "Haitian Indigenism," and from *Légitime Défense* to Negritude. But in this journey of suffering and exaltation, the writers of the Negro Renaissance were establishing the paradigm for the conscience of the race. This is why an extract of MacKay's novel *Banjo* is given in *Légitime Défense* as a model for the New Negro's literary work, as the principal objective in *Banjo* was to resist European culture by turning back to African culture.

Black American literature already contained the germs of the principle themes for Negritude, and in this respect one can claim that the real fathers of the Black cultural Renaissance in France were neither the writers in the Antillian tradition nor the surrealist poets nor the French novelists between the wars but the Black writers from the United States! They had left a deep stamp on our writers in the way they had tried to represent the whole race, and had let up a cry in which every single Black recognized himself: it was the first cry of rebellion.[11]

Indeed when black students from Africa and those from the Antilles came together in Paris it was a meeting of exiles, for they were in a double exile: both from their native countries and equally from their social and cultural context.

This experience of the black writers from Africa and the Antilles was set within a framework of colonization and cultural assimilation. Their poetry, for example, was composed of refusal and rebellion. Rebellion was made on a social level by their denunciation of the abuses of colonization and the exploitation and humiliation of the Negro. This can be seen in Senghor's *Chants d'Ombre* (''Songs from Darkness''), in this poem ''May Khoras and Balafongs Go with Me,'' in *Hosties Noires* (''Black Victims''), and in the poems ''To the Call from Saba's Race,'' ''A Preliminary Poem,'' ''Prayer of Peace,'' and finally ''Letter to a Prisoner.'' On the cultural level there was also rebellion against white culture and assimilation and toward an authentic culture drawn from African roots. This rebellion had the corollary of rehabilitation and reappraisal of precolonial Africa, as in Senghor's poem ''May Khoras and Balafongs Go with Me.'' This may also be found in later African writers such as Paul Hazoumé in *Doguicimi*, Laye Camara in *l'Enfant Noir* (''The Dark Child''), Nazi Boni in *le Crépuscule des Temps Anciens* (''Twilight of Ancient Times''), in Djibril Tamsir Niane's *Soundjata ou l'Epopee Mandingue* (''Soundjata or the Epic of Mandingue''), and Seydou Badian's *La Mort de Chaka*. All of these authors were either trying to bring to life personages from historic times or to recreate a life of tradition complete with rites and customs, the daily life in a village.

Recognition of their own values led black African writers to start questioning the West and its norms as well. This questioning is shown in novels such as *Un Vie de Boy* (''Boy's Life''), *Le Vieux Nègre et la Médaille* (''The Old Negro and the Medal'') and *Chemins d'Europe* (Paths of Europe'') by Ferdinand Oyono; *Ville Cruelle* (''Cruel Town''), *Mission Terminee* (''Mission to Kula''), *Le Pauvre Christ de Bomba* (''The Poor Christ of Bomba''), and *Le Roi Miraculé* (The Miraculous King'') by Mongo Beti; and *Les Bouts de Bois de Dieu* (''God's Bits of Wood'') by Sembene Ousmane.

This challenge to the West, together with the situation he found himself in, finally led the African to start questioning himself. And in the end there was a meeting with the West, which is what we find in Ousmane Soce's *Les Mirages de Paris* (''Mirages of Paris''), Bernard Dadie's *Un Nègre à Paris* (''A Negro in Paris''), and Ake Loba's *Kocoumbo l'Etudiant Noir* (''Kocoumbo the Black Student''). From this inner questioning there arose an existential anxiety: the translation of frustration and the rending schism between loyalty to the race and culture of the blacks and entry into a world dominated by new and strange values. This is admirably illustrated by Cheik Hamidou Kane in *L'Aventure Ambiguë* (''Ambiguous Adventure''), and in V. Y. Mudimbe's *Entre les Eaux* (''Between the Waters''). Samba Diallo, the hero of *L'Aventure Ambiguë*, sums up this painful quest of his own: ''I am not a distinct country of Diallobes, facing a West that is distinct, and understanding with a cool head what I can take from it and what I am supposed to leave behind in exchange. I have become both of them. There is no one clear way between these two choices. There is only one strange nature—one in distress at not being two.''[12] This situation of conflict was clearly summed up by W. E. B. Du Bois, though in different terms:

It is a peculiar sensation, this double-consciousness, this sense of always looking at one's self through the eyes of others, of measuring one's soul by the tape of a world that looks on in amused contempt and pity. One ever feels his two-ness: an American, a Negro; two souls, two thoughts, two unreconciled strivings; two warring ideals in one dark body, whose dogged strength alone keeps it from being torn asunder.[13]

Similarly in African poetry this expression came as a liberation that can be seen in the use of free verse and breaks in rhythm similar to the jumping rhythm of the blues, which is a special expression licensed by the sensibilities and sentiments of blacks. Senghor, David Diop, and others provide eminent examples of this kind of liberty and spontaneity of form. As Senghor wrote, black poetry is a "poetry of flesh and earth; if one is to talk like Hughes, peasant poetry which has not lost contact with the telluric forces. And this explains its cosmic rhythm, its music and its imagery of running water, rustling leaves, beating wings and twinkling stars."[14]

After *Légitime Défense*, and especially after *La Revue du Monde Noir*, the meeting together of the blacks from America, Africa, and the Antilles encouraged the dawn and rising of the great Negro poetry in French and, in a general way, the birth and development of what we today call Negro-African writing.[15] Since then the constant exchange and circulation of ideas have been established, so that the movement can be described in three stages.[16] First Africa was the point of departure for black ideas that spread from Europe to America. Second, during the decade from 1920 to 1930, Harlem-America became the center of a series of new ideas which, passing first through Paris, spread into the black world in Africa and the Caribbean. Finally today there has been established a bipolar route between Africa and the black diaspora in America and the Caribbean.

African literature, having found its examples in black American literature, takes on the same ideological character. In fact from the ideological point of view, it becomes clear that this writing has only one single aim, namely to show how black people really are, or, to take the voluntarist terms of W. E. B. Du Bois to show: "the feeling of being in at the birth of a new criterion for happiness, a new desire to be creative, a new will to exist; as if in this dawn of life of the Black group we have been woken up from some sort of sleep." The problems, the history of black Africa, its beginnings and its mythic splendors are all brought out, but on a romantic pretext, as if to contrast all the more starkly with the misery and limitations of blacks in the modern world. Both African and American writers tend in this way to insist rather strongly upon a blockage of an ideological nature, yet they do at the same time note the essential meaning of this blockage, which is both historical and sociological in nature—the history of blacks and their status and role in the contemporary world.[17]

This consideration can be reformulated with the help of a concept from literary realism, in order to indicate the importance and relevance of Negro Renaissance and Negritude.

Any society which has enjoyed a certain stability tends to corrupt those who are sensitive to the need to speak up for the groups least favored and for those in the greatest minority. Once corrupted, unionized bureaucracies and writers become integrated into the bourgeoisie, allying themselves with the interests of the dominant class which is glad to know them well and to see reflections of itself mirrored in them. But once these groups have performed their tasks their work should become a permanent questioning, a constant search for coherence, and, in the case of American society as in that of colonized Africa, there should be awkward questions raised about nationhood and law. This search would be, if Trotsky is to be believed, the essential direction of art itself, "it being fundamentally a function of the nerves demanding total sincerity."[18]

Seen in this perspective, the writer appears as a man engaged in the construction of a better world and could not in any way be a neutral observer, whether he be critical or skeptical. (Langston Hughes as well as Aimé Césaire and Lilyan S. Lenghor are examples.) The propositions put forward by the writer involved in the construction of a better world do not come from nowhere: they are born in the ups and downs of the socioeconomic world and cannot, for fear of being in contradiction with the real world, try to be original themselves. The fact is that all positive action ought to take into account both the past experience of society and contemporary norms. All great movements, wrote Trotsky, started on the "garbage dump."[19]

Here we have confirmation that an artistic movement, like any other movement, does not start at the bottom. That is to say, it does not begin with the mass of the people but is born and takes its life from the questioning of an avant-garde elite or a group—the group here being the Harlem group and the Negritude group. This questioning has both the strength and the promise of fresh action. It gets established during the process of searching, while also drawing lessons from past experience.

It is the small groups that have made the progress of art. Once the creative resources of the dominating artistic trend have been exhausted, the "garbage dump" people remain, and it is they who know how to look at the world with new eyes. The greater the daring of their conceptions and methods, the more they will be opposed to the established authorities who rely upon support from the conservative base of the masses, and the more the conventional, the skeptical and the snobs are inclined to see in them merely impotent originals or "heaps of anaemic garbage."[20]

The critical-realist approach, like the one founded by the Negro Renaissance and the Negritude movement, is characterized by this active perspective, which represents an advance for humanity. Thus when one ideology is criticized it is bound to be replaced by another ideology.

To be more precise, the only proper base to work from is from an actual acquaintance with social realities. But this is where the opposition between critical realism and social realism arises: for this acquaintance "defines a concrete perspective which above all else implies in a writer a full awareness of society as much as the reality of the contemporary world."[21] Hence no doubt the success of sociohistorical writers such as Jessie Fausset (*Iola-Leroy, There Is Confusion, The Chinaberry Tree*, and *Comedy*), and of Nella Larsen (*Quicksand*) and Langston Hughes (*Sandy*). And by the same token the bitter writing of Leon Damas, Aimé Césaire, and F. Fanon on the Negritude side. These writers have had the advantage of taking concrete facts as their pretext and this has allowed them in principle to make an analysis that may seem objective and realistic, as well as to sketch in a solution relatively close to the actual march of events.

There may be the problem of the specific features of these writings. Purely theoretical knowledge will not inspire the creation of a literary work unless it agrees with the aesthetic categories of the author.

A literary work should rest upon a correct conception of social and historical realities, and this is what allows it on the one hand to acquire an authentically realistic value and, on the other hand, what constitutes a particular and irreplaceable factor in the influence which it normally should exercise; but in the one point of view as in the other, no theoretical knowledge of the world, nor of mankind will ever inspire a writer, without it being totally incorporated into or allowed to be completely absorbed by his aesthetic categories.[22]

In what exactly does the peculiarity of literary categories consist, when these categories turn a work into an entity relatively independent of theoretical knowledge? For surely this perspective leads one to believe that any philosophical theory can inspire a literary work, which is equally true for all other kinds of social action; and this poses the precise problem of these actions regarded as reflections or effects of the evolution and structure of a society.

The writer himself is, as the evidence shows, conditioned by society and by the contradictions of the group or social class that he belongs to. But at the same time this conditioning may be drastically reduced by careful use of the rules of "authentic realism." Indeed the ideological world would, thus, no longer be a simple reflection of the economic organization of society.[23]

This call for a kind of comprehensive and radical analysis of literature is satisfactory proof that in the case of the Negro Reniassance literature, as in that of Negritude, we may find a literature that is really involved. This literature is the reflection of the material conditions of existence of black writers. It is also the ideological and spiritual expression of a group in society: the blacks.

It is fundamentally characterized by two main themes: the rehabilitation of black history; the condition of the black in contact with a white culture. On the American side there are W. E. B. Du Bois, Marcus Garvey and Carter G. Woodson; and there are Cheik Anta Diop, Th. Obenga, and J. Kizerbo on the African side.

This is a group which, because it feels itself badly integrated into another group, is clamoring for its "right to cry out and speak." It bursts out and, in declaring its differences, declares as well its right to the sun and to life. It also rises up against all received wisdom by demanding fresh judgment, by rewriting the history of the past, by interpreting in its own way the present time and its conflicts, and finally by projecting its own particular dreams into a future where it seeks to escape the dogmatism and violence of the dominant white classes in America, while in Africa it seeks to escape the white power of colonization.

The struggle of black Americans strongly attracted the first black writers from the Antilles and from Africa. The myth'created around African unity which had suggested a utopian vision of Pan-Africanism (in the writing of Padmore, for example) was constantly being reactivated throughout the struggle for political and cultural liberation in Africa. It had even inspired ideas of the most violent kind, like those of Cheik Anta Diop. The emergence of the New Negro in America lies in the political and cultural awakening of black Africa, and vice versa.

The first texts of Negro-African writing bore the influence of the poets of the Negro Renaissance, with *Pigments* by Damas, opening with an epigraph by Claude MacKay: "Be not deceived, for every deed you do I could match, outmatch: Am I not Africa's son. Black of that black land where black deeds are done." While some poems were dedicated to Mercer Cook and Louis Armstrong, Senghor also dedicated poems to Claude MacKay and Langston Hughes and translated Countee Cullen. Later these same black-American writers participated in the Congresses of Black Writers and Artists in Paris in 1956 and in Rome in 1959. They published literary texts and analytical articles in the review, *Présence Africaine*, and founded the African Society for Culture. One can perhaps now understand why so large a number of studies have been carried out about them and why one whole issue of *Présence Africaine* was published in honor of Langston Hughes. In this fact lies recognition of the important contribution made by the American Negro Renaissance toward the promotion and expression of blacks in Africa and throughout the world.

NOTES

1. Margaret Butcher, *Les Noirs dans la Civilisation Américaine* (Paris: Buchet-Chástel, 1959), p. 13. Translated into French by F. Vernan and J. Rosenthal from *The Negro in American Culture* (New York: Knopf, 1956). Based on materials left by A. Locke. The best general account is Nathan I. Huggins, *Harlem Renaissance* (New York: Oxford University Press, 1971).

2. Jean Wagner, *Les Poètes Noirs des Etats-Unis* (Paris: Librairie Istra, 1963), p. 42.

3. Arna Bontemps, *La Renaissance de Harlem* (Paris: Collection Nouveaux Horizons, 1975), p. 10.

4. Wagner, *Poètes Noirs*, p. 103.

5. *See* Bontemps, *Renaissance*, p. 55.

6. *Batouala* received the Prix Goncourt. It was quickly translated into English and had a real influence among blacks in the United States.

7. Wagner, *Poètes Noirs*, p. 105.

8. *See*, for example, V. Y. Mudimbe, *L'Autre Face du Royaume: Une introduction à la critique des langages en folie* (Lausanne: L'Age d'Homme, 1973).

9. (Paris: Editions de Seuil), 1962.

10. Lilyan Kesteloot, *Les Ecrivains Noirs de Langue Francaise: naissance d'une littérature* (Brussels: Institut Solvay, 1966), p. 63.

11. Kesteloot, *Ecrivains Noirs*, p. 64.

12. *L'Aventure Ambiguë* (Paris: Julliard, 1961), p. 175.

13. W. E. B. Du Bois, *The Souls of Black Folk* (Chicago: A. C. McLurg and Co., 1903), p. 3.

14. Kesteloot, p. 81.

15. *See* J. Jahnheiz, *A History of Neo-African Literature* (London: Faber and Faber, 1968).

16. George Shepperson, "Notes on the Negro-American Influences on the Emergence of African Nationalism," *Journal of African History* 1, no. 2 (1960): 299-312.

17. *See also* Gh. Gouraige, *La Diaspora d'Haïti et l'Afrique* (Ottawa: Ed. Naaman, 1974).

18. Leon Trotsky, *Littérature et Révolution* (Paris: Union Générale d'Editions, 1964), pp. 467-70.

19. Ibid., p. 468.

20. Ibid., p. 469.

21. Gyorgy Lukacs, *La Signification Présente du Réalisme Critique* (Paris: Gallimard, 1960), p. 176.

22. Lukacs, *Signification Présente*, p. 178.

23. *See* Lukacs, *Thomas Mann* (Paris: Maspero, 1967), p. 198.

AMERICAN INFLUENCE ON BOOKS, MAGAZINES, AND NEWSPAPERS IN SIAM _____

Sulak Sivaraksa

American missionaries made important contributions to the development of printing and intellectual life in Siam in the nineteenth century. In the preceding century, in 1767, an invading army from Burma had destroyed most of the Siamese printed materials and historical records and had taken about 30,000 Siamese as war captives back to Burma. About fifty years later an American missionary couple, the Reverend and Mrs. Adoniram Judson, who lived in Burma from 1813 to 1850, came across a Siamese colony in the Burman city of Moulmein. Ann Hazeltine Judson, in particular, was so fascinated by the Siamese language that she began to study it. She eventually translated the Gospel according to St. Matthew as well as her husband's Burmese catechism into Thai. She also translated a Siamese Jataka story (that is, an account of a former incarnation in the life of Buddha) into English.

In 1816 George H. Hough, an American printer, joined the Judsons in Burma for missionary work. He started printing Siamese and Burmese texts in Burma in early 1817. In 1819 Hough was transferred to Serampore in India (near Calcutta) and took his crude printing machine with him. Mrs. Judson's Siamese-translated catechism was printed in India in 1819 by the American Baptist Mission Press and in 1828 this same press brought out Captain James Low's *A Grammar of the Thai; or, Siamese Language*. The press with a font of Siamese type was later purchased by the Reverend Robert Barnes of Singapore. In 1835 this now famous first Siamese press was bought by the Reverend Dan Beach Bradley when he travelled from the United States to take up his first mission assignment in Siam. The first printing job was executed in Bangkok in 1838, consisting of 1,000 copies of an eight-page tract containing the Ten Commandments, with an introduction and explanation, a short prayer, and three hymns.

After less than three years in operation the press attracted the Siamese government's attention, and on 27 April 1839 Bradley turned out the first government documents ever printed in Bangkok—9,000 copies of a royal proclamation outlawing opium. His printing kept him in touch with government officials and with commerical and shipping firms, and consequently he became well known in Bangkok. For a time he published a fortnightly magazine, the *Bangkok Recorder* (1844-1867), and a newspaper, the *Bangkok Calendar* (1859-1872). Both carried material in Siamese and English and both started on July fourth. As Bradley said, "This day is regarded as the American National Day. We take this day as a symbol of the good wishes of the Americans who will share their experiences and new scientific knowledge with the people of Siam." Apart from the two bilingual periodicals, Bradley also published in English the *Siam Weekly Monitor* (1866-1868) and the *Bangkok Daily Advertiser* (1866). The Bradley's printing and publishing activities were carried on by Mrs. Bradley after her husband had passed away and until her own death in 1893.

In fact, the first Siamese book for which the author received a copyright was from the Bradley's press in 1861, when Mom Rajothai, official interpreter for the first Siamese embassy to Queen Victoria published his poetic account of the trip called *Nirat London*—the publisher's best seller. The United States minister to the court of Siam proposed to the king in 1900 that the Siamese government should pass a copyright law. The American minister was, of course, interested in protecting American interests. He was George MacFarland, the son of a missionary who had been born in Bangkok, and had written books in Thai and English as well as compiling dictionaries and inventing a Thai typewriter.

Another American couple, the Reverend and Mrs. John Taylor Jones of the American Baptist Mission, resided in Burma and were later transferred to Siam. Before leaving Burma they adopted an English boy, Sammuel John Smith, who had been born in India. At the time he was twelve years old. He was sent to be educated in the United States. There he was ordained and then joined the Baptist mission in Bangkok in 1849. From 1869 on he operated an independent printing office where he edited and published in English the *Siam Weekly Advertiser* (1869-1886), the *Siam Repository* (1869-1884), the annual *Siam Directory*, and in Siamese, *Sayam Samai* (1882-1886), an English-Siamese grammar, a Siamese-English grammar, an arithmetic textbook, a Christian catechism, a comprehensive Anglo-Siamese dictionary and a comprehensive Siamese-English dictionary (which was ready for the press at the time of his death but was never printed). He printed Siamese prose and poetry in great quantities, making the printed page very common and selling presses and fonts of type to Siamese and Chinese job printers, who opened presses everywhere in Siam.

The American pioneering missionaries not only continued their interest in Bangkok, but for years the mission published the only paper in northern Siam, the *Laos Christian News*. It is no wonder that local Thai periodicals were published in Chiengmai, the northern capital, before they were in any other town.

Siam practiced a closed-door policy toward Westerners until 1851, when King Mongkut became Rama IV. Prior to that date, he had been a Buddhist monk for twenty-six years, all through the reign of his half-brother, Rama III. During this period, Western powers were knocking at the door of Siam as they were doing in other Asian countries. Several embassies were sent from the British East India Company, from France, and from the United States. The Siamese resisted and yielded as little as they could. Protestant missionaries were finally allowed to enter Siam in 1828.

Prince Mongkut, however, realized the inevitability of encounter with the West. As a monk, he not only studied such traditional and religious subjects as the Buddhist Scriptures, astrology, and the Pali and Sanskrit languages, but he also learned Latin and English. Through the English language, he could master such subjects as geography, astronomy, and natural science, as well as the political history of the Western world. When he realized the importance of the printing press which belonged to the American missionaries, he started his own printing operation at the temple (Wat Pavaranives), asking his friends and admirers in the United States to purchase a printing machine for him.

In 1850 the Bradley's *Journal* recorded that Prince Amorit, Mongkut's cousin, ". . . really commenced printing a tract setting forth the claim of Buddhism. . . . He has obtained from us the old printing press which I brought with me from Singapore in 1835. He proposed to purchase it." Prior to that, Mr. and Mrs. G. W. Eddy of Waterford, New York, were kind enough to supply Mongkut with ink for his printing purposes. An eyewitness account by an American missionary, Samuel Reynold House, who visited the temple, recorded "several young monks working at the press. One was typesetting, another was folding, yet another was proofreading. The monks gave us a book printed in Pali, the script of which Prince Mongkut had invented. The book was about the Buddhist Ten Commandments and an explanation."

The following year when Mongkut ascended the throne, Prince Amorit was appointed printer to His Majesty, with the printing press situated in the Grand Palace itself. The king wished to send a young official to be an apprentice abroad so that he could come back to improve the royal printing facility. An American printer, a certain Mr. Cartner, was also hired from Singapore for the same purpose; but he proved a failure. The Reverend J. H. Chandler, an American missionary experienced in printing, publishing, and journalism in Bangkok, was hired for a time, but he did not get along well with the king. Dr. Caswell, another American missionary, taught English to the king while he was still a monk. Dr. Caswell was allowed to preach the Gospels to the Buddhist congregation at the temple because of the friendship between the two men. Mongkut not only attended Caswell's funeral but gave a lot of money to his widow later on. Quite a number of monks also followed the king by leaving the holy order. Some of them joined the new printing establishment.

Although King Mongkut appreciated Bradley's journalism, he was very much upset by the missionary's attack on him personally and on his country in general. In a personal memorandum, he complained that American newspapers kept praising the United States and its political regime for being advanced and civilized and looked down upon traditional Siamese culture and belief as being backward, to be condemned more than to be praised. The Americans only liked the king's innovations, which his people on the whole could not understand. They wanted to encourage him to invest his money in Western technology such as railroads, telegraphy, and engineering. He said he was tired of newspapers which, either through misunderstanding or real intention, misrepresented Siam to foreign lands. Yet the king did not suppress the newspapers, but often wrote letters to the editor and eventually started his own *Government Gazette* in 1858. The king himself was the editor and stated that whatever was printed there could really be trusted by his subjects. Unfortunately this periodical lasted only a year as the king engaged in so many other activities. The paper was revived by his son, Chulalongkorn, in 1876, and the *Government Gazette* is now the oldest weekly journal in the kingdom.

It was not only King Mongkut who was concerned with American missionaries' attacks on the Buddha's teaching. His senior official, Chao Phya Dipakarawongse, was also taken aback by such rebukes. The old savant, too, was well versed in Western sciences and foreign religions and he was much esteemed by those who knew him. Although he was minister for foreign affairs, he is best nown for having compiled historical records of the Bangkok period. He also wrote a book, extolling the excellence of Buddhism, as a superior religion to Christianity, which obviously no missionary press would print for him. Therefore, he had the text of his manuscripts cast on slabs of stone and had the book printed from them in 1861. A major part of the book was translated by Henry Alabaster and published in London in 1871 as *The Wheel of the Law*, which gives a good idea of the Siamese intellectual climate of the period. The book has recently been reprinted in Britain.

When Chulalongkorn succeeded his father to the throne in 1868 he was only fifteen years old. He and his younger brothers had received some English education within the Grand Palace and realized the importance of printed books, magazines, and newspapers. At first the king was powerless since power was in the hands of the regent and the old nobility. The younger generation formed themselves into a sort of political party which gathered momentum slowly. Its members were sufficiently strong by 1873 to take the lead in urging radical reforms. They began to issue their own newspaper, *Darunowat*, which published a considerable amount of foreign news, proverbs, science reports, and articles about fine arts, fables, poetry, and drama, as well as general news and much comment on and discussion of reforms that they felt needed to be undertaken in Siam. They formed the Young Siam Society of which Chulalongkorn's full brother, Prince Phanurangsi, was president.

Darunowat itself was published from July 1874 to June 1875 by one of the king's younger brothers, Prince Phrom. It was succeeded by the daily newspaper, *Court* (September 1875-1876), published within the palace walls by eleven of the king's younger brothers, all of whom became famous in the Siamese literary world, as well as in bringing about modern administration both for the church and the state. Without any doubt these young princes were influenced directly or indirectly by Bradley and Smith in particular. Although they were no longer interested in publishing counterattacks on the American missionaires, their books were much superior, in accuracy and scholarship, to those produced by the foreigners.

Chulalongkorn founded the Vajirañàna Library in memory of his father, who had started collecting books and archeological objects from ancient capitals like Ayuthia and Sukhothai. His younger brothers took turns in serving as committee members, and the Vajirañàna Library really became a national library and museum. Until then the history of Siam prior to the fourteenth century was practically unknown. Because of the valuable research of a small group of enthusiasts, mostly members of the royal family, who deciphered the annals of neighboring states and the lithographic inscriptions found in various parts of the kingdom, a multitude of facts bearing upon ancient Siam have been brought to light. Under Prince Damrong's presidency in particular, the national library became a storehouse for the national literature and began to foster a taste for serious reading through its periodical, the *Vajirañàna* (monthly 1884-1885 and 1894-1905, and weekly 1886-1894). The library exerted its influence on the educated public awakening the people to a knowledge of their native land and to that proper pride in national institutions and traditions which is the root of all genuine patriotism.

Books, magazines and periodicals were at first in the hands of Westerners and Siamese princes and nobility only. However, with the spread of education and modern printing techniques, commoners who were not in the employ of the royal government also became interested in publishing and journalism. The French started the *Siam Free Press*, printed also in English, in 1891. At that time both England and France were very much interested in expanding their empires towards Siam; earlier the French consul indirectly forced Bradley to give up his journalistic career. The king felt that the Thai, too, needed an English newspaper for their own cause. Hence, the *Siam Observer* was launched in 1903 by a Singhalese in the employ of the Thai government during the period of unrest just after the blockade of Bangkok by the French fleet, when news was eagerly sought after.

The *Siam Free Press* was forced out of circulation in 1908 when the French were no longer interested in annexing any more of Siam to their Indochinese empire. The paper was, however, bought by an American named P. A. Hoffman, who rechristened it the *Bangkok Daily Mail*. The *Bangkok Times* and the *Siam Observer* became friendly rivals and achieved a considerable measure of success, establishing themselves upon a firm and sound basis. Both obviously worked in complete harmony with the Siamese government and were generally kept well posted with official news. It was an open secret that they received government subsidies. Later both issued weekly mail editions in English and Siamese for transmission abroad and through the provinces. The *Observer* and *The Times* lasted all through the period of absolute monarchy in Siam, which ended in 1932. (The *Siam Observer* also ceased publication in that same year.)

What the American missionaries had started in the field of Siamese books, magazines, and newspapers, the Thai had become competent enough to run fairly smoothly by the end of the nineteenth century.

Some of Prince Vajirañàna's sermons were translated into English, published in book form, and circulated to British Burma and Ceylon. None of them contained any attacks on Christianity. In fact, it was Prince Vajirañàna who gave the idea to his nephew, King Prajadhipok or Rama VII (1925-1934), to offer a prize each for the best essay on the propagation of Buddhism among the young. An essay is still being published annually as a booklet for free distribution among school children. In the announcement for the competition, the king made it plain that essays submitted for the prize should not refer to other religions in contemptuous terms. Early American missionaries' tracts had always condemned Buddhism contemptuously. The Thai, however, followed a "more excellent way."

King Vajiravudh, known as Rama VI (1910-1925), had started editing magazines and writing essays, plays, and poems while he was the crown prince. Literature was one of his greatest loves, and he is recognized as one of the major Siamese poets of his day. Yet it must be confessed that his style was academic, and apart from patriotic songs, his poetry lacked deep feeling. His knowledge of English was perfect, since he was sent to England for education at an early age. In fact his serious writing began in that country, where he started a magazine *Samaggi Sara* (in Thai and English) in 1901 which the Siamese Students Association in England still produces regularly. He was especially impressed with the works of Shakespeare and his transla-

tions of three of the master's plays were not only close in idiom and accurate even to punctuation, but were poetical as well. He also translated
other English and French playwrights, as well as rendering Sanskrit
literature in Siamese. American literature seemed to have no influence on
him, although he visited the United States on his way home and he had a
number of American friends.

Publishing activities reached the peak in quality during Rama VI's reign.
Thai books with the best kind of paper and bindings were sought after by
the educated elites. Siamese scholars were encouraged to do research work
on Siamese and Indian language and culture, and foreign scholars were
employed in the government. When foreign residents wanted to study Siam
and her neighboring countries in depth, and to propagate their findings in
lectures and publications, Vajiravudh and Damrong encouraged them. The
Siam Society was founded under the patronage and vice-patronage of these
two members of the royal family in 1904, and the *Journal of the Siam Society*
is now fairly well known to those who are interested in Oriental studies.

Although Rama VI was an absolute monarch, he was so liberal and liked
journalism so much that he wrote many articles under various pseudonyms
in Thai and English. Attacks on the king sometimes, in newspapers and
magazines, were so strong—this time by his own subjects and no longer by
American missionaries—that he was really hurt. What K. S. R. Kulap and
Thien Wan started in the reign of his father had become common during his
period of kingship. The attacks were on him personally, on his courtiers,
and on his policy. Very often he wrote back.

The most outspoken newspaper then was the *Chino Siamese Daily News*,
published in both the Chinese and Siamese languages. Although the
Bangkok Times and the *Siam Observer* had been tamed by the end of the
last century, the *Bangkok Daily Mail*, in both its English and Siamese editions, was very vocal against the king in many respects. The American
editor, Mr. Hoffman, started a very good tradition on an ethical code of
conduct for the Thai pressmen. He refused to let his authors or columnists
be known to anyone—not even to the king—but only to himself, since those
who wrote articles criticizing the king were more often than not His Majesty's relatives and officials! However much displeased the king was with
what he called an outraged attack on him and his administration, like his
grandfather King Mongkut he read the printed words with care. In fact, it
was Hoffman's editorial that carried much weight in the king's decision to
follow the American nation in declaring war against the Central Axis
powers during World War I; and Siam derived much benefit from the war.
The *Bangkok Daily Mail*, however, outraged the king so much that he eventually bought it.

Both Kings Rama VI and VII, as their father had done before them, subsidized some newspapers and were friendly with some journalists. But journalism, then, like book publishing, was still in the hands of the educated

elite. Both kings did not care much for the popular press which they thought vulgar, but tolerated it and did not take the popular newspapers seriously. Quality journalism, of which there was quite a bit, Rama VII read attentively. He once remarked: "If any criticism is constructive, the government must act according to its suggestion. If the criticism is nonsensical, we should not take it to heart, since the writer had made a fool of himself already, and what he writes people will soon forget."

In fact it was in the United States in 1931 that King Prajadhipok announced his intention to grant a constitution to his people, and on his return to Bangkok in October of the same year he called a press conference and allowed his secretary to describe his trip to America and to outline some future policies for Siam—the first time that the Siamese royal government dealt with the press as such. Could this be attributed to the experience the king gained in the United States? Unfortunately his relatives and his American advisers thought at that time that the public was not yet ready for democracy.

When the colonels forced the king to become a constitutional monarch in June of 1932 one of the charges made against the princes was that the royal government used secretive methods in running the country. The rulers, they said, took care not to let the public know what they were doing. The people (that is, the educated military and civil servants who were not informed) felt that what was secret must be bad. Occasional public statements of policy or plans were made, but they were not of great value to the public since they were usually issued in English. The accusers felt that the king cared more for improving his image among the foreign community. For example, his intention to grant a constitution was first announced abroad, and important government statements were published in English papers and then translated into Siamese which followed the English idiom and were often unintelligible to the people. Hence, misunderstandings arose between the king and his subjects.

The irony is that after "democracy" dawned in Siam, there was less freedom for the journalists. One year after the people's government was installed, the Press Act of 1933 was passed to make the newspapers harmless to the administration. In 1932 alone, after the Revolutionary Party came to power in June, there were ten occasions in which a newspaper was closed either temporarily or permanently. From 1933 to 1934 there were seventeen occasions in which the government found it necessary to close a newspaper. An American author during that period observed: "It may be concluded, then, that Siam has very strict censorship of the press. There is no freedom of the press in Siam in the sense that there is freedom of the press in the United States. All important news is sifted through the government Press Bureau. Not only is it heavily censored, it is often quite late reaching the public."

By the 1930s there was very little American influence in the Siamese publishing world. The new regime more and more admired and imitated Germany, Italy, and Japan. British interest in the *Bangkok Times* also faded away gradually. The *Bangkok Times* had a close connection with the royal government and it ceased its operation entirely by 1941.

Up to the end of World War II, American interest in Siam was mainly for the sake of the Siamese. The missionaries were still the largest contingent. American businessmen were very few and the American legation was very small. Up to then the Siamese regarded the Americans as their best friends. Not only did American pioneers in Siam help them in publishing, medical, and educational activities, but the United States also never claimed any colonial interest in Siam. The United States, as well as an American editor in Siam, persuaded the Siamese government to enter World War I on the side of the Allies. As a result of the war, American advisers to the Siamese foreign ministry helped to persuade their government to treat Siam as an equal partner. Because of the American example other Great Powers gave up extraterritorial rights in Siam.

The Thai democratic government became more and more dictatorial. It forced the Thai people to give up their national dress in order to imitate Western fashion so that the country could be regarded really civilized. The name of the country had to have an English word attached to it since the name "Siam" reminded the new leaders of the ancient regime; hence, "Thailand" was declared the name of the country. Thailand joined the Axis Powers during World War II. The Thai minister in Washington, D.C., however, refused to deliver the declaration of war to the United States which thus did not consider that a state of war existed between the two countries. After the war, the American government tried hard to persuade the British and the French (who wanted to punish Siam for fighting the war against them) to leave the Thais alone. In fact it was the American press as well as some American citizens, concerned with the independence and integrity of Siam, who helped the Thai mission which was sent to the United States especially for this purpose. According to a member of the Thai mission, it was he who persuaded the Americans to trade more directly with Siam, not via London as hitherto, and emphasized that American capital should immediately be invested in Siam before other Western nationals had the chance to reestablish themselves there.

Soon after World War II, the Siamese dream to have the Americans become more interested in their country was really fulfilled. Former missionaries, like K. L. Landon, became advisers to the State Department. Landon's wife wrote the best-seller on Siam, *Anna and the King* (despite the fact that it was a distorted picture), which became *The King and I*. Former members of the OSS became businessmen and journalists in Bangkok and some became scholars of Thai culture.

The legation in Bangkok, with very few staff members, was raised in status to an embassy and its activities expanded as Americans became more and more involved in this part of the world.

Up to World War II, the American public hardly knew that Siam existed. Those who knew it loved it and wished it to remain an independent kingdom, preserving its friendliness, tolerance, dignity, and way of life. They would have been overjoyed if the Siamese had chosen the path of freedom and democracy, but they did not want to force their way of life on the Thai. Although Dr. Bradley sometimes criticized the Thai severely, he respected them and admired them. In his own *Journal* he kept confessing to God his own failure for not being able to convert the Thai to Christianity. In fact, as we may recall, it was the American advisers to the royal Siamese government who cautioned the king against granting a constitution to his subjects.

As the United States interest in the world grew, while great European empires were shrinking, America became a neocolonialist power whether intentionally or otherwise. Although she claimed that she did not want to extend her power, her interest in protecting the free world against communist expansion meant that she wanted to maintain and, if possible, to expand her brand of capitalism. Siam was an ideal country to be picked to be an American stronghold on the mainland of Southeast Asia. The Siamese had to be taught to fear and to hate the Communists and to admire the American way of life. To do that the United States government was even willing to back the Thai dictator who had once declared war on the United States and who was at one time a war criminal. By backing this man, Field Marshal Pibulsonggram who reentered Thai politics via on army coup in 1947, the United States began to manipulate Thai politics directly and has been doing so ever since. Three successive field marshals ran the country with full United States support until October 1973. A civilian prime minister who served a short interim period also had to be approved by Washington, D.C.

During this period, the Thai public was given information on only one side of the story. The United States Information Service was very active in supplying local editors with the latest "facts," plus ready-made commentaries in the languages of Thai, Chinese, or English. The friendly Thai editors were frequently invited to meet American VIPS, and to visit the United States and her allies in Asia. Training courses and seminars for journalists were often arranged in Bangkok and other provinces by the United States Information Service in conjunction with the Thai Public Relations Department or the Thai Press Association. A press foundation was established with American money to award prizes to Thai journalists. A John F. Kennedy Foundation, in memory of the late president, was also launched to encourage Thai authors to produce the best books possible. At one time, *Time* magazine even had a project to train future Siamese editors in the United States. Apart from the United States Information Service and *Time*, the Thai journalists were encouraged to make use of and look up to the Associated Press, the United Press, *Newsweek*, and *Reader's Digest* —not to mention shady publications and news agencies supported by CIA money. All of these were not United States government organs but they could not be said to represent anything but the American interest.

Any journalist or writer who was not friendly to the Thai or the American government could easily be branded as a Communist or fellow-traveller. In the period 1958 to 1973 no new Thai newspaper was registered, while any periodical could easily be closed down at the will of the government. The journalists had really become very tame. Those who fought for freedom of the press were either in jail (many of them without trial) or in exile abroad. Some, of course, had no other alternative but to join the Communist insurgent movement. In fact, at one time the United States Information Service had a list of friendly and unfriendly editors, and the Thai police were sometimes told by American Embassy officials to look out for or even to arrest Thai journalists. One Thai novelist whose short stories were supposed to be political could not join such a learned institution as the Siam Society, for some council members thought the author was dangerous. In fact, he was nearly arrested. The United States Information Service always managed to have at least one of its officials attached to the society and similar organizations. (A United States cultural attaché once edited the *Journal of the Siam Society*. Even today, the United States Information Service has its connection with the Siam Society.) But if any Thai author wrote anything against the Communists, such a book would receive tremendous applause. That is why the United States Information Service saw to it that Kukrit Pramoj's *Red Bamboo*, a mediocre novel, was translated into eighteen languages, while his best novel, *The Four Reigns*, and his best short story, *Many Loves*, were ignored.

The United States Information Service was, of course, active in other mass media as well. As radio, moving pictures, and television are not within the scope of this paper (although USIS and Voice of America still have a major share of "control" over the media), it should only be mentioned that the United States Information Service founded libraries in the provincial towns too, all of which were much more attractive than those run by the Thai authorities. The United States Information Service, as well as other American agencies like the Asia Foundation, supplied books in English and Thai (many translations of which were commissioned or subsidized by them) to leading editors and to almost every library, especially in schools and colleges, in the villages, and the monasteries. Some professors also received books, magazines, "information sheets" regularly through the courtesy of American "philanthropic" organizations. During this period, Thai academics and adminstrators were, on the whole, trained en bloc in the

United States. American teachers and researchers, as well as advisers and administrators—not to mention military personnel—penetrated through all Thai institutions. United States institutions of learning, established independently in this country (like the American University Alumni Association) or attached to the Thai establishment (like Indiana University), one way or the other served American interests rather than learning per se.

As the United States belongs to the great liberal and democratic tradition, however imperfect it may be, and however arrogant and selfish the government may have become, some of her citizens still think highly of the American ideals of humanity, equality, and freedom, and are willing to fight for them. Some Americans have been very vocal against their own government and even their own way of life. Some of the Thai who went to the United States for their education returned home as strong critics of United States policy and its activities in our country and in the world. Unfortunately, not many of them had been well-educated enough to see beyond the glitter of American materialism and capitalism which hide her real exploitation behind the scene. Some Americans in Siam, such as Peace Corps volunteers and even ex-GIs or those who defected from the armed forces, also informed us of their country's weak points and wickedness. Some even became first-rate journalists and writers who collaborated closely with their Thai counterparts. Again, there were not many of them around.

One good point about the Thai regimes was that they had been in power successively for so long that they became relaxed and did not take the press as seriously as they did at the beginning. In addition, the bureaucracy had never been very effective, especially in dealing with foreign literature. In the early 1960s some British and American "subversive" books, magazines, and newspapers were being sold in Bangkok fairly openly—these printed material the United States Information Service would never have dreamed of sending to their Thai friends. In 1963 some American agencies in Bangkok helped a group of Siamese-educated elite launch the *Social Science Review*. As no newspaper or magazine had been registered since 1958, this was supposed to be an academic quarterly with no social or political bearing on the Thai society. The *Review* eventually became a monthly and functioned as a platform for Thai intellectuals to express their views freely. Criticisms of Thai-American relations in the 1960s were published in the *Review*, which was the first Thai magazine to reveal the presence of American air bases in Siam. Some creative writings also first appeared in the *Review* before they were published in book form. With the *Social Science Review* as a base, a secular University Press was launched with United States Public Law 480 assistance. Some members of the Association of the American University Presses were very helpful to this new venture on a personal basis. However, the Franklin Book Program was not really interested in Siam. Finally, a bookshop was established and it became a place where liberal authors, columnists, and academics met regularly with committed students who wanted to free Siam from dictatorship and American domination. It has been claimed by some political scientists that from such a small beginning the dictatorial regime of Field Marshal Thanom Kittikhachorn was overthrown one decade later by the Thai students and people in October 1973; and the Field Marshal had to seek political asylum with the aid of his patron in Boston.[1]

Having been brainwashed by American information almost exclusively for about three decades, the public and the elites who believed in maintaining the status quo still clung to the idea that our best friend and ally would always protect us against the communist regimes, which expanded across the entire Indochinese states. They are now our next-door neighbors in the east and the northeast. American military and economic aid, as well as United States troops within our country, were all for our benefit. The bombing in Vietnam, the military intervention in Laos and Cambodia, were for the joint benefit of the free world. The capitalistic approach to development must be our solution. If only corruption among Thai officials could be eliminated, the Thai government—backed by the great American nation—would be effective in maintaining "law and order" for the benefit of our country.

Even after the events of October 1973, when the Thai government was supposed to have become more liberal and democratic, the American propaganda network was still very effective. Having been in the "game" in this country for so long, Americans knew how to spread rumors before they appeared in print. They also had many Thai propagandists on their payroll—directly or indirectly—some of whom are famous authors and authoresses. Anyone who was critical either of government or of the free world could easily be branded as a communist. Indeed any "anti-American" was normally denounced as antimonarchy also. It was claimed that those who wrote about the poverty and oppression within Siam or about the exploitation of the minorities in the United States (be it in an article or a novel) were not necessarily communists, but they paved the way for the communists to take over.

Those who were committed to freeing their country of American domination became not only fed up with such accusations (and in some cases, assassinations), but with their own experiences with the Americans during these decades. This made them realize that the United States brand of capitalism and free enterprise might only be good for the Americans and for the few local elites who were willing to trade off their country and their people for their own benefit and for the benefit of developed countries like Japan and the United States. Indeed, it was through reading some United States books and magazines written and edited by concerned American scholars that they reached this conclusion. Hence, these people sought an alternative to the American model.

As far as the printed network was concerned, the communists were at a disadvantage since they could not distribute their literature openly during the last regime. Immediately after 1973 books on Marx, Engels, Ché Guevara, and Castro as well as magazines on the New Left came mostly from the United States. It was only later that the Thai version of Mao Zedong's writings came directly from the People's Republic of China, as the law against importing anything from that country was not lifted until the Thai established diplomatic relations with Peking in 1975. By then Thai translators, authors, and editors had managed to produce a lot of local books and magazines with a strong socialistic message. There was a student newspaper which claimed to take a socialist stance, but bombs were thrown at its editorial office, so that it had to cease publication. The Americans and their friends, of course, confused the issue further, not merely by their accusations that all these people were communists, but also by producing Thai books and magazines which were supposed to be socialistic or even communistic, but which in fact distorted socialism and communism as best they could.

Those who committed themselves to the Socialist ideology, although many of them were converted, or could come out in the open only very recently, published a lot of material to propagate the success of Peking and Hanoi. Either by choice or by force of circumstances, they attacked the Thai and the American governments very strongly, seeing no single good point—not even in the remote past. To these people, the past has not been relevant; what they want is not to understand but to reform the society. Unfortunately, the Thai literature on socialism and communism thus far seems to be rather shallow. It is mostly propaganda (even in the novels), rather than containing real scholarship or literary value, and the authors rarely understand their own Thai society. They can only analyze it from the Marxist approach. They seek a quick and ready-made solution, as do their opponents who cling to the American view. These people believe that once Siam becomes a socialist state, all social ills will be easily cured. Even those who are not so naive argue that with an American presence (as it is now) we shall never be able to find our own solutions. By establishing a socialist regime, problems would not be easily solved, but at least there would be a chance of solving them. These people seem to ignore the Chinese, Vietnamese, and Russian domination, or they feel they are competent enough to deal with these foreign powers who are at least on the same ideological wave length. Or could it be that the Devil we do not know appears to be milder than the Devil we know?

The Siamese world of letters at this stage seems to be sharply divided. Even among the same religious community, strong opinions are expressed differently in print on these two lines of approach; and accusation seems to be the order of the day. We cannot minimize American negative influences on this issue. Yet what Siam needs at this stage is books, magazines, and newspapers as much as we need honest criticism of them—not to mention our own kind of creative writing free of propaganda from either camp. We need facts and information per se. The Thai should be allowed to read Marx as well as Jefferson, Thoreau, and Gandhi. The United States Information Service never had any writings of Jefferson, Adams or de Toqueville translated, not to mention Paine, Irving, Poe, or Longfellow. Dean Rusk's and Henry Kissinger's statements (while the two gentlemen were in power) were of course always translated in full. The United States Information Service only published books which said how wonderful Lincoln, Jefferson, and Washington were, not what these men actually thought and wrote.

Thai thinkers and writers should be allowed to study both liberal and communist thought and they ought to be allowed to study these ideologies in depth and dream about them. If they would be allowed to study their own society, perhaps from a Thai Buddhist and not from an American liberal or a Chinese Maoist standpoint, the Thai world of letters would be much enriched. The Thai might even be able to find their own solutions by establishing friendly relations with their communist neighbors and thus learn a great deal from them. The Thai might also be able to maintain friendly relations with the United States, as well as with the Western world and also learn to respect them. In the past, the Thai managed to preserve their independence because of their dignity, modesty, and flexibility. The United States helped them towards that end. Now the United States has said she would like to help us, but our experience has taught us that she has been a hindrance rather than an aide. And by making us its junior ally for three decades, the American government has made us lose our confidence. We have become materialistic, superficial, and lacking in self-respect. With such characteristics, we cannot produce any first-rate literature—not to mention other political, social, cultural, and spiritual aspirations. If the United States would only leave us alone or allow us to be ourselves once more, we should be able to develop our own thinking, writing, and publishing for our own benefit and perhaps for the benefit of the outside world. If we have a chance to do it ourselves and are unable to do it, then we only have ourselves to blame.

NOTE

1. The bookshop, its branch, office, and warehouse were raided after the October 1976 coup. About 100,000 copies of books were taken away by the police and the military.

INDEX

Abdou, Mohammed, 138
Acheson, Dean, 125
Adams, John, 4
Adams, John Quincy, 6
African Methodist Episcopal Church, 145-55
Agriculture, 111-18
Alabaster, Henry, 174
Al Azhar University, 138
Allende, Salvador, 121
American Bicentennial, ix, x, 144
American Council of Learned Societies, ix
American dream, The, 9, 16, 20, 24-25
American foreign policy, 9-12, 119-31
American idea of mission, 6, 14, 124-25, 133
American imperialism, 10-11, 16, 62, 119-31, 180
American influence on: Egypt, 137-44; France, 49-60; Great Britain, 61-83; Peru, 97-103; Russia, 111-18; Siam, 171-85; South Africa, 145-56; Sweden, 105-10; Yugoslavia, 39-47
Americanization of the World (Stead), 11
American Revolution, 4-5, 120
American Studies Association, ix
American Studies International Conferences, x
American trade, 10-11, 15, 100-101

American University in Beirut, 139, 142
American University in Cairo, 140
American violence, 18, 130-31
America Primo Amore (Soldati), 27, 38
America the Menace (Duhamel), 13
Anderson, Doris, 17
Architecture, 24, 27-38
Architecture Without Architects (Rudofsky), 35
Armstrong, Louis, 168
Arnett, B. W. (Bishop), 146
Art Deco, 12
Art Nouveau, 12, 31, 33
Asia Foundation, 181
Astronauts, 47-48
Attaway, Allen H. (Reverend), 151

Baker, Josephine, 162
Barlowe, Arthur, 3
Barnett, Jonathan, 30
Bartholdi, Frederic Auguste, 9
Bauhaus, 33
Beatles, The, 25, 61, 62, 67, 70, 71, 72, 74, 75, 76, 79, 82, 83
Bell, Alexander Graham, 9
Ben-David, Joseph, 18
Berendt, Joachim-Ernst, 12
Berlage, H. P., 31
Beveridge, Albert, 10
Bing, Alexander, 11
Black literature, 157-69

Boer War, 149
Boldizsar, Ivan, 17
Bontemps, Arna, 158
Boorstin, Daniel, 133
Borlaug, Norman, 117
Bradford, William, 3
Bradley, Dan Beach (Reverend), 171-72,
    174, 180
Brooklyn Bridge, 46
Brown, Courtney, 123
Brown, Denise Scott, 35
Brown, Sterling, 159
Brzezinski, Zbigniew, 14, 93
Butcher, Margaret, 157

Cambodia, 20
Caniff, Milton, 54
Carnegie Institution, 102-103
Carter, Jimmy, 93, 123
Cartier, Jacques, 3
Centennial Exposition, 9
Chandler, J. H. (Reverend), 173
CIA, 124, 130, 181
City Beautiful movement, 29-30
City planning, 27-38
Clair, René, 55
Coca-Cola, 15, 24, 42, 123
Cocteau, Jean, 55
Colt, Samuel, 9
Columbian Exposition (1893), 29, 30,
    45, 146
Comic books, 23, 25, 49-60, 62, 161
Commager, Henry Steele, 18
Connolly, Cyril, 14
Cooper, James Fenimore, 133
Coppin, Levi J., 147
Crèvecoeur, Michel-Guillaume St. Jean
    De, 6
Crumb, Robert, 55
Cubism, 33
Cullen, Countee, 159, 161, 168
Cunliffe, Marcus, 16, 134

Death and Life of Great American
    Cities, The (Jacobs), 35
Declaration of Independence, 4-5, 11,
    120

De Gaulle, Charles, 122
Democracy in America (Tocqueville), 6
"De Stijl" group, 31, 33
"Detroit Sound," 75
Dickens, Charles, 7
Dirk, Rudolph, 50
Disney, Walt, 40-42, 51, 53, 56
Downing, Andrew Jackson, 28
Drucker, Peter, 13
Dube, John L., 149-50
Du Bois, W. E. B., 151, 158, 165, 168
Duhamel, Georges, 13
Dwayne, James (Reverend), 147

Eddy, G. W., 173
Education, 137-44; women's, 140-41,
    143-44
Einstein, Albert, 13
Eliot, T. S., 133
Emerson, Ralph Waldo, 6
Expressionism, 33

Family of Man (Steichen), 39
Faulkner, William, 133
Fausset, Jessie, 159, 167
Fein, Albert, 29
Fermi, Enrico, 13
Film, 16, 18, 23-24, 40, 41, 42, 49, 55
Fisher, Rudolph, 159
Fitzpatrick, I. N. (Reverend), 147
Flynn, Errol, 40
Ford, Gerald, 123
Franklin, Benjamin, 4, 9
French Revolution, 4
Fromm, Erich, 13
Frost, Robert, 133
Fuksiewicz, Jacek, 18

Gallatin, Albert, 5
Garvey, Marcus, 158, 168
General Motors, 15
Gide, André, 160
Gilpin, Robert, 10
Glubb, J. B., 142
Grant, Madison, 158
"Green Revolution," 117-18

Gropius, Walter, 13, 32
Guevara, Ché, 41, 184
Gutheim, Frederick, 32
Guthrie, Woody, 65, 76

Haley, Bill, 64
Harding, Warren G., 12
Häring, Hugo, 31
Harlem Renaissance, 133, 157-69
Hasek, Jaroslav, 43
Haskel, Douglas, 35
Hawthorne, Nathaniel, 133
Haymarket Riot, 8
Hemingway, Ernest, 133, 161
Herzberg, Frederick, 106, 108
Higginson, Francis (Reverend), 4
Hiroshima, 42
Hiroshima, Mon Amour (Renais), 42
Hitler, Adolph, 12
Hoff, Robert van't, 31
Hoffman, P. A., 176
Hofstadter, Richard, 126
Honour, Hugh, 12
Hough, George H., 171
House, Samuel Reynold, 173
Hughes, Emmet John, 18
Hughes, Langston, 159, 163, 166, 168-69
Hull, Cordell, 130

IBM, 123
Immigration to the United States, 8-9, 105
Industrial Workers of the World, 128
Institute Geofisico del Peru, 102-103
International Style, 33
ITT, 124

Jacobs, Jane, 35
Jagger, Mick, 73
Jazz, 12, 16, 49, 65, 73, 160
Jefferson, Thomas, 5
Johansen, John, 37-38
John F. Kennedy Foundation, 180
Johnson, Edward, 4
Johnson, Lyndon, 126
Jones, John Taylor (Reverend), 172

José, Francisco, 17
Judson, Mrs. Adoniram, 171

Kahn, Louis, 24, 34, 35, 37
Kallmann, G. M., 37
Keaton, Buster, 40
Kennedy, John F., 19-20, 41-42, 120, 125
King and I, The, 179
Kissinger, Henry, 99, 123-26, 185

Landon, K. L., 179
Landscape architecture, 28-30
La Revue du Monde Noir, 162-63, 165
Larson, Nella, 159, 167
Lazarus, Emma, 8
Lea, Allen, 145
League of Nations, 12
Le Barbier, Jean-Jacques-François, 4
Le Corbusier, Charles E. J., 31, 32, 36
Leger, Fernand, 13
Le Journal de Mickey, 50, 53, 54
Lenin, Vladimir Ilyich, 113
Levi-Strauss, Claude, 13
Lewis, Sinclair, 133
Lieber, Francis, 7
Lindbergh, Charles, 13
Literature, x, 12, 17, 133-35, 159-68
London, Jack, 133
Longsworth, Richard C., 15
Luce, Henry, 13-14

McCay, Winsor, 50
McCormick, Cyrus, 9
McGregor, Douglas, 106, 108
MacKay, Claude, 159, 161, 163, 168
McLuhan, Marshall, 59
McManus, George, 50
Mahan, Alfred Thayer, 10
Maisonrouge, Jacques, 123
Marcuse, Herbert, 13
Marshall Plan, 14, 137
Martineau, Harriet, 7
Marx, Karl, 51, 111, 112, 113, 114, 121, 184-85
Marx, Leo, 3

Maslow, Abraham, 106
Media Are American, The (Tunstall), 23
Melville, Herman, 133
Mendelsohn, Erich, 31, 36
Mies van der Rohe, Ludwig, 13, 31-33
Milhaud, Darius, 12
Mills, Samuel, 6
Milosević, Milan, 41-42
Missionaries, 6, 133-35, 140-43, 145-56,
    171-74, 176
Mitchell, S. E., 146
Mobil Oil Company, 123
Moore, Charles, 37
Morris, William, 31-32
Mumford, Lewis, 28
Munger, Theodore, 8
Music, 23-25. *See also* Beatles; Jazz;
    Popular music

NAACP, 158
Nagasaki, 42
Nasser, Gamal Abdel, 122
Negro Renaissance. *See* Harlem
    Renaissance
Newsweek, 181
Niagra Movement, 151
1976 International Conference ix, x,
    13-15
Nixon, Richard, 20, 125-27
Nixon Doctrine, 126

Olmsted, Frederick Law, 24, 28, 29
Open Door Policy, 119
Opper, F. B., 50, 52
Oud, J. J. P., 31
Outcault, Richard, 50, 52

Paine, Thomas, 6
Peace Corps, 138, 182
Phillips, Wendell, 6
Pollock, Jackson, 24, 35
Pop-art, 35
Popular culture, 15-18, 23-25, 61-62,
    105. *See also* Film; Popular music
Popular music, 61-83
Pound, Ezra, 133
Presley, Elvis, 61, 64

Rauschenberg, Robert, 35
Rawson, R. C. (Reverend), 146
Raymond, Alex, 54
Reader's Digest, 181
Reich, Wilhelm, 45-46
Resnais, Alain, 42, 55, 58
Revel, Jean-François, 19
Richardson, Henry H., 29, 31
Rittenhouse, David, 9
Robbe-Grillet, Alain, 28, 38
Roberts College, 6
Robertson, Jaquelin, 30
Rockefeller, David, 124
Rock 'n' roll, 63-64, 66-67, 70, 72
Roosevelt, Theodore, 143-44
Rothko, Mark, 24
Rudofsky, Bernard, 35
Rudolph, Paul, 37
Rusk, Dean, 127, 185

Saarinen, Eero, 37
Sadoul, Georges, 57
Sadoul, Jacques, 58
Saint-Ogan, Alain, 52
Scharoun, Hans, 31
Schönberg, Arnold, 33-34
Schulz, Charles, 59
Schurz, Carl, 7
Science, 102-103
Seme, Pixley, 149-50
Senghor, Leopold, 160, 164-65, 168
Seven-Up, 24
Seward, William, 125
Sharp, Cecil, 61
Shelton, Gilbert, 55
Shenker, Israel, ix
Sinclair, Upton, 133
Singer, Isaac, 9
Slater, Samuel, 9
Smith, Norris Kelly, 30, 34
Smith, Sydney, 7
Smithsonian Institution, ix
Social Science Review, 182
Soldati, Mario, 27
Spanish American War, 11
Sports, 13, 62
Stead, William T., 11

Steichen, Edward, 39
Stein, Gertrude, 161
Stella, Frank, 24
Stewart, Gordon, 16
Stoddard, Lothrop, 158
Stravinksy, Igor, 13
Sullivan, Louis, 24, 31
Sundkler, B. G. M., 145
Sutton, S. B., 28
Sweet Movie, 42
Szyliowicz, Joseph S., 142

Taylor, Frederick, 106, 108
Technology, 9-10, 14, 16-17, 45-46,
    93-95, 97-103, 106-109
Television, 44, 47-48, 62, 66, 73
Temple, Shirley, 40
Tesla, Nikola, 44-45
Thoreau, Henry, 28
Tibawi, A. L., 142
Tillich, Paul, 13
Time, 181
Tocqueville, Alexis de, 6
Toomer, Jean, 159
Toscanini, Arturo, 13
Trotter, W. M., 151
Truman, Harry, 14, 125
Truman Doctrine, 14
Tunstall, Jeremy, 17, 23
Turgot, A. Robert Jacques, 5

Uniroyal Incorporated, 123
United Nations, 117

Unites States Constitution, 19
United States Information Service,
    181-85
United Nations, 117

Venturi, Robert, 35
Verne, Jules, 48
Vietnam War, 43, 121, 126-27, 130, 183
Voice of America, 181

Wagner, Jean, 158, 160
Walker, Francis, 8
Washington, George, 120, 126
Webster, Daniel, 5
Weinstein, Richard, 30
Whitney, Eli, 9
Wilberforce Institute, 151-53
Wilberforce University, 146, 148
Williams, William Appleman, 125

Williams, William Appleman, 125
Wilson, Woodrow, 12, 14, 119
Winston Cigarettes, 24
Without Marx or Jesus (Revel), 19
Woodson, Carter G., 158, 168
World War I, 11-12, 44, 50, 160, 179
World War II, 13, 15, 16, 41-43, 50, 107,
    179-80
Wright, Frank Lloyd, 24, 30-34, 36, 38
Wright, R. R. (Bishop), 152

Ziman, John, 16

ABOUT THE CONTRIBUTORS _____

EQBAL AHMAD has been a fellow at the Institute for Policy Studies (Washington) and at the Transnational Institute (Amsterdam and Washington). He is a member of the editorial board of *Afrique-Asia*, a mass circulation magazine published in Paris, and *Race and Class*, London. A citizen of Pakistan, he has lived in South Asia and the United States, North Africa, and western Europe. He is currently at work on a book on United States foreign policy after Vietnam.

ALLEN F. DAVIS is professor of history at Temple University and formerly the executive secretary of the American Studies Association. He is the author of *Spearheads for Reform* and *American Heroine* and the co-author of *Generations* and *Conflict and Consensus in American History*. He served as coordinator of the conference.

SAHAIR EL CALAMAWY has been professor of modern Arabic literature at Cairo University since 1956. She has been chairman of the General Organization for Publishing and Editing, Ministry of Culture, secretary general of the All Arab Federation for Women, and president of the Cairo Federation of University Women. She is the author of *Criticism, Imitation in Art, The Modern American Novel*, and *Tahtawi, Egyptian Reformer*.

ISAIAS FLIT STERN is Director-general, Instituto de Investigacion Tecnologicia Industrial y de Normas Tecnicas, Lima, Peru.

CHARLIE GILLETT was born in Lancashire, England, in 1942. He received a degree in economics from Cambridge University and a master's degree from Teachers College, Columbia University. A lifelong fan of America and its culture, he has made his living from his particular enthusiasm for its music, tracing the history of rock and roll in his book, *The Sound of the City* (1970), playing records on various BBC radio shows (1972-1978), and currently as a partner in an independent record label in South London, Oval Records.

PEHR G. GYLLENHAMMAR is president of AB Volvo and the Volvo Group in Sweden. He has studied law and has also been president of the Skandia Insurance Company and the Swedish Ships Mortgage Bank in Gothenburg.

MAURICE C. HORN is the author of more than fifty mysteries, espionage and science fiction novels, radio and television plays, and short stories. He is the author of *A History of the Comic Strip* and *75 Years of the Comic Strip*, and editor of *World Encyclopedia of Comics*. He was the organizer of the exhibition "Bande Dessinée et Figuration Narrative" at the Louvre in 1967 and he organized "75 Years of the Comics" at the New York Cultural Center in 1971. He was also the organizer of the First International Comics Convention in New York in 1968.

DUŠAN MAKAVÉJEV is a film maker and author who was born in Belgrade, Yugoslavia. He is the author of *Kiss for Komradess Slogan*, a book of essays on the young generation; a satirical play, *New Man on the Flower Market* (with R. Popov); and a dozen film scripts for feature films. He has directed 20 short films and five features. His social documentaries include *Smile 61*, *Parade*, and *New Domestic Animal*. Feature films: *Man Is Not a Bird, Love Affair or a Case of a Missing Switchboard Operator, Innocence Unprotected, W. R. Mysteries of the Organism,* and *Sweet Movie*. He has received the Silver Bear Award, Berlin, 1968; International Film Critics Award, Berlin, 1968; Golden Hugo Award, Chicago, 1968; October Award, Belgrade, 1968; Silver Hugo Award, Chicago, 1971; Luis Buñuel Award, Cannes, 1971; L'Age d'Or Award, Cinematheque Royale de Belgique, Bruxelles, 1973. He taught at New York, Harvard, and McGill universities.

MARINA MENSHIKOVA was with the United Nations Secretariat in New York (until her death in November 1979). She has been a senior research member of the Institute of World Economy, Academy of Sciences Moscow and at the Institute of Economics and Industrial Engineering, Siberian Department, Academy of Sciences, Novosbirsk. She has also been affiliated with the Institute of International Relations, Moscow and the Economics Department, Moscow University. Her books (in Russian) include *Structural Change in U.S. Agriculture, Problems of Agriculture in Developed Capitalist Countries, Capitalist Accumulation and Technical Revolution in U.S. Agriculture,* and *Economic Ties Between Agriculture and Industry.*

MBULAMWANZA MUDIMBE-BOYI is professor of languages and literature at the National University of Zaire. She has also taught at Lovanium University and has been chief editor of the DIA Press Agency and executive secretary of the Research Center for African Literature. She is the author of *L'oeuvre Romanesque de Jacques-Stephen Alexis, Ecrivain Haitien.*

ANTONY NGUBO is a professor of sociology, University of California at San Diego.

SULAK SIVARAKSA is the coordinator of the Asian Cultural Forum on Development (ACFOD)—a regional nongovernmental organization based in Bangkok. He has been visiting professor at the Universities of Toronto and Hawaii. His latest book is *Siam in Crisis.*

BRUNO ZEVI has been professor of architectural history in the Faculties of Architecture of the Universities of Venice and Rome. Co-editor of *Metron-architettura*, a Rome monthly from 1945 to 1955, since 1955 he has been publisher and editor of *L'architettura—cronache e storia*, a monthly issued in Rome and Milan. He is president of the International Committee of Architectural Critics. Among his numerous books, the following have been translated into English: *Towards an Organic Architecture, Architecture as Space,* and *The Modern Language of Architecture.*